NUMBER 227

THE ENGLISH EXPERIENCE

ITS RECORD IN EARLY PRINTED BOOKS
PUBLISHED IN FACSIMILE

JOANNES BOEMUS

THE FARDLE OF
FACIONS

LONDON 1555

DA CAPO PRESS
THEATRVM ORBIS TERRARVM LTD
AMSTERDAM 1970 NEW YORK

The publishers acknowledge their gratitude
to the Syndics of Cambridge University Library
for their permission to reproduce
the Library's copy

(Shelfmark: Syn. 8.55.88)

S.T.C. No. 3197

Collation: *⁴, A-Y⁸, Z⁴

Published in 1970 by
Theatrum Orbis Terrarum Ltd.,
O.Z. Voorburgwal 85, Amsterdam

&

Da Capo Press
- a division of Plenum Publishing Corporation -
227 West 17th Street, New York, 10011
Printed in the Netherlands
ISBN 90 221 0227 0

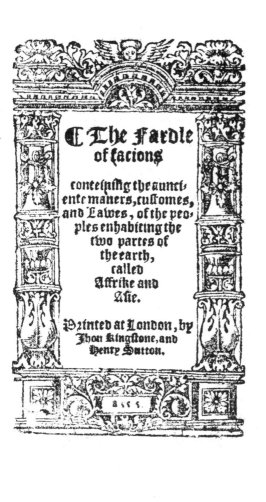

¶ The Fardle of facions

conteining the aunciente maners, custſomes, and Lawes, of the peoples enhabiting the two partes of the earth, called Affrike and Aſie.

Printed at London, by Jhon Kingstone, and Henry Sutton.

1555.

¶ To the righte honoura-
ble the Erle of Arundel, Knight of
the ordre, and Lorde Stewarde of
the Quenes maiesties moste
honourable house-
holde.

Ftre what time
the barrein tra-
ueiles of longe
seruice, had dri-
ne me to thinke
libertie the best
rewarde of my
simple life, right
honozable Erle
and that I had
determined to leaue wrastlyng with fortune, and to giue my self wholie to liue
vpon my studie, and the labours of my
hand: I thought it moste sitting with the
duetie that I owe to God and manne, to
bestowe my time (if I could) as well to
the profite of other, as of my self. Not co-
ueting to make of my floudde, a nother
mânes ebbe (the Cancre of all commune
wealthes) but rather to sette other afloate,
where I my self rake on groud. Tourning me thereto, to the searche of wise-

*.ij.   dome

dome and vertue, for whose sake either
we tosse, or oughte to tosse so many pa-
pers and tongues: although I founde a-
boute my self, verie litle of that Threasu-
re, yet remembred I that a fewe yeres
paste, at the instaunce of a good Citezein
(who might at those daies, by authoritie
commaunde me) I had begonne to trau-
slate, a litle booke named in the Latine,
Omnium gentium mores, gathered longe
sence by one Iohannes Boemus, a manne
as it appereth, of good iudgemente and
diligence. But so corrupted in the Prin-
ting, that aftre I had wrastled a space,
with sondrie Printes, I rather determined to lose my labour of the quartre tran-
slacion, then to be shamed with the haulf.
And throwing it a side, entended no further to wearie my self therwithall, at the
leaste vntill I mighte finde a booke of a
bettre impressió. In searching wherof at
this my retourne to my studie, although
I found not at the full that, that I sought
for: yet vnderstanding among the booke
sellers (as one talke bringes in another)
that men of good learning and eloquéce,
bothe in the Frenche, and Italien tonge,
had not thought ..   ne to bestowe their
time

time aboute the tranſlacion therof, and
that the Emperours Maieſtie that now
is, vouchedſaulſe to receiue the preſenta-
cion therof, at the Frenche tranſlatours
hande, as well appereth in his booke: it
kindled me againe, vpon regard of mine
owne profite, and other mennes moe, to
bring that to ſome good pointe, that earſt
I had begonne. For (thought I) ſeing the
booke hath in it, muche pleaſant bariette
of thinges, and yet more profite in the
pitthe: if it faile to bee otherwiſe rewar-
ded, yet ſhal it thankefully of the good be
regarded. Wherefore ſetting vpon it a
freſſhe, where the booke is deuided acording to thaunciente deuiſion of the earth,
into thre partes, Affrique, Aſie, and Europe: hauing brought to an ende the two
firſte partes, I found no perſone in mine
opiniō ſo fitte as your honour, to preſent
them vnto. For ſeing the whole proceſſe
ronneth vpon gouernaunce and Lawes,
for thadminiſtracion of commune wealthes, in peace and in warre, of aunciente
times tofore our greate graundfathers
daies: to whom mighte I bettre preſente
it, then to a Lorde of verie nobilitie and
wiſedome, that hath bene highe Mare-
                ſti.   ſhall

halle in the fielde abrode, deputie of the locke and keie of this realme, and a counsailour at home, of thre worthie princes. Exercised so many waies in the waues of a fickle Commune wealthe: troubled sometime, but neuer disapoincted of honourable successe. To your good Lordeshippe then I yelde & committe, the firste fruictes of my libertie, the firste croppe of my labours, this firste date of the Newe yere: beseching the same in as good parte to receiue it, as I humblie offre it, and at your pleasure to vnfolde the Fardle, and considre the stuffe. Whiche euer the farder in, shall sieme I truste the more pleasaunte and fruictefulle. And to conclude, if I shall vndrestade, that your honour delighteth in this, it shal be a cause sufficiente, to make me go in hande with Europe, that yet remaineth vntouched. Almightie God giue vnto your Lordeshippe prosperous fortune, in sounde honour and healthe.

Your Lordshippes moste humblie at commaundemente.

William Watreman.

I HAVE *sought* out at times, as laisure hath serued me, Good reader, the maners and faciōs the Lawes, Customes and Rites, of all suche peoples, as semed notable, and worthy to be put in remembráce, together with the situaciō & descripciō of their habitatiōs: which the father of Stories Herodotus the Greke, Diodorus, the Siciliane, Berosus, Strabo, Solinus, Trogus Pompeius, Ptolomeus, Plinius, Cornelius the still, Dionysius the Afriane, Pōponius Mela, Cæsar, Iosephus, and certein of the later writers, as Vincentius, and Aeneas Siluius (whiche aftreward made Pope, had to name Pius the seconde) Anthonie Sabellicus, Ihon Nauclerus, Ambrose Calepine, Nicholas Perotte, in his cornu copiæ, and many other famous writers eche one for their parte, as it ware skatered, & by piece meale, set

furthe

furthe to posteritie. Those I sate haue I
sought out, gathered together, and acordyng to the ordre of the storie and tyme,
digested into this litle packe. Not for the
hongre of gaine, or the ticklyng desire of
the peoples vaine brute, and vnskilfulle
commendacion : but partly moued with
the oportunitie of my laisure, & the wondrefull profite and pleasure, that I conceiued in this kinde of studie my self, and
partly that other also delightyng in stories, might with litle labour, finde easely
when thei would, the somme of thynges
compiled in one Booke, that thei ware
wonte with tediousnes to seke in many.
And I haue shocked theim vp together,
aswell those of aunciente tyme, as of later yeres, the lewde, aswell as the vertuous indifferentlie, that vsyng thē as present examples, and paternes of life, thou
maiest with all thine endeuour folowe
the vertuous and godlie, & with asmuche
warenes eschewe the vicious & vngodly.
Yea, that thou maiest further, my (reader)learne to discerne, how men haue in
these daies amended the rude simplicitie
of the first worlde, frō Adam to the floud
and many yeres after, when men liued
                                    skateryng

skateryng on the earthe, without knowe
lege of Money, or what coigne ment, or
Merchauntes trade : no maner of ex-
chauge, but one good tourne for another
When no man claimed aught for his seueralle, but lande and water ware as cōmune to al, as Ayer and Skie. Whē thei
gaped not for honour, ne hunted after richesse, but eche man contented with a litle, passed his daies in the wilde fielde,
vnder the open heauen, the couerte of
some shadowie Tree, or slendre houcile,
with suche companion or companiōs as
siemed them good, their diere babes and
childzen aboute them. Sounde without
careke and in restfull quietnesse, eatyng
the fruictes of the fielde, and the milke of
the cattle, and dzinking the waters of the
chzistalline spzinges. First clad with the
softe barcke of trees, or the faire bzoade
leaues, ₹ in pzocesse with rawe felle and
hide, full vnwozkemanly patched together. Not then enuironed with walles,
ne pente vp with rampers, and diches of
deapthe, but walking at free skope i mōg
the wanderyng beastes of the fielde, and
where the night came vpon theim, there
takyng their lodgyng without feare of

murth exer oz thief. Mery at the fulle, as
without knowledge of the euilles ý aftre
ensued as ý wozlde waxed elder, thzough
diuers desires, and contrarie endeuours
of menne. Who in pzocesse foz the insuffi-
cientie of the fruictes of the earthe, (whiche she tho gaue vntilled) and foz default
of other thynges, ganne falle at disquiete
and debate emong themselues, and to a-
uoied the inuasion of beastes, and menne
of straunge bozders, (whom by themselues thei could not repelle) gathered into
companies, with commune aide to with-
stande suche encursions and violence of
wzong. And so ioynyng in confederacie,
planted themselues together in a plotte,
assigned their boundes, framed vp cotages, one by anothers chieque, diked in thē
selues, chase officers and gouernours,
and deuised lawes, that thei also emong
theimselues might liue in quiete. So beginnyng a rough paterne of tounes and
of Cities, that aftre ware laboured to
moze curious finesse.

AND now ware thei not contented,
with the commodities of the fieldes and
cattle alone, but by diuers inuencions of
handecraftes and scieces, and by sondzie
labours

labours of this life, thei sought how to
winne. Now gan thei tattempte the seate
with many deuices, to transplante their
progenie, and offspring into places vnen-
habited, and to enioye the commodities
of eche others countrie, by mutuall traf-
ficque. Now came the Oxe to the yoke,
the Horse to the draught, the Metalle to
the stampe, the Apparel to handsomnes, the
Speache to more finesse, the Behauour
of menne to a more calmenesse, the fare
more deintie, the Buildyng more gorgeous, thenhabitours ouer all became mil-
der and wittier, shaking of (euen of their
owne accorde) the bruteshe outrages and
stearne dealinges, ŷ shamefully mought
be spoken of. Nowe refrained thei from
sleayng one of a nother, frō eatyng of ech
others flesh, from rape and open defiling
of mother, sister, and daughter indifferētly, and fro many like abhominacions to
nature and honestie. Thei now marieng
reason, with strength: and pollicie, with
might: where the earthe was before forgrowen with bushes, and wooddes, stuf-
fed with many noisome beastes, drouned
with meares, and with marshe, vnfitte to
be enhabited, waast and vnhandsome in

A. iij.   euery

euery condition: by wittie diligence, and labour, ridde it from encombraunce, planed the roughes, digged vp trees by the rootes, dried awaie the superfluous waters, brought all into leauelle, banished barreinesse, and vncouered the face of the earth, that it might fully be sene, conuerted the champeine to tillage, the plaines to pasture, the valley to meadow, the hilles thei shadowed with wooddes and with Vines. Then thruste thei in cultre and share, and with wide woundes of the earthe, wan wine and corne plenteously of the grounde, that afore scarcely gaue them Akornes and Crabbes. Then enhabited thei more thicke, and spred themselues ouer all, and buylte euery where. Of Tounes, thei made cities, and of villages, Tounes. Castles vpon the rockes, and in the valleis made thei the temples of the goddes. The golde graueled springes, thei encurbed with Marble, & with trees right pleasauntlie shadowed them aboute. From them thei deriued into cities and Tounes, the pure freshe waters a greate distaunce of, by conduicte of pipes and troughes, and suche other conueyaunce. Where nature had hidden the

waters

waters, out of sighte, thei sancke welles
of greate deapth, to supplie their lackes.
Riuers, and maigne floudes, whiche a-
fore with vnbridled violence, oftymes
ouerflowed the neighboured aboute, to
the destruction of their cattle, their houses, and themselues: thei restrained with
banckes, and kept them in a course. And
to the ende thei might not onely be vada-
ble, but passed also with drie foote, thei
deuised meanes with piles of Timbre,
and arches of stone, maulgre the rage of
their violent streames, to grounde brid-
ges vpon them. Yea, the rockes of the sea
whiche for the daungier of the accesse,
thoughte themselues exempte from the
dinte of their hande, when thei perceiued
by experience thei ware noyous to sai-
lers, with vnspeakeable labour did thei
ouerthrowe & breake into gobettes. He-
wed out haues on every strond, enlarged
crieques, opened rodes, and digged out
herborowes, where their shippes mighte
ride saulfe fro the storme. Finally thei so
laboured, beautified, and perfeighted the
earthe, that at this daie compared with
the former naturalle forgrowen wasten-
nesse, it might well sieme not to be that,

but rather the Paradise of pleasure, out of the whiche, the first paternes of mankinde (Adam and Eue) for the trangression of Goddes precept, ware driuen.

MEN also inuented and founde many wittie sciences, and artes, many wondrefull workes, whiche when by practise of lettres, thei had committed to bookes, and laied vp for posteritie, their successours so woundered at their wisedomes, and so reuerenced their loue and endeuours (whiche thei spied to be meant toward them, and the wealth of those that shuld folow of thē) that thei thought thē not blessed enough, with theestate of men mortalle, but so aduaunced their fame, and wondered at their worthinesse, that thei wan theim the honour and name of Goddes immortall.

THO gan the Prince of the worlde, when men so gan to delight in thadournyng of the worlde, to sowe vpō the good siede, the pestilente Dernell, that as thei multiplied in nombre, so iniquitie might encrease, to disturbe and confounde this blessed state.

FIRST, therefore when he had with all kinde of wickednes belimed ẙ world, he he put into their heades, a curious searche of the highest knowledge, and suche as dependeth vpon destenie of thynges. And so practised his pageauntes, by obscure and doubtfully attempzed Respocions, and voices of spirites, that after he had settred the wozlde in the trauers of his toies, and launced into their hartes a blinde superstition, and feare: he trained it whole to a wicked wozship of many goddes and Goddesses, that when he ones had wiped cleane out of mynde the knowlege and honour of one God euerlastyng, he might practise vpon manne, some notable mischief. Then sette he vp pilgrimages to deuilles, fozeshewers of thynges, that gaue aduertisemente and answere to demaundes in sondzie wise. In the Isle of Delphos one, in Euboea another, at Nasamone a thirde, and emong the Dodonians, the famous okes, whose bowes by the blastes of the winde resounded to the eare, a maner of aduertisemente of deuellishe delusion. To the whiche Idolles and Images of deuelles he stirred vp men to do the honour (Helas) due onely to God. As to Saturne in Italie, to Jupiter in Candie, to Juno in

A.b.　　Samos,

Samos, to Bacchus in India, & at Thebes: to Iris, and Osiris in Egipte: in old Troie to Vesta : aboute Tritona in Aphrique to Pallas, in Germanie and Fraunce to Mercurie, vnder the name of Theuthe: to Minerua at Athenes and Himetto, to Apollo in Delphos, Rhodes, Chio, Patara, Troade and Cymbra. To Diane in Delos and in Scythia, to Venus in Paphos, Ciprus, Gnydon, and Cithera. To Mars in Thraria, to Priapus in Lampsacho of Hellespontus, to Vulcane in Lyppara and Lênos, and in diuers other places to sondrie other, whose remembraunce was then moste freshe in the memorie of their people, for the benefaites and merueilous inuencions bestowed emong them.

AFTERVVARD, also when Jesus Christe the verie sonne of the almightie father, shewyng hymself in the fleshe of our mortalitie, was conuersaunte in the worlde, pointyng to the same, as with his fingre, the waie to immortalitie, & endelesse blessednesse, and bothe with woorde and example, exhorted and allured them to vprightnes of life, to the glorie of his father, sendyng his disciples and scolers

into

into the vniuersall woꝛlde, to condemne Superstition and all errour of wickednes, with the moste healthsome woozde: to plante true Religion, and geue newe pꝛeceptes, and directions of the life, and had now set the matier in suche foꝛwardnesse and poincte, that the Gospell beyng generally of all nacions receiued, there lacked but continuaunce to perfeicte felicitie: The deuell eftesones retournyng to his naturall malice, desirous to repossesse that, that constrainedly he foꝛsooke, betrappyng again the curious conceipte of man, some he reuersed into their foꝛmer abuses and errours, and some with newe Heresies he so coꝛrupted, snarled, and blynded, that it had bene muche bettre foꝛ them, neuer almoste to haue knowen the waie of truthe, then after their entraunce, so rashely and maliciously to haue foꝛsaken it.

AT this daie in Asia the lesse, the Armenianes, Arabians, Persians, Sirias, Assirians, and Meades: in Aphꝛique, the Egipcians, Numidians, Libiens, and Moozes. In Europe, the whole coūtrie of Grecia, Misia, Thꝛacia, ⁊ all Turquie thꝛowyng awaie Chꝛiste, are become the folowers

folowers and worshippers of Mahomet
and his erronious doctrine. The people
of Scithia, whom we now cal Tartares
(a greate people and wide spred)parte of
them worshippe the Idolle of their Emperour Kamme, parte the Sonne, the
Moone, and other Starres, and part according to the Apostles doctrine, one onely God. The people of Inde, & Ethiope,
vnder the gouernaunce of Presbiter Ihō
perseauer in Christiane godlinesse, howbeit after a sort, muche different frō ours.

The sincere and true faithe of Christ,
wherwith in time it pleased God to illu-
mine the worlde, remaineth in Germanie, Italy, Fraunce, Spaine, Englande,
Scotland, Ireland, Denmarke, Liuon,
Pruse, Pole, Hungarie, and the Isles
of Rhodes, Sicilie, Corsica, Sardinia,
with a fewe other. This bytter ennemie
of mankinde hauyng thus with his subtilties enueiled our mindes, and disseue-
red the christiā vniō, by diuersitie of maners and factions of belief, hath brought
to passe thorough this damnable wyc-
kednes of Sacrifices, and Rites, that
whilest euery people (vndoubtedly with
religious entent)endeuour theim selues
to

to the worshippe of God, and echeone ta=
keth vpō him to be the true and best wor=
shipper of him, and whilest echone thinke
theim selues to treade the streight pathe
of euerlastyng blessednes, and contēdeth
with eigre mode and bitter dispute, that
all other erre and be ledde farre a wrie:
and whilest euery man strugglethe and
striueth to spread and enlarge his owne
secte, and to ouerthrowe others, thei doe
so hate and enuie, so persecute and annoy
echone an other, that at this daie a man
cannot safely trauaill from one countrie
to another: yea, thei that would aduen=
ture saufely or vnsaufely, be almost eue=
ry where holdē out. Wherof me thinkes
I see it is like to come to passe, that whi=
lest one people scant knoweth the name
of another, (and yet almost neighbours)
all that shall this daie be written or re=
ported of theim, shalbe compted and re=
fused as lyes. And yeat this maner of
knowledge and experience, is of it self so
pleasant, so profitable & so praise worthy,
that sundrie (as it is wel knowen) for the
onely loue and desire thereof, leauyng
their natiue countrie, their father, their
mother, their wiues and their children,
yea,

yea, throwyng at their heles their caul-
tie and welfare, haue with great troubles, vexations, and turmoilynges taken
vpon theim for experience sake, to cutte
through the wallowyng seas, and many
thousande miles, to estraunge theimselues fro their home. yea, and those men
not in this age alone, but euen from the
first hatchyng of the worlde haue been
reputed and founde, of mosse wisedome,
authoritie, and good facion, sonest chosen
with all mennes consent, bothe in peace ⁊
warre, to administre the comune wealth
as maisters and counsaillours, Iudges
and Capitaines. Suche ware thancient
sages of Grece and of Italy, Socrates,
Plato, Aristotle, Antisthenes, Aristippus
Zeno, ⁊ Pythagoras, who through their
wisedomes and estimacion for trauailes
wan them great nombres of folowers,
and brought furthe in ordre the sectes named Socratici, Academici, Peripateci, Cy-
nici, Cyrenaici, Stoici, and Pythagorici,
echone cholyng name to glorie in his
maister. Suche ware the prudente lawe-
makers of famous memorie, Minois and
Rhadamanthus emōg the Cretenses, Orpheus emong the Thraciens, Draco and
                                    Solon

Solon emõg the Athenienses, Licurgus
emong the Lacedemoniãs, Moses emõg
the Iewes, and Zamolxis emong the
Scythians, & many other in other tredes
Whiche dreamed not their knowledge
in the benchehole at home, but learned
ot the men in the worlde moste wise, the
Chaldees, the Brachmanni, the Gym-
nosophites & the priestes of Egipte, with
whõ thei had for a space bene couersant.
Like glorie, & y̆ like trauaill happened to
the worthies of the worlde, as to Iupiter
of Crete (reported fiue times to haue sur-
ueied the whole worlde) and to his twoo
sonnes Dionisius (otherwise called Bacchus) and Hercules the mightie. Likewise to Theseus and Iason, and the rest
of that voiage, To the vnlucky sailer Ulis-
ses, and to the banished Eneas, to Cy-
rus, Xerxes, and Alexander the Greate,
to Hanniballe and Mithridate, kyng of
Pontus, reported able to speake fiftie so-
drie languages, to Antiochus, the greate
and innumerable Princes of Roome,
bothe of the Scipioes, Marii, and Len-
tuli. To Pompeius the greate, to Iulius
Cesar, Octauian, and Augustus, to the
Constantines, Charles, Conrades, He-
rickes,

rickes and Frederickes . Whiche all by
their exploictes vpon straunge nacions,
haue gotten their immortall and euerlastyng renoume. Wherefore,seyng there
is in the knowledge of peoples,& of their
maners and facions, so greate pleasure
and profite, and euery man cannot, yea,
fewe men will,go traueile the countries
themselues: me thinkes gentill reader,
thou oughtest with muche thanke to re-
ceyue at my hande these bookes of the
maners and facions of peoples most notable and famous,togyther with the places whiche thei enhabite : And with no
lesse cherefulnes to embrase theim, then
if beyng ledde on my hande from coun=
trey to countrey,I should poynct the at
eye, how euery people liueth,and where
they haue dwelte, and at this daye doe.
Let it not moue the,let it not withdrawe
the, if any cankered reprehendour of o-
ther mens doynges shall saie vnto the :
It is a thyng hath bene written of,ma-
ny yeares agone,and that by a thousand
sondry menne,and yet he but borowyng
their woordes, bryngeth it foorthe for a
mayden booke, and nameth it his owne.
For if thou well considre my trade, thou
shalt

of the Authour.

shalt fynd, that I haue not only brought
thee other mennes olde store, but opened
thee also the treasury of myne owne
witte and bokes, not euery where
to be found, and like a liberall
feaster haue set before thee
much of myne owne,
and many thynges
newe. Farewell
and thanke-
fully take
that,
that with labour is
brought thee.

B.I.

¶ The first Chapter.

¶ The true opinion of the deuine, concernyng the beginnyng of man.

Hen God had in. V. daies made perfecte the heauens and the earth, and the furniture of bothe: whiche the latines for the goodlinesse and beautie therof, call Mundus, and we (I knowe not for what reason) haue named the worlde: the sixth daie, to the extent there mighte be one to enioye, and be Lorde ouer all, he made the moste notable creature Man. One that of all earthly creatures alone, is endowed with a mynde, and spirit from aboue. And he gaue him to name, Adam: accordyng to the colour of the molde he was made of. Then drawyng out of his side the woman, whilest he slept, to thende he should not be alone, knitte her vnto hym, as an vnseparable compaignion, and therwith placed them in the moste pleasaunt plot of the earth,

B.ij.   fostered

foftered to flourifhe with the moifture of floudes on euery parte. The place for the frefhe grieneffe and merie fhewe, the Greques name Paradifos. There lyued they a whyle a mofte bleffed life without bleamifhe of wo, the earth of the own accorde bringing forth all thing. But when they ones had tranfgreffed the precepte, they ware banyffhed that enhabitaunce of pleafure and driuen to fhift the world. And fro thenceforth the gratioufnes of the earth was alfo abated, & the francke fertilitie therof fo withdrawen, that labour and fwette now wan leffe a greate deale, then ydle lokyng on before tyme had done. Shortly crepte in fickenes, and difeafes, and the broyling heate and the nipping cold began to affaile their bodyes. Their firft fonne was Cayin, and the feconde Abell, and then many other. And as the world grewe into yeares, and the earth began to ware thicke peopled, loke as the nombre did encreace, fouices grew on, and their lyuing decaied euer into woors. For gilteleffe dealyng, wrong rame in place, for deuoutenesse, cõtempte of the Goddes, and fo farre outraged their wickednes, that God fkarcely fyndyng

ding one iuſte Noha on the earth (whom
he ſaued, with his houſholde, to repayre
the loſſe of mankind and replenyſſhe the
woꝛlde) ſente a floude vniuerſall. whiche
couering all vnder water, killed all fleſhe
that bare lyfe vppon earth, excepte a fewe
beaſtes, birdes, and woꝛmes that ware
pꝛeſerued in the miſticall arke. In the
ende of fiue Monethes aftre the floude
began, the Arque touched on the moũtei-
nes of Armenia. And within foure Monethes aftre, Noas and all his beyng re-
ſtoꝛed to the earth , with Goddes fur-
theraunce in ſhoꝛte ſpace repeopled the
woꝛlde. And to thende the ſame myghte
euery wheare again be enhabited, he diſ-
perſed his yſſue and kyndꝛedes into ſondꝛie coaſtes. After Beroſus opynion he
ſent Cham otherwyſe, named Cameſes
and Chameſenuus with his offſpꝛing, into Egipte. Into Lybia and Cirene, Tri-
ton . And into the whole reſidewe of Affrike the ancient Japetus called Attalus
Pꝛiſcus. Ganges he ſent into Eaſte Aſia
with certeine of the ſonnes of Comerus
Gallus. And into Arabia the fertile, one
Sabus, ſirnamed Churifer. Ouer Arabia the Waaſte he made Arabus gouer-

nour, and Petreius ouer Petrea. He
gaue vnto Canaan, all that lyeth fro
Damasco to the outemost bozdze of Pa-
lestine. In Europe he made Tuisco king
of Sarmatia, from the floude of Tanais
vnto the Rhene. And there were ioyned
vnto him all the sonnes of Istrus, and
Mesa, with their brethren, fro the moun-
teyne of Adula to Mesemberia pontica.
Archadius and Emathius gouerned the
Tirianes, Comerus Gallus, had Italie
and Fraunce, Samothes, Brtteigne and
Normandie, and Iubal, Spayne. That
spiedie and vnripe puttyng forthe of the
chyldren from their progenitours, befoze
they had throughly learned and enured
them selues with their facions and maners , was the cause of all the diuersitie
that after ensued. For Cham, by the reason of his naughty demeanour towarde
his father, beyng constrayned to departe
with his wyfe and hys chyldzen, planted
him selfe in that parte of Arabia, that after was called by his name. And lefte no
trade of religion to his posteritie, because
he none had learned of his father. Wherof it came to passe, that when in processe
of tyme they ware encreased to to many

ny for that londe : beyng sent out as it
ware, swarme aftre swarme into other
habitations, and skatered at length into
sondzy partes of the wozlde (for this banysshed progeny grewe aboue measure)
some fel into errours wherout thei could
neuer vnsnarle themselues. The tongue
gan to altre & the knowledge of the true
God and all godlie wozshippe banysshed
out of mind. Into muche that some liued
so wildely (as aftre thou shalt here) that
it ware harde to discerne a difference betwixte them and the beastes of the felde.
Thei that flieted into Egipt, wonderyng
at the beautie and course of the Sonne, &
the Moone, as though there had been in
them a power deuine, began to wozshyp
them as Goddes: callyng the lesse, Isis
and the bigger Osiris. To Jupiter also
thei Sacrificed, & did honour as to y principall of life. To Vulcan for fire, to Pallas, as Lady of the skie, to Ceres as go-
uerneresse of thearth, and to sondzy other
for other sondzy considerations . Neyther staied that darkenesse of iniquitie in
Egipte alone, but where so euer the progeny of Cham stepte in from the begyn-
nyng, there fell true godlines, all oute of

B.iiij.   minde

minde and abōdage to the deuell entred
his place. And there neuer was countrie,
mother of moe swarmes of people, then
that part of Arabia, that he, and his, chase
to be theirs. So greate a mischief did the
vntymely banishemente of one manne,
bring to the whole. Cōtrarily the progenie of Iapheth, and Sem, brought vp to
full yeres vndre their elders, and rightly enstructed: contentyng thē selues with
a litle circuite, strayed not so wide as this
brother had doen. Whereby it chaunced
that the zeale of the truthe, (I meane of
good liuyng and true worshippe of one
onely God) remained as hidden in one
onely people, vntill the tyme of Messias.

☞ The seconde Chapitre.

☞ The false opinion of the Philosophre concernyng the be-
gynnyng of man.

BUt the aunciente Philosophers, whiche without
knowledge of God, and
his truthe, many yeres a-
go, wrate vpon the natu-
res of thinges, and thistories of times had another opinion of the
originall

oꝛiginall of man. Foꝛ certain of them, belieued the woꝛlde euer to haue been, and
that euer it ſhould be, and man together
with it to haue had no beginnyng. Certaine did holde that it had a beginnyng,
and an ende it ſhould haue, and a time to
haue been, when man was not. Foꝛ ſaie
thei, the begynner of thynges viſible,
wꝛapped vp bothe heauen and earth at
one inſtant, togither in one paterne, and
ſo a diſtinction growyng on betwixte
theſe meynte bodies, the woꝛlde to haue
begon in ſuche oꝛdꝛe as we ſee. The aire
by nature to be cōtinually mouyng, and
the moſte firie parte of theſame, foꝛ the
lighteneſſe thereof, moſte highe to haue
climbed. So that ſonne and Moone, and
the planetes all, participatyng of the nature of that lighter ſubſtaunce: mone ſo
muche the faſter, in how muche thei are
of the moꝛe ſubtile parte. But that whiche was mixed with waterie moiſture,
to haue reſted in the place, foꝛ the heaui-
neſſe therof, and of the watery partes, the
ſea to haue comen: and the matier moꝛe
compacte to haue paſſed into a clammi-
neſſe firſte, and ſo into earth. This earth
then bꝛought by ẙ heate of the ſonne into

a moze fastenesse. And after by the same
power puffed and swollen in the vpper-
mosse parte, there gathered manye humours in sondzy places, which dzawing
to ripenesse enclosed them selues in sly-
mes ano in filmes, as in the maresses of
Egipt, and other stondynge waters we
often se happen. And seynge the heate of
thaier sokyngly warmeth the cold groud
and heate meint with moissure is apt to
engendze: it came to passe by the gentle
moissure of the night aire, and the com-
fozting heate of the daie sonne, that those
humours so riped, dzawyng vp to the
rinde of thearth, as though their tyme of
childbirthe ware come, bzake out of their
filmes, and deliuered vpon the earth all
maner of liuyng thinges. Emog whiche
those that had in the mosse heate, became
soules into the aire: those that ware of
nature moze earthie, became wozmes
and beasses of sondzie kindes: and where
water surmounted, thei dzewe to the e-
lemente of their kinde, and had to name
fisshes. But afterwarde the earth beyng
moze parched by the heate of the Sonne,
and the dzouthe of the windes, ceased to
bzing furthe any mo greate beasses: and
                                    those

those that ware alreaby bꝛought furthe,
(ſaie thꝛi) mainteined, and encreaſed by
mutualle engendꝛure, the barietie, and
nombꝛe. And they are of opinion that
in the ſame wiſe, men ware engendꝛed
in the beginning. And as nature putte
them foꝛth emong other beaſtes, ſo lined
they at the firſt an vnknowen lyfe wyl-
dely emong them, vpon the fruittes, and
the herbes of the fieldes. But the beaſtes
aftre a while waring noyſome vnto
them, they ware foꝛced in commune foꝛ
echeothers ſauftie to dꝛawe into companies to reſiſte their anoyaunce, one hel-
ping another, and to ſieke places to make
their abiding in. And where at the firſte
their ſpeache was confuſe, by litle and
litle they ſayed it dꝛewe to a diſtincte-
neſſe, and perſeighte difference: in ſoꝛte
that they ware able to gyue name to all
thinges. But foꝛ that they ware diuerſely ſparckled in diuers partes of the
woꝛlde, they holde alſo that their ſpeache
was as diuers and different. And herof
to haue aftreward riſen the diuerſitie of
lettres. And as they firſte aſſembled into
bandes, ſo euery bande to haue bꝛoughte
foꝛthe his nacion. But theſe men at the

firſt

firste voide of all helpe and experience of
liuyng, ware bittrely pinched with hongre and colde, before thei could learne to
reserue the superfluous plenty of the Somer, to supply the lacke of Winters barreinesse, whose bitter blastes, and hōgrie
pinynges, consumed many of them. whiche thing whē by experiēce dere bought,
thei had learned : thei soughte bothe for
Caues to defende them fro colde, and began to hourde fruictes. Then happe foūd
out fire, and reason gaue rule of profite,
and disprofite, and necessitie toke in hand
to sette witte to schoole. Who gatheryng
knowledge, and perceiuyng hymself to
haue a helpe of his sences, more skilfull
then he thought, set hande a woorke, and
practised connyng, to supplie all defaul-
tes, whiche tōgue and lettres did enlarge
and distribute abrode.

THEI that had this opinion of the o-
riginall of manne, and ascribed not the
same to the prouidence of God, affirmed
the Ethopiens to haue bene the firste of
all menne. For thei coniectured that the
ground of that countrie liyng nierest the
heates of the Sonne musse nedes first of
all other waxe warme. And the earth at
that

that tyme beyng but clammie and softe, through the attemperaunce of that moysture and heate, man there first to haue bene fourmed, and there to haue gladlier enhabited (as natiue and naturall vnto him) then in any other place, whē all plaçes ware as yet straunge, and vnknowen, whiche aftre men soughte. Beginnyng therfore at them, after I haue shewed how the worlde is deuided into thre partes (as also this treatise of myne) and haue spoken a litle of Aphrique, I wyll shewe the situacion of Aethiope, and the maners of that people, and so forthe of al other regions and peoples, with suche diligence as we can.

❡ The thirde Chapitre.

❡ The deuision and limites of the Earthe.

Hose that haue bene before our daies, (as Orosius writeth) are of opinion, that the circuite of the earth, bordered about with the Ocean Sea: disroundyng hym self, shooteth out thre corner wise, and is also

diuided

deuided into thre seuerall partes, Afrike,
Asie, and Europe. Afrike is parted from
Asie with the floude of Nilus, whiche comyng fro the Southe, ronneth through
Ethiope into Egipte. where gentiy shea-
dyng hymself ouer his banckes, he leaueth in the countrie a meruellous fertilitie, and passeth into the middle earth sea,
with seuen armes. From Europe it is seperate with the middle earth sea. whiche
beginnyng fro the Ocean aforesaied: at
the Islande of Gades, and the pilours of
Hercules, passeth not tenne miles ouer.
But further entryng in, semeth to haue
shooued of the maigne lande on bothe
sides, & so to haue won a more largenesse.
Asie is deuided from Europe, with Tanais the floude, whiche comyng fro the
North, ronneth into the marshe of Meotis almoste midwaie, and there sinckyng
hunself, leaueth the marshe and Pontus
Eurinus, for the rest of the bounde. And
to retourne to Afrike again, the same hauyng Nilus as I saied on the Easte, and
on all other partes, bounded with the sea,
is shorter then Europe, but broader towarde the Ocean, where it rileth into
mounteigne. And shoryng towarde the
West,

weſte, by litle and litle wareth moze
ſreighte, and cometh at thende to a na=
rowe poincte. Aſmuche as is enhabited
therof, is a plentuous ſoile, but the great
parte of it lieth waſte, voide of enhabi=
tauntes, either to whote foz menne to a=
bide, oz full of noiſome and venemous
vermine, and beaſtes, oz elles ſo whel=
med in ſande & grauell, that there is no=
thing but mere barreineſſe. The ſea that
lieth on the Moorthe parte, is called Libi=
cum, that on the Southe Aethiopicum,
and the other on the weſt Atlanticum.

AT the firſt the whole was poſſeſt by
ſower ſondzie peoples. Of the whiche,
twaine (as Herodotus wzriteth) ware
founde there, tyme out of minde, and the
other twaine ware alienes and incom=
mes. The two of continuaunce, ware the
Poenj, and Ethiopes, whiche dwelte, the
one at the Moorthe of the lande, the other
at the South. The Alienes, the Phœnices
the Grekes, the old Ethiopians, and the
Aegipcianes, if it be true that thei repozt
of thēſelues. At the beginnyng thei ware
ſterne, and vnruly, and bzutiſhely liued,
with herbes and with fleſhe of wilde bea=
ſtes, without lawe oz rule, oz faciō of life,
roiſlyng

roſtyng and rowmyng vpon heade, heather and thether without place of abode,
where night came vpon them, there lai-
yng their bodies to reſte. Aftrewarde (as
thei ſaie) Hercules paſſyng the ſeas out
of Spaine, into Libie (a countrie on the
Northe ſhore of Afrike) and bringyng
an ouerplus of people thence with hym,
ſomewhat bettre factioned and manered
then thei, trained them to muche more
humanitie. And of ȳ troughes thei came
ouer in, made themſelues cotages, and
began to plante in plompes one by another. But of theſe thinges we ſhall ſpeake
here afire more at large.

Afrike is not in euery place a like enhabited. For toward the Southe it lieth
for the moſte part waſte, and vnpeopled,
for the broilyng heate of that quartre.
But the part that lieth ouer againſt Europe, is verie well enhabited. The frute-
fulneſſe of the ſoile is excedyng, and to
muche meruetllous: as in ſome places
bringyng the ſiede with a hundred folde
encreaſe. It is ſtraunge to beleue, that is
ſaied of the goodneſſe of the ſoile of the
Moozes. The ſtocke of their vines to be
moze then two menne can fadome, and
their

their cloufters of Grapes to be a cubite
long. The coronettes of their Pasnepes,
and Gardein Thiftles (whiche we calle
Hortichockes)as also of their Fenelle,to
be twelue Cubites compaffe. Thei haue
Cannes like vnto thofe of India,whiche
may contein in the compaffe of the knot, or
iointe, the meafure of. ij. buſhelles. Ther
be sene also Sparagi, of no leſſe notable
biggueneffe. Coward the mounte Atlas
trees bee founde of a wondzefull heigth,
smothe, and without knaggue oz knotte,
vp to the hard toppe, hauyng leaues like
the Cyppzes, but of all other the moſte noble Citrus, wherof the Romaines made
greate deintie . Affrike hath also many
sondzie beaſtes , and Dzagones that lye
in awaite foz the beaſtes, and when thei
see time, fo bewzappe and wzeathe them
aboute , that takyng fro theim the vse of
their iopnctes,thei wearie them and kille
theim . There are Elephantes, Lyons,
Bugles,Pardales,Roes,and Apes, in
some places beyonde nombze, There are
also Chamelopardales and Rhizes,like
vnto Bulles . Herodote wzitteth , that
there be founde Affes with hoznes, Hie-
nas Pozpetines,wilde Rambes,a beaſt

engendꝛed of the Hiene and the Woulfe
named Thoas, Pantheres, Stoꝛckes,
Oistruthes, and many kindes of ſerpen-
tes, as Cerastes, and Aspides, againſt
whom nature hath matched the Ichneu-
mon (a berie litle beast) as a moꝛtall ennemie.

¶ The. iiij. Chapter.

¶ Of Ethioꝑe, and the auncient maners of that nation. Cap. iiij.

Two countreies there
ware of that name
Ouerlanders, and
Netherlanders. The
one pertaynyng to A-
phꝛique, the other to
Asie. The one whiche
at this daie is called
Inde, hath on the east the redde sea, and
the ſea named Barbaricum, on the noꝛthe
it toucheth bpon Egypte, and bpon that
Libie that standeth on the vtter boꝛder
of Afrike toward the sea. On the west it
is bounded with the other Libie that sta
deth moꝛe into the mayne londe. The residue that runneth toward the south, ioy-
neth bpon the netherland Ethioꝑe, whiche

the lyeth more southerly, and is muche
greater. It is thought that these Æthi-
opes toke name of Æthiopus Uulcanes
sonne, that (as Plinie saieth) was gouernour there. Or els of the Greke wordes
aythoo and ops, whereof the former si-
gnifieth to broyle, or to bourne vp with
heate, and the other, in the eye or sight.
Whiche sheweth in effecte, that the coun-
treie lyeng in the eye of the Sonne, it
must nedes be of heate almost importa-
ble. As in diede it lyeth in the full course
of the sonne, and is in continuall heate.
Toward the weast it is hilly, in the middes grauell and sande, and on the easte
waste and deserte. There be in it dyuers
peoples of sondry phisonomy and shape,
monstruous and of hugly shewe. They
are thought (as I saied) to haue bene the
fyrst of all men, and those whiche of all
other maye truelyest be called an home-
borne people. Neuer vnder the bondage
of any: but euer a free nacion. The first
waie of worshippyng God (say thei) was
deuised and taught emonge theim: with
the maners and ceremonies there to ap-
pertinent. They had two kyndes of letters, one, whiche ware knowen onely to

　　　　　their

their priestes for matters of Religion,
whiche they called misticall, and another
for the vse of the people hidden fró none.
Peat ware not their Letters racioned to
ioyne together in sillables like ours, but
Ziphres, and shapes of men and of beastes, of heades, and of armes, and artificers tooles, whiche signified in sondrie
wise echone accordyng to his propertie.
As by the picture of an hauke swiftenes
and spiede, by the shape of a crocodile displeasure or missfortune, by the figure of
an eye, good watche or regarde, and so
forthe of other. Emong their priestes,
loke whome they sawe startle aboute as
haulfe wood, him did they iudge of all o-
ther moosse holy, and making him their
king, they fall dowñe and worship him,
as thoughe there ware in him a God-
head, or as thoughe at the least he ware
by goddes prouidence giuen them. This
king for al that, must be gouerned by the
lawe, and is bounde to all thinges after
thordre of the contry. He his selfe maye
neither punishe or guerdon any manne.
But loke vpon whome he wyl haue exe-
cución done, he sendeth the minister appoincted for the purpose, to the person

with

with a token of deathe: whiche when he
hath shewed, the officier retourneth, and
the persone what soeuer he be, inconti-
nent foɔdoeth him self. So greatly ware
they giuen to thee honour of their kynges, suche a feruencie had they towarde
them, that if it foɔtuned the king thɔough
any mishap, to be maymed oɔ hurte in a-
ny parte of his bodye, as many as ware
towarde him, namely of housholde, vo-
luntarily woulde giue them selues the
lyke hurt, thinckingit an vnsitting thing
the kynge to lacke an eye oɔ the vse of a
legge, and his frindes neither to halt, ne
yet to lacke parte of their sight. They say
it is the manier also, that when the king
dieth, his friendes should wilfully dispatche theim selues and die with hym,
foɔ this compte they gloɔious and a testi-
mony of very frendship. The moste part
of them, foɔ that they lye so vnder the
Sonne, go naked: couering their pɔuiti-
es with shiepes tayles. But a feawe of
them are clad with the rawe felles of beastes. Some make them bɔieches of the
heares of their heades vp to the waeste.
They are comenly bɔeeders and grasiers
in communs together. Their shepe be of

very

very small body, and of a harde & roughe
coate . Their dogges also are neuer a
whitte bigger, but thei are fierce and har
die. They haue good store of gromel and
barly, wherof they vse to make drincke.
All other graine and fruictes thei lacke,
excepte it be dates whiche also are verye
skante. Some of them lyue with herbes
and the tender rootes of cannes or Riedes. Other eate sleshe, milke, and chese.
Meroe, was in time past the heade citie
of the kyngdome, whiche stondeth in au
Isle of the same name factioned like a shi-
elde, stretching it selfe thre thousand fur-
long alongest by Nilus. Aboute that Islande do the cattle masters dwelle, and
are muche giuen to hunting, and those
that be occupied with tilthe of the grounde
haue also mines of gold. Herodotus writeth that thethiopians named Macrobij,
do more estieme latton then thei do golde
whiche thei put to nothyng that thei cōpt
of any price . In so muche that the Ambassadours of Cambises, when thei came
thether, found the prisoners in the gaole
fettred and tied with Chaines of golde.
Some of theim sowe a kinde of graine
called Sesamus , and other the delicate
Lothon,

Lothõ. Thei haue greate plenty of Hebe꞉
num, a woode muche like Guaiacum, and
of Siliquastrum. Thei hunte Elephantes
and kyll them to eate . There be Lions,
Rhinocerotes, Basiliskes, Pardales,
and Dragones, whiche I said enwrappe
thelephauntes, and sucke them to death,
for their bloude. There be found the pre꞉
cious stones called the Iacinthe, and the
Prasne. There is also cinamome gathe꞉
red. Thei occupie bowes of woode seaso꞉
ned in the fire, of foure cubites lõg. Wo꞉
men be also trayned to the warres, and
haue for the moste parte a ring of latton
hanging throughe their lippe. Certeine
of theim worshippe the Sonne at his vp꞉
rishe, and curse him moste bittrely at his
doune gate . Diuers of thẽ throwe their
dead into Riuers, other coser them vp
in earthen cofres, some enclose them in
glasse, and kepe them in their houses a
yeare, and in the meane season worship
them deuoutly, and offre vnto them the
first of all their encreace. In the naming
of a newe king, they giue ther voice chie꞉
fly to him that is moste goodly of stature,
moste conning in breeding of catile, and
of strengthe and substaunce passing the

L.iiii.   reast.

reaſſ. The lawe hath bene, that the prieſtes of Memphis ſhoulde haue the auc-
thozitie to ſende the Ringe the token of
deathe, & to ſet vp another in the place of
the deade, whome they thoughte good.
They haue an opinion that ther are two
Goddes, one immoztall, by whome all
thinges haue their beginning, and continuaunce vnder his gouernement, and a-
nother moztall, and he is vncerteine.
Their king, and him that beſt deſerueth
of the city next vnto him, they honour as
Goddes. This was the ſtate of Ethiope
from the beginning, and many yeares
ſence.

BVT at this daye as myne Authour
Sabellicus ſaieth ÿ he learned of thoſe that
are enhabitantes in ÿ contrey: The king
of Ethiope (whome we commonly calle
Pretoianes oz Presbiter Jhon) is a man of
ſuche power, that he is repozted to haue
vndze him thze ſkoze and two other kinges. If the heade Byſſhoppes of the
Realme deſire to do, oz to haue aughte
done, al is referred vnto him. Of him be
giuen al benefices, and ſpiritual promo-
rions, which prerogatiue the Pope hath
giuen, to the maieſtie of kinges. Yet is
he

he him selfe no priest, ne hath any maner
of ordres. There is of Archebisshoppes
(that is to say of superiour and head bisshoppes) a great nombre, whiche haue e-
uery one vndre them at the least twenty
other. The Princes, Dukes, Earles,
and head Bisshoppes, and suche other of
like dignitie, when they come abrode,
haue a crosse, & a basine of golde filled ful
of earthe caried befoze them: that thone
maye put them in remembraunce that
earth into earth must again be resolued,
and ŷ other renewe the memozy of Chzistes suffering. Their priestes to haue ys-
sue, mary one wyfe, but she ones beyng
dead, it is vnlawfull to mary another.
The temples & churches ther, are muche
larger, much richer, and moze gozgeous
then ours, for the moste part boulted frō
the flooze to the toppe. They haue many
ordres of deuout men, moche like to our
ordres of Religious: as the ordre of S,
Anthony, Dominique, Calaguritani,
Augustines, and Machareanes, whiche
are bound to no colour but weare some
suche one as Tharchebysshoppe shall allowe. Next vnto the supreame and soue-
reigne GOD, and Mary the virgin his
    C.v.   mother,

mother, they haue moste in honour Thomas sirnamed Didimus. This king, of
all other the worthiest, whome they call
Gias (a name giuen him of his mighti-
nesse and power) is of the bloud of Dauid, continued from one generation to a-
nother (as they are perswaded) by so many yeres of successio. And he is not as the
moste of the Ethiopians are, blacke, but
white. Garama the chiefe citie, and as
we terme it the châbre of the king, stondeth not by building of masonrie, & car-
pentrie as ours, but striried with tentes
and pauilions placed in good ordre, of
veluet and saten, embrauded with silkes
and purples of many diuers sortes: By
an auncient ordre of the realme, the king
liueth euer in presence and sighte of his
people, and neuer soiourneth within the
walles aboue two daies. Either for that
they iudge it an vncomely thing, and a
token of delicate slouthfulnes, or elles for
that some lawe doth forbid it. His army
in the warres is ten hundred thousande
men, fiue hundred Elephantes, and horses, and Cameles, a wonderfull nomber,
and this is but a meane preparacion.
Ther are throughout the whole nacion
certeine

certeine houses and stockes, that are pē=
cionaries at armes, whose issue is as it
ware branded with the marcke of the
crosse, y skinne beyng pretely slitte. Thei
vse in the warres, Bowe, Pique, Ha=
bregeon, and helmette. Their highest di=
gnitie is priesthode, y next, shordre of the
Sages, whiche thei cal Balsamates, arD
Táquates. They attribute moche also to
the giltelesse and vprighte dealing man,
whiche vertue they estieme as the firste
staier to climbe to y dignitie of the sages.
The nobilitie hath the thirde place of di=
gnitie, and the pēcionaries aforesaid, the
fourthe. Whē the iudges haue giuen sen=
tence of life, or of deathe, the sentence is
brought to the headborough of the Citie
(whom we call the Mayour) and they
Licomegia: he supplieth the place of the
King. Lawes written thei occupy none,
but iudge accordyng to reason and cōsci=
ence. If any man be conuict of adulterie
he forfeicteth the fourtieth parte of his
goodes, but thadulteresse is punished at
home, accordyng to the discretion of the
partie offended. The men giue dowrie to
those whom thei mary withal, but not to
those y thei purchase besides. Their wo=
mens

mens attire is of Golde, (whereof that
country hathe plentie) of pearle, and of
Sarsenette. Bothe men and women are
apparelled in long garmentes downe to
the foote, slieued, and close rounde about
of al maner of colours, sauig only blacke
for that in that contry is proper for morning. They bewaile their dead. xl. dates space. In bancquettes of honour, in
the place of our frnicte (which the latine
calleth the seconde boorde) they serue in
rawefleshe very finely minced and spi-
ced, wherbpō the gestes fiede very licou-
ricely. They haue no maner of wollen
webbe, but are eyther cladde in sarsenet-
tes, or in linnen. One maner of speache
serueth not throughout the whole contry, bnt sondry & diuerse, aswel in phrase
as in namig of thinges. Thei haue twise
in the yere haruest, and twise in the yere
somer. These Ethiopians or Indianes
excepted, al the reste of the people of Li-
bia westward, are worshippers of Mahomet, and liue aftre the same sorte in
maner, that ȳ Barbariens do in Egipte
at this present, and are called Maures,
or Moores as I thincke of their outlea-
pes and wide rowming. For that people
was

was no lesse noysome to Lybie in those cursed tymes (when so greate mutacion of thinges happened, when peoples ware so chaunged, suche alteration of seruice, and religion bꝛoughte in, and so many newe names giuen vnto contries) then the Sarasens ware.

❧The.v.Chapiter.

❧Of Aegipte, and the auncient maners of that people.

Egipte is a Countrie lyyng in Affrike, oꝛ as some hold opiniõ, boꝛderyng thervpõ, so named of Aegiptus, Danaus bꝛother, where afoꝛe it was called Aeria. This Aegipte (as Plinie recoꝛdeth in his siueth boke) toucheth on the East, vppon the redde Sea, and the land of Palestine. On the west fronteth vppon Cirene, and the residue of Afrike. On the South it stretcheth to Aethiope: And on the Noꝛthe is ended with the sea, to whom it giueth name.

The notable Cities of that Countrie, ware

ware in tyme past, Thebes, Abydos, Alexandrie, Babilon, and Memphis, at this
daie called Damiate, alias Chairus or
Alkair, and the seate of the Solda, a citie
of notable largenesse. In Aegipt as Plato affirmeth, it was neuer sene rain, But
Nilus supplieng that defaulte, yerely a-
boute sainct Barnabies tide, with his o-
uerflowynges maketh the soile fertile.
It is no where of the moste parte of writers, emong the Ilandes: For that Nilus so parteth hymself aboute it, that he
fashioneth it triangle wise.

The Aegiptians firste of all other, deuised the names of the twelue Goddes,
builte vp Altares, and Images, erected
Chappelles, and Temples, and graued
in stone the similitude of many sondrie
beastes. All whiche their doynges, dooe
manifestly make, that thei came of the
Aethiopes, who (as Diodore the Sicilian
saieth) ware the firste inuentours of all
these. Their women in old tyme, had all
the trade of occupieng, and brokage a-
brode, and reuelled at the Tauerne, and
kepte lustie chiere: And the men satte at
home spinnyng, and woorkyng of Lace,
and suche other thynges as women are
wonte

wonte. The men bare their burdeins on
the heade, the women on the shulder. In
the easemente of vrine, the men rowked
doune, the women stoode vpzighte. The
easemente of ordure thei vsed at home,
but commonly feasted abzode in the stretes. No woman tooke ozdzes, either of
God, oz Goddesse. Their maner of ozdzes, is not to make seuerally foz euery
Goddesse and God, a seuerall pziest, but
al at a shuffe, in generall foz all. Emong
the whiche, one is an heade, whose sonne
enheriteth his roume by succession. The
men childzen, euen of a custome of that
people, did with good wil kepe their fathers and mothers, but the women childzen (of they refused it) ware compelled
The moste part of men in solempne burialles, shaue their heades and let theyz
beardes growe, but Thegiptians shaued
their beardes and let their heades grow.
They wzought their doughe with their
fiete, and their claye with their handes.
As the Grecians do beleue, this people,
and their offspzing, are they that vsed circumcision. Thei ozdze their wzityng frō
their right hande towarde their left, contrary to vs. It was the maner emonge
                                        them

them, that the menne should weare two
garmentes at ones, the women but one.
As the Aethiopes had, so learned they of
them, two maner of lettres: the one seuerall to the priestes thother vsed in commune. Their priestes, euery thirde daye
shaued their bodies, that there might be
none occasio of filthinesse whe they shold
ministre, or sacrifie. Thei did weare garmentes of linnen, euer cleane wasshed,
and white: and shoes of a certeine kinde
of russhes, named Papyrus, whiche aftre
became stuffe, to geue name to our paper
They neither sette beane their selues, ne
eate them where oeuer they grewe : no
the priest may not loke vpon a beane, for
that it is iudged an vncleane puls They
are wasshed euery daye in colde water
thrise, and euery nighte twise. The heades of their sacrifices (for that they vsed
to curse them with many terrible woozdes) did they not eate, but either the priestes solde them to such strangiers as had
trade emonge them, or if there ware no
suche ready in time, they threwe them in
to Nilus.

All the Egiptians offer in sacrifice, neither cowe, ne cowe calfe, because they are
halowed

hallowed to Isis their goddesse, but bulles, and bulle calues, or oxen, and steres.
For their meate they vse, moche a kynde
of pancake made of rye meale. For lacke
of grapes they vse wyne made of Barly.
They liue also with fisshe, either dried in
the Sonne and so eaten rawe, or elles
kept in pikle. They fede also vpō birdes,
and foules, firste salted, and then eaten
rawe. Quaile, and mallard, are not but
for the richer sorte. At all solempne sup-
pers, when a nomber is gathered, and
the tables withdrawen, some one of the
company carieth aboute in an open case,
the image of death, caruen out of wodde,
or drawē with the pencille as niere to the
biue as is possible, of a cubite, or two cubites long at the moste. Who shewyng it
aboute to euery of the gestes, saieth, loke
here: drinke, and be mery, for aftre thy
death, suche shalt thou be. The yonger yf
they miete their auncient, or bettre, vpon
the waye, giue them place, going somewhat aside: or yf the aunsiente fortune te
come in place where they are sitting, they
arise out of their seate. Wherin they agre
with the Lacedemoniēs. Whē thei miete
in the waye, they do reuerence to eche o-

ther

ther, bowing their bodies, and letting fal
their handes on their knees. They weare
longe garmentes of lynnen, denimed a-
bout the skirtes beneth, whiche they calle
Casiliras: ouer the which they throwe on
another white garment also. Wollen apparelle thei neither weare to the churche,
ne bewry any man in.

Nowe forasmoche as they afore time
that euer excelled in anye kinde of learning, or durste take vppon them to pre-
scribe lawe, and rule of life vnto other, as
Orpheus, Homere, Museus, Melampode,
Dedalus, Licurgus, Solon, Plato, Pithago-
ras, Samolxis, Eudoxus, Democritus, Ino-
pides, and Moses the Hebrue, with manye other, whose names the Egiptians
glorie to be cronicled with theim: trauei-
sed first to the Egiptians, to learne emõ-
gest them bothe wisedome, and politique
ordre (wherein at those daies they passed
all other) me thinketh it pleasaunte and
necessarie also, to stande somewhat vpon
their maners, ceremonies and Lawes,
that it may be knowen what they, & sondry moe haue borowed of thẽ, and translated vnto other. For (as Philip Bero-
alde writeth in his commentary vpon A

puleius

puleius booke, entituled the Golde Aſſe)
the moſte parte of the deuices that we vſe
in our Chziſtian religion, ware bozowed
out of the maner of Thegiptians. As ſur-
pluis and rochet, and ſuche linnen garmentes: ſhauen crownes, tourninges at
the altare, our maſſe ſolempnities, our oz
ganes, our kneelinges, crouchinges, pzai-
ers, and other of that kinde. The kinges of Ægipte (ſaieth Diodoze the Sicilian in his ſeconde booke) liued not at ro-
uers as other kinges doe, as thoughe me
luſteth ware lawe, but bothe in their mo-
nie collections, and daily fare and apparell, folowed the bzidle of the lawe. They
had neither ſlaue that was homebozne,
ne ſlaue that was fozein bought, appointed to attende oz awaite vpon them. But
the ſonnes of thoſe that ware pzieſtes of
honour, bothe aboue thage of twenty yeres, ⁊ alſo ſingulerly learned. That the
king hauing theſe attendant foz the body
both by daie and by night, reſtrained by
the reuerence of the company about hym
might commit nothing that was vicious,
oz diſhonourable. For men of power are
ſeldome euil, where they lacke miniſtres
foz their vnlawfull luſtes. There ware

appointed houres, bothe of the daie and
the night, in the whiche the kinge mighte
lawfully doe, what the Lawe did permit.
In the mozning, assone as he was ready,
it behoued him to peruse al lettres, suppli-
cations, and billes : that knowing what
was to be done, he might giue aunswer
in tyme : that all thinges might rightlie,
and ozdzely be done. These being dispat-
ched, whē he had washed his bodie emõg
the Pieres of y Realme, he put on some
robe of estate, and Sacrified to the goddes. The maner was, that the Pzimate,
oz head of the spiritualty (the beastes appoincted foz the sacrifices being bzought
harde to the altare, and the Kyng standing by) should with a loude voice, in the
hearing of the people, wysshe to the king
(that bare him selfe iustely towarde his
subiectes) pzosperous healthe, and good
foztune in all. And should further parti-
culerly recite the vertues of the king, his
deuoutnes and reuerence towarde God,
and clemency towarde men. Commende
him as chaste, tuste, and vpright: of noble
and great courage, sothfaste, liberal, and
one that well bzideled al his desires. Pu-
nisshing thoffendour vnder his desertes,

and

and rewarding the well doer aboue his
merites. Making a processe of these, and
such other like: in the ende with the rehersalle of the contrary vices, he cursed the
wicked & euil. Then absoluing the King
of his offences, he laied all the faulte vpon
the ministres, and attendauntes, y should
at any time moue the king to any thing
vnright, or vnlawfull. These thinges beinge done, he preached vnto the King the
blessednes of the life, led accordyng to the
pleasure of the goddes, and exhorted him
thervnto : as also to frame his maners &
doinges vnto vertue, & not to giue eare to
that, that lende men should counsaile him,
but to followe those thynges that led vnto honour and vertue. In thende, whan
the King had sacrificed a bulle, the priest
declared certain preceptes and examples
of exellente, & moste worthy men: written
in their holy scripture. To thende that the
Kynge admonisshed by the example of
theim, might ordre his gouernaunce iust-
lye, and godly, and not geue hym selfe to
couetous cloinyng, and hourdyng of tre-
sure. He neither satte to iudge, ne toke his
vacacion, ne walked abrode, ne wasshed
at home, ne laye with his Quiene, ne fi-

nally did any maner of thing, but vpōthe
prescripte of the lawe.

Their fare was but simple, nothing but
veale, and goose, and their wine by measure appoincted. So that thone should nether ouerlade the bealy, ne the other the
heade. To conclude, their whole life so
bounde vpon temperaunce, that it might
be thoughte raither to haue bene prescri-
bed them by a discrete Phisicen to preserue heithe, then by a politique Lawyer.
It semeth wondrefull that the Egiptians mighte not rule their owne priuate
life, but by the Lawes. But it semeth
more wonderfull that their King had no
liberty of him selfe, either to sitte in iudge
ment, to make collections of money, or to
punishe any man, vpon wilfulnes, stoute
stomacke, angre, displeasure, or anye vniuste cause: But to be holden vnder lawe
as a commune subiecte, and yet not to be
agreued therwith, but to thincke them sel
ues moste blessed in obeyeng & folowyng
the lawe, and other in folowing their lustes most vnhappy. As being led by them
into many dauncters, and damages.
For suche oftentimes, euen when they
know them selues to do euil, either ouer-

come with malice, and hatred, oz some
other mischiefe of the minde, are not able
to witholde them selues from the euille.
But they which by wisedome and discrecion, gouerne their liues, offende in fewe
thinges. The kinges vsing suche an equitie, and vprightnes towarde their subdi-
tes, are so tendzed againe of them, that
not onely the priestes, but all the Egiptians in generall, haue moze care foz the
health and the welfare of the Ring, then
foz their wiues, their childzens, oz any o-
ther princes.

He that to his death continueth in this
goodnesse, him being dead, do they in ge-
neral lamente. They teare their clothes,
they shut vp ý churche dozes, they haunte
no place of wonte cómune cócourse, they
omytte all solempne holy daies: and gir-
ding them selues vnder the pappes with
bzode Ribbond of Sarsenet, two oz thze
hundzed on a company, men and women
together, renewe euery daye twise, thze
skoze & rij. daies together, the buriall be-
wailing, casting dirte on their heades,
and singing in rithme the vertue of the
Ringe. They absteine from al flesshe of
beastes, all meates ý touche fire, all wine

and

and all preparation of seruice at the table. They bathe not, thei smel of no swee-
tes, they goe to no beddes, they pleasure
not in women: but as folkes that had buried their beste beloued childe, all that cō-
tinuaunce of time they lamente. During
these seuenty and two daies (hauyng prepared all thinges necessarie for the fune-
rall pompe: the laste daye of all, the bodie
beyng enbaulmed and cofred, is sette before the entrie of the Toombe. There,
aftre the custome, one redeth an abridge-
mente of all the thinges done by the king
in his life. And if there be any man disposed to accuse the deade, libertie is giuen
him. The priestes are present, & euer giue
praise to his well doinges, as they be reci-
ted. Ther stondeth also rounde about the
Toombe a multitude of the cōmunes,
which with their voices allowe asmuche
as is trew, and crie out vpon that, that is
false, with vehemēt gainsaienges. Wher
by it hath happened, that sondry kynges
by the repugnynges of the people haue
lien vntoombed: and haue lacked the honoure of bewrialle, that the good are
wonte to haue. That feare, hath driuen
the kynges of Aegipte, to liue iustly, and
vprightly,

vprightly, lesse the people aftre their dea
thes, might shewe them suche dishonour,
and beare them perpetuall hatred. This
was the maner specially, of the auncient
kynges there.

The whole realme of Egipte was diuided into Shieres: and to euery Shiere
was appoincted a Presidente, whiche
had the gouernaunce of the whole Shiere.
The reuenewes of the realme ware diuided into iii. partes: wherof the companie
of the priestes had the first parte, whiche
ware in greate estimacion emong them,
bothe for the administracion of Goddes
Seruice, and also for the good learnyng,
wherin thei brought vp many. And this
porcion was giuen theim, partely for the
administracion of the Sacrifices, & partely for the vse and commoditie of their
priuate life. For thei neither thincke it
mete, that any parte of the honour of the
Goddes should bee omitted, or that thei,
whiche are Ministres of the commune
counsaill and profecte, should be destitute
of necessary commodities of the life. For
these menne are alwaie in matters of
weighte, called vpon by the nobles, for
their wisedome and counsaille: And to
shewe

shewe(as thei can by their cónyng in the
Planettes, and Starres, and by the maner of their Sacrifices)the happe of thinges to come. Thei also declare vnto thē,
the stories of men of olde tyme, regestred
in their holy Scripture, to the ende that
accordyng to thē the kynges maie learne
what shall profighte, or disprofighte. For
the maner is not emong them, as it is e-
mong the Grecians, that one manne, or
one woman, should attende vpon the sacrifices and Ceremonies alone: but thei
are many at ones aboute the honour of
their Goddes, and teache thesame ordre
to their childrē. This sorte of menne is
priuileged, and exempte from all maner
of charges, and hath next vnto the kyng,
the second place of dignitie and honour.

The second porcion cometh to the king
to maintein his owne state, and the charges of the warres: and to shewe liberali-
tie to men of prowesse accordyng to their
worthinesse. So that the Communes
are neither burdoned with taxes nor tri-
butes.

The thirde parte do the pencionaries
of the warres receiue, and suche other as
vpō occasions are moustered to the warres,

res: that vpon the regard of the ftipende, thei maie haue the better good wille and courage, to hasarde their bodies in battaile. Their communaltie is deuided into thre sortes of people. Husbande men, Brieders of cattle, and men of occupacio The Husbandmen buyeng for a litle money a piece of grounde of the Priestes, the king, or the warriour: al daies of their life, euen from their childhode, continually applie that care. Whereby it cometh to passe, that bothe for the skoolyng that thei haue therin at their fathers handes, and the continuall practisyng fro their youthe, that thei passe all other in Husbandrie.

The Brieders, aftre like maner, learnyng the trade of their fathers, occupie their whole life therabout. We see also that all maner of Sciences haue bene muche bettred, yea, brought to the toppe of perfection, emong the Egiptians. For the craftes men there, not medlyng with any commune matiers that mighte hindre theim, emploie theim selues onely to suche sciences as the laiwe doeth permit them, or their father hath taught the. So that thei neither disdaine to be taughte,

nor

nor the hatred of eche other, ne anything elles withdraweth them frõ their crafte.

Their Judgementes and Sentences of lawe, are not giuen there at aduēture, but vpon reason: for thei surely thought that all thinges well done, muste niedes be profitable to mannes life. To punishe the offendours, and to helpe the oppressed, thoughte thei the best waie to auoide mischiefes. But to buye of the punishemente for money or fauour, that thought thei to be the very confusion of the commune welfare. Wherefore thei chase out of the chief cities (as Heliopole, Memphis, and Thebes) the worthiest men, to be as Lordes chief Justice, or Presidentes of Judgemētes, so that their Justice benche did sieme to giue place, neither to the Areopagites of the Athenienses, ne yet to the Senate of the Lacedemonians that many a daie after theim ware instituted. Aftre what tyme these chief Justices ware assembled (thirtie in nõbre) thei chase out one that was Chauncellour of the whole: and when he failed, the citie appoincted another in his place. All these had their liuynges of the kyng: but the Chauncellour more honorably then

the

the reſt. He bare alwaie about his necke a tablette, hangyng on a chaine of golde, and ſette full of ſundꝛie pꝛecious ſtones, whiche thei called Veritie and Truthe. The courte beyng ſet and begunne, and the tablet of Truthe by the Chauncellour laied furthe, & theight bookes of their lawes (foꝛ ſo many had thei) bꝛought furth into the middes emong them: it was the maner foꝛ the plaintife to putte into wꝛityng the whole circumſtance of his caſe, and the maner of the wꝛong doone vnto him, oꝛ how muche he eſtemed himſelf to be endamaged thereby. And a time was giuen to the defendant to wꝛite anſwere again to euery poinct, and either to deny that he did it, oꝛ elles to alledge that he rightfully did it, oꝛ elles to abate the eſtimate of the damage oꝛ wꝛog. Then had thei another daie appointed, to ſaie finally foꝛ thē ſelues. At the whiche daie whē the parties on bothe ſides ware herd, and the iudges had conferred their opinions, the Chauncellour of the Judges gaue ſentence by pointyng with the tablet of Veritie, toward the parte ÿ ſemed to be true. This was ÿ maner of their iudgemētes.

And foꝛaſmuche as we are fallen into mencions

mencion of their iudgementes, it shall
not be vnfyttyng with myne enterprise,
to write also the aunciente Lawes of the
Egiptians, that it maie be knowen how
muche they passe, bothe in ordre of thynges, and profite.

Fyrst to be periured was heading: for
they thought it a double offence. One in
regarde of consciece not kept toward god,
and an other in gyuynge occasion to destroy credite among men, whiche is the
chiefest bonde of their felowship. If any
wayfaryng man shuld espy a man sette
vppon with thieues, or otherwyse to be
wronged, and dyd not to his power succour & ayde hym, he was gyltie of death.
If he ware not able to succour and to re-
skewe hym, then was he bounde to vtter
the thieues, and to prosecute the matter
to enditement. And he that so dyd not,
was punyshed with a certayne nombre
of stripes, and was kept thre days without meate. He that shuld accuse any mā
wrongfully, if he fortuned afterward to
be broughte into iudgement, he suffered
the punishement ordeyned for false accu-
sers. All the Egyptians ware compelled to brynge euery man their names to
the

the chiefe Justices, and the facultie or science wherby they liued. In the which behalfe if any man lyed, or lyued with vnlaufull meanes, he felle into penaltie of death. If any man willyngly had slaine any man free or bond, the lawes condemned hym to die, not regardynge the state of the man, but the malicious pourpose of the diede. Wherby they made men afrayd to doe mischief, and death beynge erecuted for the death of a bondman, the free myght goe in more sauftie. For the fathers that slewe their chyldren, there was no punyshement of death appoynted, but an iniunction that they shoulde stande thre daies and thre nyghtes togither at the graue of the deade, accompanied with a common warde of the people to see the thyng done. Neyther dyd it seme them iuste, that he that gaue life to the childe, should lose his life for the childes death, but rather be put to continual sorowe, and to be pyned with the repentance of the diede, that other myght therby be withdrawen from the like wycked nes. But for the chyld that kylled either father or mother, they deuised this kynd of synguler torment. They thruste hym

through

through with riedes sharpned for the noses, in euery toynt all ouer his body, and
caused hym quicke to be throwen vpon a
heape of Thornes, and so to bee burned.
Judgyng that there could not be a greater wickednes emong men, then to take
awaie the life, from one that had giuen
life vnto hym. If any woman with child
ware condempned to dye, thei abode the
tyme of her deliueraunce notwithstan-
dyng: for that thei iudged it farre from
all equitie, that the gilteles should dye together with the giltie. Or that it should
be punished, where but one had offended.
Who so had in battaille or warre, withdrawen hymself from his bande, forsaken his place in the arraie, or not obeied
his capitaigne: was not condempned to
dye, but suffred for his punishemente a
notable reproche emong the whole armie.
As estiemed but a villaine, vntill with
his forwardnes and wel doyng, he could
weare into estimacion again, & at length
be restored to his former estate. And that
lawe so grewe into mennes stomacques
that thei thought suche kind of reproche,
of all punishementes the woorste, & more
greuous then death. Who so had disclo-
                                                      sed

sed any secrete to the ennemie, the Lawe
commaūded his tongue to be cutte out of
his heade. And who so clipped the coigne
oz countrefaced it, oz chaunged the shape
oz diminisshed the weighte: oz in lettres
and wzitinges, shoulde adde any thing,
by entrelinyng, oz otherwise: oz should
guelde out any thyng, oz bzyng a fozged
euidence, Obligacion oz Wille, bothe his
handes ware cutte of. That suche parte
of the bodie as had offended, mighte foz
euer beare the punishemente therof: and
the residue takyng warnyng by his ensample, might shonne the like.

There ware also sharpe punishementes
constitute, in offences concernyng women. Foz he that had deflowzed a free
woman, had his membzes cutte of, because in one offence, he had cōmitted thze
no smalle wickednesses. That is to saie,
wzong, made the woman an whoze, and
bzought in a doubte the lausulnes of her
issue. But thei that ware taken in adulterie, bothe partes byeng agreed the mā
was whipped with a thousande stripes
by tale: and the woman had her nose cut
of, wherwith beside ÿ shame she had, the
whole beautie of her face was disgraced,

and disfigured.

The Lawes that apperteigned to the trade and occupieng of men, one with another: ware made (as thei saie) by one Bocchorides. It is commaunded in them, that if money haue bene lent any manne without wzityng, vppon credite of his woozde: if the bozower deny it, he should be put to his othe, to the whiche the creditour muste stande. For thei so muche esteemed an othe, that thei thoughte no man so wicked, as wilfully to abuse it. And again, because he that was noted to sweare very ofte, lost vtterly his credite, and name: many menne affirme, that for the regard of their honesties, it happened very seldome, that any man came to his othe. Their Lawe maker also, iudgyng that vertue was the engēdzer of credite, thoughte it good by good ozdzes to accustome men to good liuyng and honestie, vpon feare to seme vnwozthie of all reputaciō. He thought it also to be against conscience, that he that without an othe had bozowed, should not nowe for his own, bebeleued with an othe. The fozfect for non paiment of the lone, mought not bee aboue the double of the somme that

was

was borowed. And paiement was made
onely of the gooddes of the borower, the
body was not arreſſable. For the Lawe-
maker thought it conueniente, that onely the gooddes ſhould bee ſubdite to the
debte, and the bodies (whoſe ſeruice was
required bothe in peare and in warre)
ſubiecte to the citie. It was not thoughte
to bee Juſtice, that the manne of warre,
whiche haſardeth his bodie for the ſauftie of his countrie, ſhould for an entereſt
of lone, bee throwen into priſone. The
whiche lawe, Solon ſeemeth to haue trā-
ſlated to the Athenienſes, vndre the name
of the lawe, Siſarea decreyng that the body of no citezein, ſhould for any maner of
entereſt be empriſoned.

The giptians alſo for thieues, had this
lawe alone, and no people els. The lawe
commaunded that as many as would
ſteale, ſhould entre their names with the
chief Prieſte: and what ſo euer was ſtol-
len, incontinente to carp the ſame vnto
hym. Likewiſe, he that was robbed was
bounde to entre with the ſaied Chieſe
Prieſt, the daie, time and houre, when he
was robbed. By this meanes the thefte
being eaſely founde out, he that was rob-

bed, loste the fourthe parte and receiued the residue, the whiche fourthe was giuen to the thiefe. For the Lawe maker (seing it was impossible vtterly to be withoute thieues) thought it moche bettre by this meanes that men bare the losse of a piece then to be spoiled of the whole.

The ordre of Mariage emong the Egiptians is not vniforme, for the priest might mary but one onely wife. All other haue as many as they wille, acording to their substaunce. Ther is no child emong them, though it be borne of a bought woman slaue, that is compted illegitimate. For they onely compte the father to be the authour of his kynde, and the mother onely but to geue place and nourishemēt to the childe. When their childrē be borne they bring them vp with so lytle coste, as a man would skantly beleue. They fiede them with the rootes of mererusshes, and other rootes, rosted in the embries, and with marshe Caubois, and colewortes which partly they seathe, and partly they roste, and parte giue them rawe. They go for the moste parte withoute hosen or shoes, all naked, the contry is so temperate. All the coste that the Parentes be-

stowe

ſowe on their children til they be of age
to ſhift for themſelues, ſurmounteth not
the ſomme of a noble.

The prieſtes bring vp the childrē, both
in the doctrine of their holye ſcriptures,
and alſo in the other kindes of learning
neceſſary for the commune life, and chiefly in Geometry and Arithmetique. As
for the roughe exerciſes of wraſteling,
ronning, daunſing, playeng at weapons,
throwyng ẏ barre or ſuche like, thei train
not their youth in, ſuppoſyng that the daily exerciſe of ſuche, ſhoulde be to roughe,
and daungerous for them, and that they
ſhould be an empeiryng of ſtrēgth. Mu-
ſique they doe not onely compte vnprofi-
table, but alſo hurteful: as making mens
courages altogether womanlyke. When
they are ſicke, they heale them ſelues, eyther with faſting or bomiting : ẏ that eyther euery eche other daye, or euery third
daye, or fourthe. For they are of opinion
that all diſeaſes growe of ſuperfluite of
meate, and that kinde of cure therfore tʊ
be beſte, that riddeth the grounde of the
griefe. Men goyng to the warres, or traueillyng the countrie, are healed of free
coſt. For the Phiſicens, ẏ Chirurgiens.

haue a ſtipende allowed them of ordenary at the charge of the communes.

In curing, they are bounde to folowe the preceptes of the auncient and allowed writers, regeſted in their holy ſcripture. If a man folowing the preſcripte of the ſcriptures can not ſo heale ý ſicke, he is not blamed for that: But yf he fortune to heale him by any other meanes then is in the ſcripture appointed, he dieth for it. For the lawe giuer thoughte that it was harde to finde a bettre waye of curing, then that ý which of ſuche antiquitie was by longe practiſe founde oute and allowed, and deliuered vnto them by ſuche a continuaunce. The Egiptians do worſhip aboue meaſure certeine beaſtes, not onely whileſt they be onliue, but alſo when they are dead. As the Catte, the Icneumon the dogge, the hauke, the Woulfe, the Cocodrille, and many other like. They are not onely not aſhamed to profeſſe the worſhip of theſe openly, but ſetting them ſelues out in the honouring of them to the vttermoſte: they compte it aſmuch praiſe and glory to them ſelues, as yf they beſtowed the like on the Goddes. And they go about on proceſſiõ with the

the propre Images of them, from citie,
to citie, and from place, to place: holding
them vp and shewing them a farre of
vnto other, which fall on their knees, and
euery one worship them. When any one
of them dieth, they couer it with Sarcenet, and houling, and crieng, and beating
of their breastes they all to bestrawe the
carckesse with salte. And aftre they haue
enbalmed it with the licour of the Cedre
and other fragraunt oyntmentes, and
oyles, to preserue it the longer: thei bewrye it in holy sepulture . If a man haue
slayne any of these beastes willingly: he
is condempned to death. But yf he haue
slaine a catte or a snyte, willingly or vnwillingly : the people ronneth vpon him
vppon heapes, and withoute all ordre of
Iustice or lawe, in moste miserable wise
torment him to death. Vpon feare of the
which daungier who soeuer espieth one
of those lyeng dead: standing a farre , he
howleth and crieth professing that he is
not giltie of y death. These beastes with
great attendaunce and chardge are kept
vp aboute the cloistres of the Temple, by
men of no meane reputation : whiche
siede them with floure and otemeale,

and diuers deinties, sopped and stieped in milke. And they set euery daie before them goose, bothe sodde and rosted. And before those that delight al in raw meate they sette birdes and rawe foules . Finally as I said they kiepe them all with great diligence and coste. They lament their death asmoche as the death of their owne childzen, & bury them moze sumptuously then their substance doth stretch. In so moche that Ptolomeus Lagus reigning in Egipt, when there chaunced a cowe to die in Memphis, foz very age: he that had taken charge of the kepyng of her, bestowed vpon the buriall of her (beside a greate some of mony that was giuen him foz the keping) siftie talentes of siluer, that he bozowed of Ptolome. Peraduenture these thynges will seme vnto some men to wondzeful: but he wil wondze asmoche yf he cō sidze what communely is done emonge euery of the Egiptians in the funeralle of their deade.

When any man is departed his lyfe, all his niere friendes and kindesfolke, chzowing dirte vpō their heades, go wieping and wailing rounde about the citie vntie the Cozps be buried . And in the

meane

meane season they neyther bathe, ne
drincke wine, or eate any meate, but that
that is most base & vile, ne weare any apparell that is gorgeous or faire . They
haue thre sortes of Sepulchres, Sumptuous, meane, and basse. In the firste sorte
they bestowe a talente of siluer . Aboute
the seconde, twenty Markes, and aboute
the thirde litle or nothing. There be certaine Pheretrers, whose facultie it is to
sette forthe the burialles, whiche learne it of
their fathers and teache it their childre.
These when a funeral happeneth, make
vnto him that is doer for the deade, an
estimate of the exequies in writing, whiche the doer may at his pleasure enlarge
or make lesse. When thei are ones fallen
at appoyncte, the bodye is deliuered to
the Pheretrer to bee enterred acordyng
to the rate that they agreed vpon. Then
the bodie beyng laied foorthe, commeth
the Pheretrers chiefe cutter, and he ap-
poincteth his vnder cutter a place on the
side haulfe of the paunche, wher to make
incision, and how large. Then he with a
sharpe stone (whiche of the country fro
whence it commeth, they call Æthiopicus)
openeth the left side as farre as the lawe
C.b.   permitteth.

permitteth. And freight with all spede
ronneth his waye frõ the compãny ſtanding by, which curſe him and reuile him
and throwe many ſtones aftre him. For
they thincke there yet remaineth a certeine hatred due vnto him that woũdeth
the body of their frinde. Thoſe that are
the ſeaſoners and embalmers of the body (whome they calle poulderers) they
haue in greaſe honour and eſtimacion,
for that they haue familiaritie with the
prieſtes, and entre the temples together
with them. The bodye nowe commen to
their handes, one emõg all (the reſte
ſtanding by) vnlaceth the entrailes, and
draweth them out at the foreſaid inciſi-
on, all ſauing the kidneis, and the harte.
Theſe entrailes are taken by another at
his hande, and waſſhed in wine of the
rountry Phenicea, wherin are enfuſed
many ſoote odours and drugges. Then
enoincte they the whole bodye ouer, firſte
with Cedze, and then with other oynte-
mētes. xxx. daies & aboue. Then do thei
ceare it ouer with Mirrhe & Cinamome
and ſuche other thinges as wil not onely
preſerue it to cõtinuaunce, but alſo make
it ſoote ſmelling. The Corps thus being
                                        trimmed

trimmed, is deliuered to ye kindesfolke of
ye deade, euery parte of it kepte so whole
(not an heare of his browes or eye liddes
being hurte) yt it raither lieth like one being in sleepe then like a dead corpse. Before ye body be enterred, ye kindesfolke of
the deade signesse to the iudges, and the
friendes of this passed, ye day of ye burial.
Whiche (accordyng to the maner then v-
sed) thei terme the deades passaige ouer
the mere. The maner wherof is this.

The iudges, aboue. xl. in nomber, sittinge on the farther side of the mere, on
a cōpassed benche wheeling haulfe roūde
and ye people standing about them: The
body is put intc a litle boate made for the
nones, and drawen ouer to the iudges
by a chorde. The body then standing before the iudges in the sight of the people,
before it be cofred, if ther be any manne
that haue aught to saye against the dead,
he is permitted by the lawe . If any be
proued to haue liued euyll, the iudges
geue sentence that the bodye shall not be
buried. And who so is founde vniustke-
lye to haue accused, suffreth greate pu-
nyshemente therfore. When no manne
wyll accuse, or he that accused is knowen
to

to haue slaunderously done it, the kinsfolke endyng their mournyng: tourne
them selues now to the prayse of ẏ dead,
nothing aftre the maner of the Grecians, for that the Egiptians thinke them
selues all to be gentlemen alike. But be
ginnyng at his childehode, in the whiche
thei reherse his bringing vp, nourtering
and scholyng, thei passe to his mannes
age, their commending his godlines, his
iustice, his temperaunce, ẏ the residewe
of his vertues. And calling vpon the vndre earthe, goddes, they beseche them to
place him emonge the godlye and good.
To the which wordes allthe whole multitude crieth Amen: showtyng oute, and
magnifieng the glorye of the deade, as
thoughe they shoulde be with the vnder
earth goddes, among ẏ blessed for euer.
This done euery man burieth his dead,
some in Sepulchres made for the purpose, and other that haue no suche preparacion, in their strongest wall at home in
their house, setting vp ẏ cofre ther taber-
bernacle wyse. But they that for some
offence, or debte of enterest, or suche like,
are denied their bewrtall, are sette vp at
home without any cofre, vntle their successours

teſſours growyng to abilitie canne diſchardge their debtes and offeces, and honourably bewrie them.

There is a maner emong them, ſometyme to borowe money vpon their parētes corpſes, deliueryng the bodies to the creditours in pledge. And who ſo redemeth theim not, ronneth into vtter infamie, and is at his death, denied his bewriall. A manne (not altogether cauſeles) mighte merueile, that thei could not be contente to conſtitute lawes for the framyng of the maners of thoſe that are on liue, but alſo put ordre for the exequies, and Hearſes of the deade. But the cauſe why thei bent them ſelues ſo muche herevnto, was for that thei thought ther was no bettre waie poſſible, to driue men to honeſtie of life. The Grekes, which haue ſet furthe ſo many thynges in fained tales, and fables of Poetes (farre aboue credite) concernyng the rewarde of the good, and puniſhment of the euill: could not with all their deuices, drawe men to bertue, and withdrawe them from bices. But rather cōtrariſwiſe, haue with them that be leudely diſpoſed: broughte all together in contempte and deriſion. But
amonge

emong the Egiptians, the punishemente
due vnto the wicked and lewde, and the
praise of the godlie and good, not heard
by tales of a tubbe, but sene daiely at the
eye: putteth both partes in remembraunce
what behoueth in this life, & what fame
and opinion thei shall leaue of them selues, to their posteritie. And hervppon it
riseth, that euery man gladly emong thē,
ensueth good ordre of life. And to make
an ende of Thegiptiãs, me siemeth those
Lawes are of very righte to be compred
the beste, whiche regarde not so muche to
make the people riche, as to aduaunce
theim to honestie and wisedome, whers
riches of necessitie must folowe.

¶ The. vj. Chapitre.

¶ Of the Poent, and thother
peoples of Iphrique.

F the Penois there
are many and sondrie
natiõs. Adrimachidæ
lieng toward Egipte,
are like of maners to
Thegiptiãs, but their
apparell is like to the
other Penois. Their
wiues

wiues haue vpon ethe legge, a houpe of
Latton. Thei delight in long heare, and
looke what lyce it fortuneth any of them
to take aboute them: thei bite theim, and
throwe theim awaie, the whiche propretie, thei onely of all the Poeni haue. As
also to present their maidens that are v-
pon mariage, to the kyng, whiche choo-
syng emong them the maiden that liketh
hym beste, sieketh in her lappe, that aftre
can neuer bee founde. The Nasamones
(a greate and a terrible nacion, spoilers
of suche Shippes as fortune to bee throwen vpon the Sandes in the streightes)
towarde Sommer, leauyng their cattle
vpon the Sea coaste, goe doune into the
plaine countrie to gather Dates, whiche
are there very faire, and in greate plentie. Thei gather the boughes with the
fruicte, not yet perfectely ripe, and laie
them a Sonnyng to ripe. Afterward thei
stiepe theim in Milke, and make soupin-
ges and potages of theim. It is the maner emong theim, for euery man to haue
many wiues: and the felowship of their
wiues, that other vse in secrete: thei vse
in open sighte, in maner aftre the facion
that

that the Massagetes vse. It is also the maner of the Nasamones, when any man marieth his first wife, to sende her about to euery one of the ghestes, to offer hym her body. And asmany as receiue her into armes, and shewe her the curtesie she comes for, must giue her some gifte, whiche she hath borne with her, home to her house. Their maner of takyng an othe, & foreshewyng of thinges to come, is thus.

Thei sweare by the menne that ware (by reporte) the best and moste iustemen emong thē, layeng their handes on their Graues, or Tumbes. But for the foreknowledge of thynges, thei come to the Graues of their kyndreade, and there when thei haue praied their stinte, laye them doune vpon them to slepe: and loke what thei dreame, that doe thei folowe. Where in cōfirmyng of our promise, we vse to strike hādes (as we calle it) thei vse to drincke one to another: or elles if thei lacke liquour, to take dusse fro the earth, and one to licke parte of that to another. The Garamantes shonne the felowship and the sighte of all other peoples: and neither vse any kinde of weapon, or armour, ne yet dare defende them selues a‐
    gainst

gainſt other that vſed them. They dwell
ſomwhat aboue the Naſamones, moze
vp londe. Aboute the ſea coaſte towarde
the weſte, ther bozdereth vpon them the
Maces: whiche ſhaue their heades in the
crowne, and clyppe them rounde by the
ſides. The Gnidanes (nexte neighbours
to the Maces) when they giue battaylle
to the oſtruthes, their bzieding vnder the
grounde, are armed with rawe felles of
beaſtes. Their women ware pzety weal-
tes of leather, euery one a greate manye
whiche (as it is ſayde) they begge of
ſuche menne as haue lien with them. So
that the moe ſhe hath, the moze ſhe is eſtemed, as a deinty derling beloued of many. The Machlies dwalling aboute the
merſhe of Tritonides, vſe to ſhaue their
fozeparte of their heade, and the Anſes
their hindze parte . The maydens of
the Anſes, at the yerely feaſtes of Minerua, in the honoure of the goddeſſe
their country womã: deuiding them ſelues into two companies, vſe to giue battaile, one parte to another with ſtaues,
and with ſtones: ſayeng that thei obſerue
the maner of their country in the honour
of her that we calle Minerua . And the
maiden

maiden.that departeth the battayle with
out wounde,thei holde her for no maide.
But before ther battayle be fought,they
determine that what maydē so euer beareth her selfe mooste valeaunte in the
fielde, all the other maydens with commune consente shall garnishe her, and
arme her,both with the armour of Grecia,and the helmet of Corinthe.And shal
sette her in a chariot, & carye her rounde
about the mershe.The same menne ksen
their women as indifferētly commune,
as kyen to the bulle . The childzen remaine with the women ontil they be of
some strengthe . Ones in a quartre the
men do assemble wholy together,& then
looke with whome the childe fantasieth
mooste to abide, him do they compte for
his father.

There is a people named Atlantes,of
the mounte Athlas, by the whiche they
dwell.These giue no names one to another as other peoples do,but echeman is
namel sse.When the sonne passeth ouer
their heades, they curse him,and reuyle
him with all woozdes of mischiefe: for
that he is so bzoiling hote,that he destroi
eth bothe them and ther countrye.

They

They eate of no kinde of beaste, neither dreame in their sliepe. The Aphres (whiche are all brieders of catteile) liue with flesshe and milke, and yet absteine they fro cowes milke, and all cowe flesshe, according to the maner of the Egiptians, and therfore kepe they none vp. The women of Cyrene thincke it not lawfull to strike a cowe, for Isis sake that is honoured in Egipt, to whome also they appointe fasting, and feastfull daies, and obserue them solempnly. But the wome of Barcea absteine bothe fro cowe flesshe and sowe flesh. When their children are iiii. yeare olde they vse to cauterise them on the coron vaine (and some on the temples also) with a medecine for that purpose, made of woolle as it is plucked fro the shiepe: because thei should not at any time be troubled with rheumes or poses, and by that meanes they say they liue in very good health. Thei sacrifise after this maner. When in the name of their firste frutes they haue cutte of the eare of the beaste, they throwe it ouer the house. That done, they wring the necke on the one side. Of all the goddes they offre sacrifice to no more but Sonne & Mone.

All

All the Aphres burye their deade as the Grecians doe, sauing the Nasamones, which bury them as thoughe they ware sitting: wayting well when any man lieth in drawing on, to set him on his taile, leaste he should giue vp the ghoste lieng vpright. Their houses are made of wickers, and withes, wrought aboute trees, moch like vnto those that we calle fräckencëce trees, and in suche sorte that they may tourne them rounde euery waye. The Maries, shaue the lefte side of their heade, and lette the heare growe on the right. They die their bodie in redde, and vaunte that they come of the Troianes. The women of the Zabiques (which are the nextneighbours to the Maries) drie the cartes in the warres, in the which the men fight. Ther are a people called Zigantes, wher beside the great plentye of hony that they gather fro the Bies, they haue also certeine men that are makers of honye. They all die them selues with red, and eate apes fleshe, wherof thei that dwel in the mounteines haue great plentye. These al being of the part called Libye, liue for the moste parte a wilde lyfe abrode in the fieldes like beastes, ma-

king

king no household prouission of meate, ne
wearing any maner of appareil but gotes felles. The gentlemē, and men of honour emong thē, haue neither cities nor
townes, but Turrettes builte vpon the
waters side, in the which they laye vp the
ouerplus of that that they occupy. They
sweare their people euery yere to obeye
their Prince, and that they that obey in
diede, shoulde loue together as felowes
and companions: but that the disobedi-
ente shoulde be pursued like felons and
traitours Their armour and weapō, are
bothe acording to the nature of the country and contrimen: for wher thei of them
selues are very quicke, and deliure of bodye, and the country champaine, and
playne, they neither vse swearde, dag-
ger, ne harneis, but onely cary thre Iauelines in their hande, and a nombre of
piked and chosen stones, in a case of stiffe
leather hāging aboute them. With these
they vse bothe to fight and to skirmishe.
In his coming towarde the ennemy, he
throweth his stone, fetching his ronne,
and maketh lightlye a narowe mysse,
thoughe it be a good waye of: suche continuall practise they haue of it . They

kepe

kiepe neither lawe ne faithe.

The Troglodites (whiche are also named of the Grecians pastours, for their fieding and breding of catteille) a people of Ethiope, do lyue in companies, & haue their heade ouer them, whome they call Tiraunte. But not meaninge in him so much tirany in diede, as some time some of our gouernours vndre a fayrer name do erecute. None of them hathe any seuerall wife, and therfore no seueral children, but bothe those in commune, the tiraunte excepted : who hathe but one wyfe onely. To the whiche yf any manne do but approche or drawe nighe : he is condempned in a certeine nombre of cattalle to be paied to the Tiraunte.

From ye beginning of July vntle about midde August (at ye which time thei haue great plenty of raine) thei nourishe them selues with milke, and bloude, sodden a litle together. The pasture vplod being, dried away with the heate of the Sonne: They sieke downe to the marshe, & lowe groundes, for the whiche onely they be often at debate. When their catteil wareth olde or sicke, they kyll them, and eate them, & altogether liue vpon such. They

do

do not giue the childe the name of the father, but name him aftre a bull, a rambe
oz an eawe. And those call thei father (the
beastes I meane of the masse kinde) and
thother of the femel kynde, they call mother, because ther daily fode is giuen by
them. The people called Idiote, vse for
their dzincke the iuyce of a whinne named Paliurus. But the men of wozshyp
and gentlemen vse the iuce of a certeine
floure they haue emonge them, whiche
maketh dzincke moche like the wozste of
ſ Reniſhe muste. And because thei cary
great dzoues of cattelle with them, they
chaunge their soile often. Their bodies
are all naked, sauing their pziuities, whiche they hide with felles of beastes. All
the Troglodites are circucised aftre the
maner of the Egiptians, sauing only the
Claudians: which they so terme of clau-
dicacion oz limping. They onely, dwellinge from their childehode within the
country of the Hesternes, are not touched with rasour oz knife. The Troglodites that are called Magaueres, carye
for theyz armour and weapon, a rounde
buckler of a rawe ore hide, and a clubbe
shodde with yzon. Other haue bowes, ⁊
Iauelins

Iauelines . As for graues or places of
buriall, they passe not. For they binde the
heade, and the fiete of the dead together
with witthes of Palurus, & then setting
it vp vpon some hilly place, haue a good
sporte to all to bethwacke it with stones,
vntle they lie heaped ouer the corps. The
laye they a gostes horne on the toppe
and departe, biddinge sorrowe go plaie
him. They warre one with another, not
as the Griekes vpon rancour and Am-
bicon, but onely for foode sake. In their
skirmishes, firste they go to it with stones, as afore ye haue hearde, vntle it fortune some nombre to be hurte. Then occupieng the bowe (wherin they are very
sure handed) thei kille one another vpon
hepes. Those battayles are attoned by
the women of mooste auncient age. For
when they be ones comen into the middle emonge them (as they maye do withoute harme, for that is compted abhomi-
nacion in any wise to hurte one of them)
the battaille sodenly ceaseth . They that
are nowe so fiebled with age, that they
can no longer folowe the heard: winding
the tayle of an ore aboute their throte
& hoke vp & die . But he that differreth to
rydde

riaoe him felfe in ths forte: It is laweful
for another(aftre a warninge)to doe it.
And it is there compted a friendly bene∙
faicte. Men also diseased of feures, or a∙
nye other incurable malady, they doe in
lyke maner dispatche: iudginge it of all
griefes the woorsse, for that manne to
liue, that canne nowe nothinge doe,
why he shoulde desyre to lyue. Herodo∙
te writeth, that the Troglodites myne
them selues caues in the grounde, wher∙
in to dwell. Men not troubled with anye
desire of riches, but raither giuing them
selues to wilfull pouertie They glory in
nothing but in one litle stone, wherin ap∙
pere thre skore sondry colours: which we
therfore calle Exaconthalitus. They eate
sondry kindes of benemous vermyne.
And speake any distincte worde they can
not, but sieme rather to busse or churre be
twene the tiethe, then to speake.

There is another people dwelling in
that Ethiope that lyeth aboue Egipte,
called Ryzophagi, whiche bestowe muche
time in digging vp of the rootes of Rie∙
des growing niere aboute them, and in
wasshing and clensing of the same. whi∙
che afterward they bruse betwixt stones

F.v.   till

til thei become clämie, & so make swiete
cakes of thē, muche facioned like a bzick
a hande bzoade. Those bake thei by the
Sonne, and so eate them. And this kinde
of meate onely, serueth them all their life
tyme, plentifully and enough, and neuer
wareth fulsome vnto theim. Thei neuer
haue warre one with another, but with
Lions, whiche comyng out of the deserte
there, partly foz shadowe, and partly foz
to pzaie vpon smaller beastes, doe oftymes wourie diuers of the Aethiopes, comyng out of the Fennes. In so muche
that that nacion had long sences bene vt-
trely destroied by the Lions, excepte nature of purpose, had shewed thē her aide.
Foz toward the dogge daies, there come
into that coaste, infinite swarmes of
Gnattes, without any dzifte of winde to
enfozce them. The men then fleing to the
fennes, are not harmed by thē. But thei
dziue the Lions with their stingyng and
terrible huszyng, cleane out of that quartre. Next vpon these, bozdze the Ilophagi
and Spermatophagi, the one liuynge by
suche fruicte as falleth from the trees, in
Sommer, and the restdew of the yere by
suche herbes as thei picke vp in the shadowed

dowed groundes. The other, the Ilopha=
gi, ſtickynge to the plaines with their wi=
ues and their childꝛen, climbe trees, and
gather, eate, and cary home: the tendꝛe
croppes and buddes of the boughes. And
thei haue by continualle pꝛactiſe, ſuche a
nimblenes in climbyng, that (a wondꝛe=
full thynge to be ſpoken) thei wille leape
from boughe to boughe, and tree to tree
like Cattes oꝛ Squirelles, and by reaſon
of their ſlendꝛenes and lightenes, wille
mounte vp on bꝛaunches and twigges,
without daunger oꝛ hurte. Foꝛ thoughe
their ſiete ſlippe, yet hang thei faſt by the
handes: and if thei bothe faile theim, yet
falle thei ſo light, that thei be harmeleſſe.

These folkes go naked, and hold their
wiues and chíldꝛe in commune. Emong
them ſelues they fighte foꝛ their places
without weapon : but againſt foꝛeiners
with ſtaues. And wheare thei ouercome,
there chalenge thei Loꝛdeſhippe. Thei
communely dye foꝛ hongre, when their
ſight faileth them: whiche was their one=
ly inſtrumente to finde their foode. The
reſidewe of the countrie there aboute, do
thoſe Aethiopians holde, whiche are na=
med Cynecy, not very many in nombꝛe,
but

but muche differing in life from the reff.
For their Countrie beyng wooddie, and
wilde, fulle of thicquettes, and skante of
watre, thei are forced by night, for feare
of wilde beaftes, to flepe in trees; and to
ward the mornyng, all weaponed together, to drawe doune to the waters, wher
thei shroude them felues into couert, and
fo abide clofe till the heate of the daie. At
the whiche tyme the Bugles, Pardales,
and other greate beaftes, what for the
heate, and what for thriffe, flocke toguether to the watres. Affone as thei haue
drunken, and haue well laden their bealies with watre, the Ethiopes ftartynge
out vpõ them with ftakes, sharpened and
hardened in the fire, and with ftones, and
with arrowes, and fuche like weapon, at
this aduauntage flea them vpon heapes,
and deuide the carkeffesby compaignies
to be eaten. And fometyme it happeneth
that thei them felues are flaine by fome
beaft of forre, howbeit very feldome. For
thei euer by their pollicies and traines,
doe more damage to the beaftes, then the
beaftes can do vnto them. If at any time
thei lacke the bodies of the beaftes, then
take thei the rawe hides of fuche as thei
latelieft

lateliest before had slaine, and clensyng
them cleane fro the heare, thei sokyngli e
laie them to a softe fire, and when thei be
throughly hette, deuide them emong the
compaignie, whiche very griedely fille
them selues of them.

They exercise their children whilest
thei be boies, to throw the darte at a sette
marke, and he that hitteth not the marke
receiueth no meate. By the whiche maner of trainyng, hongre so worketh in the
boies, that thei become excellent darters

The Acridophagie (a people border-
ryng vpon the deaserte) are somwhat lower of stature then the residewe, leane, &
exceding blacke. In the Spring time, the
weste, and Southwest winde, bringeth
vnto them out of the Deaserte, an houge
nombre of Locustes, whiche are of verie
greate bodie, and of wynge very filthily
coloured. The Ethiopians well accustomed with their maner of slighte & trade,
gather together into a lōg slade betwixte
two hilles, a great deale of rubbeshe and
mullocke, from places nighe hande, apte
for firyng, and all the grasse and wiedes
there aboute. And laieng it ready in heapes aforehande, a long the slade, whē thei
see

ſee the Locuſtes come with the winde like cloudes in the aire, thei ſet al on fire, and ſo ſwelte theim in the paſſyng ouer, that thei bee ſkante full out of the ſhade, but thei fall to the grounde in ſuche plentie, that thei be to all the Acridophagi, a ſufficient victuallyng. For thei poudre them with ſalte (wherof the countrie hath plétie) and ſo continually from yere to yere, liue by none other foode. For thei neither haue any kinde of catteille, ne fiſſhe can haue, beyng ſo farre fro the ſea. And this maner of meate ſiemeth to theim, verie pleaſaunte and fine.

Of bodie thei are very lighte, ſwifte of foote, and ſhorte liued, as not paſſyng xl. yeres, he that liueth lógeſt. Their ende is not more incredible, then it is miſerable. For whé thei drawe into age, their briedeth a kinde of winghed lice in their bodies, of diuers colours, and very horrible, and filthie to beholde: whiche firſte eate out their bealies, and thé their breſt, and ſo the whole body in a litle ſpace. He that hath this diſeaſe, firſt as thoughe he had on hym ſome tickelyng ytche, all to beſkratcheth his bodie with ſuche pleaſure, as is alſo mingled with ſome ſmart

And

And within a litle while aftre, when the lyce beginne to craule, and the bodie beginneth to mattre, enraged with the bitrenes and grief of the disease, he teareth and mangleth his whole bodie with his nailes, putting furth in the meane while many a greuous grone. Then gusheth there out of hym, suche aboundaunce of lice, that a mainne would thinke they had bene barelled in his body: & that the barel now broken, the swarme plomped out. And by this meanes, whether throughe the enfectious aire, or the corrupcion of their fieding, thei make a miserable ende

Upon the Southe border of Affrike, dwell there menne called of the Grekes Cynnamie, & of their neighbours Sauluages: Bearded, and that with aboundaunce of heare. Thei kiepe for the saufegarde of their liues, greate compaignies of wilde Mastiues: for that from midde June, till midde Winter, there entreth into their countrie, an innumerable sorte of Kine of Inde. Whether thei flie thether to saue them selues from other beastes, or come to sieke pasture, or by some instincte of nature vnknowen to manne, it is vncertaine. Against these, when the
menne

men of their owne force, are not able to
refift:thei defende themfelues by the helpe
of their dogges,and take many of them.
wherof thei eate parte whileft thei are
freffe, and parte referue thei in pouldze,
foz their aftre.niede. Thei eate alfo many
other kindes of beaftes,whiche thei hunt
with their dogges.

The laffe of all the Affriens Southe-
warde, are the Ichthiophagi . A people
boꝛderyng vpon the Troglodites, in the
Goulfe called Sinus Arabicus: whiche vnder the fhape of man, liue the life of beaftes . Thei goe naked all their life tyme,
and make compte of their wiues and their
childzen in commune.Thei knowe none
other kindes of pleafure, oꝛ difpleafure,
but like vnto beaftes , fuche as thei fiele:
neither haue thei any refpecte to vertue,
oꝛ vice, oꝛ any difcernyng betwixte good
oꝛ badde . Thei haue litle Cabanes not
farre from the Sea, vpon the clieues ſides: where nature hath made great car-
fes,diepe into the grounde, and hollowe
Guttres, and Criekes into the maigne
lande, bowtyng and compaffyng in and
out,to & fro,many fondzie waies.whofe
entringes thenhabitauntes vfe to ſtoppe
vp

vp with great heapes of calion and stones, wherby the criekes serue them now
in the steade of nettes. For when the sea
floweth (which happeneth there twise in
the daye, aboute the houres of thre, and
of nyne) the water swelleth so highe, that
it ouerfloweth into the maygne shore,
and filleth those crieques with the sea.
And the fisshe folowing the tide, and dis-
persinge them selues abrode in the maigne
londe to seeke their foode: at the ebbe
when the water withdraweth, retiring
together with it alway to the dieper places, and at laste remaining in these gut-
ters & crieques, they are stopped in with
the stone heapes, and at the lowe water
lye drie. Then come the enhabitauntes
with wyfe and children, take them, and
laye them oute vpon the rocques against
the midday sonne, wher, with the brotling
heate of the same, they be within a while
skorched and parched. Then do they remoue them, and with a litle beating seperate the fysshe fro the bones. Then put
they the fisshe into the hollowes of the
rocques, and beate it to pomois, ming-
linge therewith the siede of the whynne
Paliurus. And so facion it into lumpes

G.i.　　　much

muche like a bꝛicke, but somewhat longer. And when they haue baken them a-
gaine a litle by the sonne, they sitte them
downe together, and eate by the bealy.
Of this haue thei alway in stoꝛe, accoꝛ-
dinge to the plenty that Neptune gyueth
them. But when by the reason of tempest
the sea ouerfloweth these places aboue
his naturall course, and tarieth longer
then his wonte, so that they can not haue
this benefight of fisshing, and their stoꝛe
is all spent: they gather a kynde of great
shelle fysshe, whose shelles they grate o-
pen with stones, and eate the fisshe rawe,
in taste muche like to an oyster. If it foꝛ-
tune this ouerflowing by the reason of
the winde, to continue longe, and their
shellefysshe to fayle them: then haue they
recours to the fysshebones (which they do
of purpose reserue together in heapes)
and when thei haue gnabeled of the sof-
test and grislely partes with their tiethe,
of those that are newest and beste, they
beate the harder with stones into pieces,
and eate thē. Thei eate as I haue said in
the wilde field together abꝛode, reioising
with a semblaunte of merinesse, & a maner of singyng full vntuned. That done
they

they falle vppon their women, euen as
they come to hande withoute any choyse:
vtterly voide of care, by reason they are
alwaye sure of meate in good plentye.
Thus foure daies euer continual, busied
with this bealy bownsing chiere, the. v.
daie thei flocke together to go dzincke, al
on a dzoue, not vnlike to a heard of kiene
to the waters, shouting as they go with
an yzishe whobub. And when they haue
dzonke till their bealies stonde a strutte,
so that thei are skåt able to retourne: eue
rye bodie layes him downe dzonckarde-
like to rest his water bolne bealy, and
that daye eateth nothing. The next daye
agayne they fail to their fysshing: And so
passe they their lyfe continually.

Thei seldome falle into any diseases, foz
that they are alway of so vnifozme diete
Neuerthelesse they are shozter lyued thē
we are. Theyz nature not cozrupted by
any perswasion taken of other, compteth
the satisfieng of hōgre, the greatest pleasure in the wozld. As foz other extraozde-
nary pleasures, they seke them not. This
is the maner of liuing propze vnto them
that lye within the bosome of the sayde
Arabique sea. But the maner of them

G.ii.   that

that dwell without the bosome, is moche
more mervueilous. For thei neuer drinke
ne neuer are moued with any passion of
the mynde. These beynge as it ware by
fortune throwen oute into the desertes,
farre from the partes miete to be enhabited, giue them selues altogether to fyſ-
ſhing, which they eate haulfe rawe. Not
for to auoyde thirſte (for they desire no
moyſte thinges) but raither of a nature
saulvage and wilde, contented with such
victualle as commeth to hande. They
compte it a principal blessednes to be with
oute those thinges what so euer they be,
that bringe sorowe or griefe to their ha-
uers. Thei are reported to be of such pa-
cience, that thoughe a manne ſtrike them
with a naked sweard, thei wil not ſhonne
him, or flye from him. Beate them, or do
theim wronge, and they onely wil looke
vppon you, neither ſhewinge token of
wrathe, nor countenaunce of pitie. Thei
haue no maner of speache emong them:
But onely ſhewe by signes of the hande,
and nodding with the heade, what they
lacke, and what they would haue. These
people with a whole consent, are mayn-
teners of peace towarde all men, ſtraun-
ger,

ger and other. The whiche maner al
thoughe it be wondzefull,they haue kept
time oute of mynde. Whether thzoughe
longe continuaunce of custome, oz dzi
uen by necessitie,oz elles of nature: I can
not saye. They dwell not as the other,
Icthiophagi doe, all in one maner of ca
banes,but sondzy in diuers. Some haue
their dennes,and their cabanes in their
opening to the Nozth: to the ende they
might by that meanes be the bettre sha
dowed fro the sonne,and haue the colder
ayze. Foz those that are open toward the
southe,by the reason of the greate heate
of the sonne,caste fozthe suche a bzeathe,
foznais like, that a manne can not come
niere them. They that open towarde
the nozthe,builde them pzeaty Cabanes
of the ribbes of whales (whiche in those
seas they plentuously finde)compassing
them aboute by the sides, accozdynge to
their naturall bendinge, and fasteninge
them together at bothe endes with some
maner of tyenge. Those do they couer
with the woose and the wiedes of the sea
tempered together. And in these they
shzoude them selues fro the sonne: na
ture by necessitie deuising a way how to

helpe

helpe and defende her selfe.

Thus haue ye hearde the lyfe of the Icthiophagi, and now remaineth there for Aprique onely the Amazones to be spoken of, which menne saye in the olde tyme dwelte in Libye. A kinde of warlike women, of greate force, and hardinesse, nothing lyke in lyfe vnto our women. The maner amonge them was to appointe to their maidens a certein space of yeres to be trayned, and exercysed in the feictes of warre. Those beynge expired, they ware ioyned to menne for yssues sake. The women bare all the rule of the commune wealthe. The women ware princes, lordes, and officiers, Capiteines, and chiefteines of the warres. The menne had noughte to doe, but the drudgery at home, and as the women woulde appointe them. The children assone as thei ware borne, ware deliuered to the men to nourysche vp with milke, and suche other thinges as theyr tendrenes required. If it ware a boye, they eyther brake the right arme assone as it was borne, that it mighte neuer be fytte for the warres, or slue it, or sente it oute of the countrye. If a wenche, they
streighte

ffreight ceared ẏ pappes, that theī might
not growe to hindꝛe them in the warres
Therfoꝛe the Grecians called theim A-
mazones, as ye woulde saie, pappelesse.
The opinion is, that theī dwelt in the I-
londe named Hespera, which lieth in the
marsshe, named (of a riuer that ronneth
into it) Tritonis, ioyning vpon Æthiope,
and the mounte Atlas, the greatest of
all that lande. This Ilonde is very
large and greate, hauyng plentie
of diuers soꝛtes of fruictes,
whereby the enhabi-
tauntes liue. Theī
haue many
flockes of shiepe, and
goates, and other
smalle catteile,
whose milke
and flesshe they eate. They
haue no maner of graine,
ne knowe what
to doe ther-
with.

¶The firſt Chapitre.

¶Of Iſie and the peoples
moſte famous therin,

Sie, the ſe=
conde part of
the thꝛe wherin
to we haue ſaid
that the whole
erth is diuided :
tocke name as
ſome hold opini
on, of the dough
ter of Oceanus, and Tethis, named Aſia,
the wife of Japhetus, and the mother of
Pꝛometheus. Oꝛ as other affirme, of A-
ſius, the ſonne of Maneye the Lidian.
And it ſtretcheth it ſelf from the South,
bowtyng by the Caſte into the Noꝛthe:
hauyng on the Weſt parte the two ſloud-
des, Nilus and Tanais, and the whole
Sea Eurinum, and parte of the middle
earth ſea. Upon the other thꝛe quarters,
it is lyſſed in with the Oceean, whiche
where he cometh by Caſte Aſie, is called
       G.b.   Eous

Eous (as ye would saie toward the daw-
nyng) by the South, Indicus (of the countrie named India) and aftre the name of
the scoure Scithiane , vpon the Northe
Scythicus. The greate mounteine Taurus
ronnyng East and West, and in a maner
equally partyng the lande in twaine: leaueth one parte on the Northe side, called
by the Grekes the outer Asie: and another on the South, named the inner Asie.
This mountein in many places is foūd
thre hundred. lxxv. miles broade: and of
length equalle with the whole countrie.
About a fiue hundred thre skore and thre
miles. From the coast of the Rhodes, vn
to the farthest part of Inde, and Scithia
Eastwarde. And it is deuided into many
sondrie partes , in sondrie wise named,
wherof some are larger, some lesse. This
Asie is of suche a sise, as auchours holde
opinion, that Affrike and Europe ioyned
together: are scante able to matche it in
greatnes. It is of a temperate heate and
a fertile soile, and therfore full of all kindes of beaste, foule, and worme, & it hath
in it many countries and Seignouries.

On the other side of the redde Sea, o-
uer against Egipte in Affrike: lieth the
tripartite

tripartite region, named Arabia, whose
partes are, Petrea: boundyng West and
Northe vpon Siria: and right at frontes
before hym Eastwarde, Deserta: and A-
rabia Felix by Southe. Certein writers
also adioyne to Arabia: Panchria, and
Sabea. It is iudged to haue the name of
Arabus, the sonne of Appollo & Babilons

   The Arabiens beyng a greate people,
and dwellyng very wide, and brode : are
in their liuyng very diuers, and as soun-
drie in religion. Thei vse to go with long
heare vnrounded & forked cappes, somewhat mitre like, all aftre one sorte, and
their beardes partie shaue. Thei vse not
as we doe, to learne faculties and sciences one of another by apprenticehode, but
looke what trade the father occupied, the
same doeth the sonne generally applie
hymself to, and continue in. The mooste
aunciente and eldest father that can be
founde in the whole Countrie, is made
their Lorde and Kyng. Looke what possessions any one kindrede hath, the same
he commune to all those of that bloude:
Yea one wife serueth theim all. Wherefore he that cometh firste into the house,
laieth doune his faulchon before the dore,
                   as

as a token that the place is occupied. The
seniour of the stocke enioieth her alnight.
Thus be thei al brethren and sistren one
to another, throughout the whole people.
Thei absteine fro the embrasinges neither of sister ne mother, but all degrees
are in that poynct as indifferent to them,
as to beastes of the fieldes. Yet is adulterie death emong them And this is adulterie there: to abandon the body to one of
another kindred. And who so is by suche
an ouerthwarte begotten: is iudged a ba-
stard, and otherwise not. Thei banquet
not lightly together, vndre the nombre of
thirtie persones. Alwaie foreseene that,
two of the same nombre at the leaste, be
Musicens. waiters haue thei none, but
one kinsman to minister to another, and
one to helpe another. Their tounes and
cities are wallesse, for thei liue quietly &
in peace one with another. Thei haue no
kinde of ople, but that whiche is made of
Sesama, but for all other thynges, thei
are most blessed with plentie. Thei haue
Shiepe greater then Kien, and verie
white of woulle. Horses haue thei none,
ne none desire, for that their Chamelles
in all niedes serue thē aswell. Thei haue
siluer

siluer and golde plentie, and diuerse kindes of spices, whiche other coūtries haue
not. Laton, Brasse, Iron, Purple, Sa-
fron, the pretious rote costus, and all coruen woorkes, are brought into theim by
other. They bewrie their kyng in a dong-
hille, for other thei wille skante take so
muche laboure. There is no people that
better kiepeth their promise and coue-
naunt, then thei do, & thus thei behight it

When thei wille make any solempne
promise, couenaunte, or league, the two
parties commyng together, bryng with
them a thirde. who standyng in the middes betwixte theim bothe, draweth bloud
of eche of them, in the palme of the hand,
along vnder the rote of the fingres, with
a sharpe stone: and then pluckyng from
eche of their garmentes a litle taggue, he
enoynteth with that bloude seuen other
stones, lieng ready betwixte theim for
that purpose. And whilest he so doeth, he
calleth vpon the name of Dionisius and
Vrania, whom thei accompt emong the
nombre of goddes, reuengers of faithe-
lesse faithes. This done, he that was the
sequestrer of the couenaunte, becometh
suretie for the parties. And this maner of
contracte

contracte, be that standeth moste at libertie, thinketh mēte to be kepte.

Thei haue no strynge but broken endes & chippes of Myrrhe, whose smoke
is so vnholsome, that excepte thei with-
stode the malice therof with the perfume
of Styrax, it would brede in them vncu-
rable diseases. The Cinamome whiche
groweth emong theim, none gather but
the priestes. And not thei neither, before
thei haue sacrificed vnto the goddes. And
yet further thei obserue, that the gatheryng neither beginne before the Sonne
risyng, ne cōtinue aftre the goyng doune
He that is lorde and gouernour emong
them, when the whole gather is broughte
together, deuideth out vnto euery man
his heape with a Iauelines ende, whiche
thei haue ordinarily consecrate for that
purpose. And emongest other, the Sonne
also hath a heape deuided out for hym,
whiche (if the deuision be iuste) he kinde-
leth immediatly with his owne beames,
and brenneth into asshes. Some of the A-
rabiens that are pinched with penurie,
without all regard of body, life, or helth,
doe eate Snakes, and Addres, and suche
like vermine, and therefore are called of
the

the Grekes Ophyophagi.

The Arabiens named Nomades, occupie much Chamelles, bothe in warre,
and burden, and all maner cariage, farre
and nighe. The floude that ronneth a-
longe their bordes, hathe in it as it ware
small of golde in great plentie. Whiche
they neuertheles for lacke of knowledge
do neuer fine into masse.

Another people of Arabia named De-
boe, are for the great part shepemasters,
and brieders. Parte of thē notwithstan-
ding, occupie husbandrie, & tilthe. These
haue suche plētie of gold, that oftetimes
emōg the cloddes in the fieldes thei finde
litle peables of gold as bigge as akeror-
nes, whiche thei vse to set finely with stones, and weare for owches aboute their
necke & armes, with a very good grace.
They sell their golde vnto their borde-
rers for the thirde parte of Laton, or for
the halfe parte of siluer. Partly for that
they nothing estieme it, and specially for
the desire of the thinges that foreiners
haue. Nexte vnto them lie the Sabeis,
whose riches chiefely consisteth in encence, Myrrhe and Cinamome, howbeit some holde opinion also that Baulme
groweth

groweth in some places of their borders.
Thei haue also many date trees very re-
dolente of smelle, and the roote called
Calamus.

There is in that contry a kinde of ser-
pentes lurking in the rootes of trees, of
haulfe a foote lengthe, whose bitinge is
for the moste parte death. The plenty of
swiete odours, and sauours in those quarters, doeth verely stuffe the smelling. And
to auoyde that incommoditie, they often
times vse the fume of a stincking gōme,
and gotes heare chopped together. Ther
is no man that hath to do to giue sentēce
vpon any case but the king. The mooste
parte of the Sabeis apply husbandrye.
The residewe gatheringe of spices, and
drugges. They sayle into Ethiope for
trade of marchaundise, in barkes couered with leather. The refuse of their cinamome and Cassian they occupy for fi-
ring. Their chiefe citie is called Saba,
and stondeth vpon a hyll. Their kynges
succede by discent of blonde, not any one
of the kindred certeine, but su he as the
people haue in moste honour, be he good
be he badde. The king neuer dare be sent
oute of his Palace, for that there goeth
                                    an

an olde prophecie emong them of a king
that shoulde be stoned to deathe of the
people. And euery one feareth it shoulde
lighte on him selfe. They that are about
the king of the Sabeis:haue plate bothe
of siluer and golde of all sortes, curious-
ly wrought and enkallied. Tables,four-
mes, trestles of siluer,and all furniture
of household sumptuousaboue measure
They haue also Galeries buylte vppon
great pillours,whose coronettes are of
golde and of siluer. Cielinges, voultin-
ges,dores and gates couered with siluer
and golde,and set with precious stones:
garnisshinges of puorpe, and other rare
thinges whiche emong men are of price.
And in this bounteous magnificece haue
thei continued many yeres. For why the
gredy compasse how to atteyne honoure
with the vniuste rapine of other mennes
goodes,that hath tombled downe headel-
ling so many commune wealthes,neuer
had place emong them. In richesse equal
vnto them,are the Garres,whose imple-
mentes of household are all of golde and
siluer. and of those and yuorie together,
are their portalles, their cielinges, and
rophes,made.The Nabatheens of all o-
ther

H.i.

ther Arabiens are the beſte huſbandes, and thriftieſt ſparers. Their caſte is wittye in winning of ſubſtaunce, but greater in kepinge it. He that appaireth the ſubſtaunce that was lefte him, is by a commune lawe puniſhed: and contrariwiſe he that encreaſeth it, muche praiſed and honoured.

The Arabiens vſe in their warres ſwerde, bowe, launce, ſlinge, and battle are. The rable of helhoundes (whom we calle Saraſines) that peſtilent murreine of mankinde, came of this people. And as it is to be thoughte, at this daye the great parte of Arabia is degenerate into that name. But thei that dwell towarde Egipte, kepe yet their olde name, & lyue by butin, like prickers of the bordre, wherin, the ſwiftenes of their camelles doeth them good ſeruice.

The ſeconde Chapitre.

Of Panchaia, and the maners of the Panqueis.

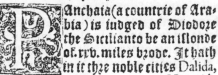

Anchaia (a countrie of Arabia) is iudged of Diodore the Siciliā to be an iſlonde of .xxb. miles brode. It hath in it thre noble cities Dalida, Hyracida

Hyractda, ⁊ Oceanida. The whole contrie
(excepte a litle vaine of sandie grauelle)
is fertile and plenteous: chiefely of wine
and encence. Whiche groweth ther in
suche aboundaunce, that it sufficeth the
whole worlde for the francke sume of-
feringe. There groweth also good store
of Myrrhe, and diuers other redolente
thinges, whiche the Panqueis gather,
and selle to the merchauntes of Arabia.
At whose hande other busienge them a-
gaine, transporte them into Ægipte, and
Sirie. And fro thence they are spred a-
brode to al other peoples. The Panqueis
in their warres vse wagons aftre the
maner of menne in olde time.

Their commune wealth is deuided into thre sondry degrees. The firste place
haue the priestes, to whome are ioyned
the artificers. The seconde the housebād
men. And the thirde the menne of warre:
with whom the catteile maisters or bree-
ders be coupled. The priestes are ỹ heades, and chiefe of all the residewe, and
haue aucthoritie aswell in sentence of
lawe, as to put ordre in al ciuile affaires:
the sentence of deathe onely excepted.

The housebandemen, tille the grounde,
and

and attende vpon the fruictes, and bring all into the commune store. And thei that shalbe founde moste diligente in that laboure and occupation: are chosen by the priestes (but not aboue the nombre of ten at one time) to be iudges ouer the distributió of the fruictes, vpon consideracion that other by their aduauncement might be stirred to like diligence. The catteile maisters, yf ther be any thing either apperteining to the sacrifices, or commune affaires, touching nombre, or weight, do it with all diligence.

No man amonge the Panchais hath any thinge that he can call proprely his owne: his house, and his gardein excepted. For bothe the customes, & reuenewes, and all other profectes, are deliuered into the priestes handes. Who acordinge as they finde necessarie and expediente, iustely distribute them. But they them selues are graunted double share. Their garmentes by the reason of the finesse of the wolle of their shiep specially aboue other, are verye softe and gentle clothe. Bothe menne and women vse ther, to sette oute them selues with Iuelles of golde, as cheines, braselettes,

tes, earringes, tablettes, owches, ringes, Annuletes, buttons, broches and
shoes embraudred, and spangled with
golde, of diuers colours. The menne
of warre serue onely for the defence of
their country.

The priestes aboue all other, giue them
selues vnto plesaunte life, fine, nette and
sumptuous. Their garmentes are rochet-
tes of fine linnen, and sometime of the
deintiest wollen. Upon their heades thei
weare mitres embraudred, and garnished with golde. They vse a kinde of bar-
ded shoes (whiche afterwarde the Grie-
ques toke vp, and called sandalium) very
finely made, and of sondry colours. And
as the women weare, so do they, all ma-
net of Iuelles sauing earinges. Their
chiefe occupacio is to attende vpon goddes seruice, settinge forthe the worthie
diedes of the goddes, with hymnes, and
many kindes of commendacion. Yf thei
be founde without the halowed grounde,
it is lawfull for any manne to slea them.
They saye that they came of the bloude
of Iupiter Manasses, at suche time as he
came firste into Panchaia, hauinge the
whole worlde vndre his dominion. This

B.iii.   country

countrie is full of golde, siluer, latton, tinne, and yron, of the whiche it is not lawful to carie any one out of y realme. The giftes both of siluer & golde, whiche in greate nombre of longe time, haue bene offred to their goddes, are kepte in the temple: whose dores are by excellent workemanship garnished with golde, siluer and puorle. The couche of their God is. vi. cubites longe, and foure cubites brode, all of golde, gorgeous of worcke, and goodly to beholde. And by that, is there sette a table of like sorte in euerie pointe: for sise, stuffe, and gorgeousnes. They haue but one temple, all of white stone, builte vpon pilours, grauen, and embossed, thre hundred and. xxxviii. taylours yardes square. that is to saye, euen of lengthe and brodthe, euery waye so muche. And somewhat according to the syse of the temple, it is sette full of highe ymages very precious: coruen and grauen. Rounde about the temple haue the priestes their habitacion. And all the grounde aboute them. xxb. myle compasse: is halowed to their goddes. The yerely rente of that grounde is bestowed vpon sacrifice.

The

¶ The .iij. Chapitre.

¶ Of Aſſiria and Babilonia, and the maners of thoſe peoples.

S ſaieth ſaint Auguſtine, the countrie called Aſſiria, was ſo named of Aſſur, the ſonne of Sem. And at this daie, to the ende that time might be founde an appatrer of al thinges, with the loſſe of a ſillabe is becomen Siria: Hauyng for his bounde, on the Eaſt, the countrie called Inde, and part of Media. On the Weſt the floude Tygris, on the Southe Suſiana, and on the Northe the maigne mounteigne Caucaſus. It is a deintie to haue in Aſſiria a ſhowre of raine: and therefore are thei conſtreined for the due moiſtyng of their lande, to tolle in the riuers by pollicie of trenching and damming: wherwith thei ſo plentiſie their grounde, that thei communely receiue two hundred buſſchelles for a buſſhell, and in ſome ſpeciall beſre, three hundred for one. Their blades of

D.iiij.   their

their wheate and Barlie are sowze fin-
gers bzode. Their Sesamum, and Milium
(Somer coznes) are in groweth like vnto trees. All the whiche thinges Herodotus the histozien, thoughe he knoweth the
(as he wziteth) be to vndoubtedly true,
yet would he that men toke aduisemente
in the repoztyng of theim: foz that thei
mighte seme vnto suche as neuer sawe
the like, incredible. Thei haue a tree called Palma, that beareth a kinde of small
Dates. This fruicte thei fede muche vppon, and out of the bodie of the tree, thei
dzaw at one time of the yere a liquour oz
sappe, wherof thei make bothe wine and
hony. In their fresh waters thei vse boates facioned round like a buckler. which
the Armenians that dwelle aboue them,
do make of salowe wikers wzought one
within an other, and couered with rawe
leather. The appareile of the Assyzians
is a shirte downe to the foote, and ouer
that a shozt garment of wollen, and last
of al a saize white pleicted cassaque doun
to the foote agayne. Their shoes are not
fastened on with lachettes, but lyke a
poumpe close about the foote. Which also the Thebans dydde vse, and but thep
twaine

twayne, no moe. They suffre theyr heares to growe and couer them with pre-
ty forked cappes somwhat mytrelyke.
And when they goe abroade, they be-
sprinkle them selues with fragraunt oyles, to be swete at the smelle. They haue
euery man a ryngs with a signet, and also a sceptre finely wrought: vppon whose
toppe thei vse to sticke either an apple, or
a rose, or a lillye, or some lyke thynge.
For it is a dishonour to beare it bare.

Emongest all the lawes of that people
I note this chiefly as worthie memorie.
Whē their maidens came to be mariage
able, thei ware frō yere to yere, brought
foorthe into the Marquette, for suche as
would buye them to be their wiues. And
because there ware some so hard fauou-
red, that menne would not onely be loth
to giue money for them, but some menne
also for a litle money to take theim: the
fairest ware first solde, and with the prices of theim brought into the communs
Treasourie, ware the fowler bestowed.
Herodote writeth that he heard by reaporte, that the Heneti (a people on the bordre of Italie towarde Illiria) ware wonts
to vse this maner. Whervppon Sabellicus

takyng an occasion, wꝛiteth in this maner. whether there ware suche a maner
vsed emong that people (saieth he) oꝛ not
I haue litle moꝛe certaintie to saie foꝛ
my self then Herodote had. But thus
muche am I able to saie: that in Uenice
(a citie of famous woꝛthines, and whose
power is well knowen at this daie, to be
greate, bothe by Sea and by lande) suche
maner as I shall saie, was sometyme v-
sed. There was in the Citie of Uenice, a
place dedicate, as ye would saie to our
Ladye of Pietie. Befoꝛe whose dooꝛes it
happened a child oꝛ twaine, begotten by
a skape (whiche either foꝛ shame oꝛ necessitie could finde no mother, oꝛ foꝛ the
nombꝛe of parteners, no one pꝛopꝛe father) to bee laide. And when by the good
Citezeins suche tendꝛeues had been shewed to two, oꝛ thꝛe, as the mothers loked
foꝛ, and manhode (to saie the truthe) doth
require: the doꝛe of pitie became so fruict-
full a mother, that she had not now one
oꝛ twoo in a yere, but thꝛee oꝛ fower in a
quarter. Whiche thyng when the gouernours of the citie perceiued, thei toke oꝛdꝛe by commune consente, that frõ thens
fooꝛthe suche women childꝛen onely, as
  theuld

should fortune so to bee offred to Pietie, should bee nourished at the commune charge of the citie, & none other. And for those acordyngly, thei ordeined a place wher thei ware brought up, hardly kepte in, and diuersly enstructed acordyng to their giftes of witte and capacitie, untill thei ware mariage able. At the whiche tyme, she that had beautie and good qualities bothe, found those a sufficient dowrie to purchase her choyse of husbandes. And she that hadde but beautie alone, thoughe her qualities ware not so excellente, yet for her honestie that beside forth was singuler in theim all, founde that beautie and honestie could not be unmaried. These therfore ware not permitted to euery mannes choise, but graunted to suche as ware thoughte menne worthie of suche women. If there ware any that lacked the grace of beautie, yet if she ware wittie, and endewed with qualities (together with her honestie) a small dowrie purchased her a husbad in good time. But if there ware any in who there happened neither commendacion of beautie nor wit, but onely bare honestie: for her bestowyng was there a meane found by

waye

wase of deuocio, as we terme it whe we
signifie a respecte of holines in the dede.

Menne vnmaried beyng in daungier
vpon Sea o2 on Lande, o2 veyng so2e di-
stressed with sickenes, makyng a vowe
fo2 the recouerie of healthe, where vnto
thei holde them selues bounden in conscience (if it fo2tuned theim at that tyme to
be deliuered) fo2 satisfactio of their vowe
in that case not vp2ightly perfourmed, v-
sed to take fo2 their wiues, suche of the
simplest as other had left. So that in p2o-
cesse thei alwaie founde husbandes, and
the commune wealthe a diminishyng of
charge.

Another Lawe of the Babilonians
there was, mo2e wo2thie of memo2ie a
greate deale, fo2 that it impo2ted mo2e
weight. And that was this. Thei had fro
their beginnyng no Phisicens emong
theim, but it was enacted by the consente
of the Realme, that who so was diseased
of any malady, should comon with other
that had bene healed of the like afo2e.
And acco2dyng to their counsaille, p2actise
vpon himself. But he that vsed o2 attempted any other waie, to be punished fo2 it.
Other w2ite that the sicke ware b2ought
out

out into the Marquet place, where suche
as had bene deliuered of the like grief
afoze: ware bounde by the lawe, to go fro
persone to persone, and shewe theim by
what meanes thei had bene remedied.

Thei bewzie their dead in Honie, and
obserue the same maner of mournyng
that the Egiptians do. If any man haue
medled with his wife in the nighte, neither of theim bothe toucheth any thyng
the nert mozning, befoze thei be washed:

There was in Babilon a Temple ve-
dicate to Venus, & it hath bene the maner in tyme paste, that when their came
any straunger to visite this Temple, all
the women of Babilon should come vnto hym oz them, with greate solempnitie
and fresshely appareiled, euery one hauing a garlande on her heade, with some
seueralle knowledge or distinction one
frô another, and offre their seruice to the
straungier. And looke whom he liked, he
must laie doune in her lappe, suche sôme
of money as pleased him. That done thei
bothe withdzew themselues fro the temple a greate distaunce, and laie together.
That money was consecrate to Venus.

There ware certein kindzedes emong
theim

theim, that liued with none other thyng but fisshe dryed against the Sonne, and brused in a mortare, and so laied vp till nede ware. And then did thei mingle it, and kneade it with water into a maner of paaste, and so baked it, & eate it. There ware thre sortes of menne that bare rule and office emong them. The king, the nobles with the Seniours, and thole that had serued in the warres and ware now exemute. Thei had also menne skilfull in the secretes of nature, whiche thei calle Magi, and Chaldej, suche as ware the priestes of Egipte, institute to attende vpon the seruice of their Goddes. These men all their life daies, liued in the loue of wisedome, & ware connyng in the cours of the Sterres. And sometyme by foretokenyng of birdes flight, and somtyme by power of holy verses and nombres, tourned awaie the euilles fro menne, and benefited the with thinges that ware good. Thei could expounde Dreames, and declare the significacions of vncouth wondres. So that men ware certein of suche successe, as thei had foresshewed. Thei wente not into straunge scholes to learne their knowledge, as the Grecians doe,

but

but learned the science of these thynges
at their fathers hādes, as heiritage from
one generacion to another, euen from
their childhode at home in their houses.
Whereby it came to passe that beyng so
kingly learned, it was bothe the more
groundedly learned, and also without
tediousnes. Thei had one vniforme and
constaunt waie of teaching, and one constantnes of doctrine, not waueryng and
almoste contrary to it self, as the doctrine
of the Grekes: where eche Philosopher
almoste had his waie, and iudgemente,
of the principles and causes of thynges.
But these menne agre al in one, that the
worlde is eternall and euerlastyng, with
out beginnyng and without ende. And
that the ordre of the whole, was disposed
by the prouidence of the highest. The bodies aboue to haue their course, not at all
aduentures and without rule, but by an
inuiolable lawe of God, acordyng to his
ordenaunce and will moste certein. Thei
haue learned by long markyng and no-
tyng of thynges tyme out of mynde, one
aftre another: how by the course of the
Starres, to prognostique, that is to foreshewe vnto men, many thynges to come
Thei

Thei holde that of all other Sterres, the planetes are strongest of Influence, namely Saturnus. To the sonne thei attribute brightnes and vertue of life. Mars Jupiter, Mercurie, and Uenus, thei obserue moste (for that thei haue a course propre by them selues) as interpretours of the mindes of the goddes to foresignifie thinges vnto men. Which opinion is so grounded in them, that they haue called all those foure planetes, by the one name of Mercurius. as ye woulde saye commune currours or messengers. Thei also do warne menne of many thinges, bothe hurtefull and abaileable: by the marking, and knowledge of winde and weather, of raine and droughte, of blasing sterres, of the eclipses of the Sonne and Mone, of earthquakes, and manye suche like.

Furthermore thei ymagine in the firmament other sterres, subiecte in influence vnto these former. wherof some are in the haulfe heauen continually in our sighte, and some in the other haulfe continually oute of our sight. And as the Egiptiens haue feigned them selues. xii. goddes, so likewyse haue thei. To euerie of the whiche they referre one moneth, and one signe of the Zodiaque. Thei haue prophecied vnto kinges, many aduentures. As vnto Alexandre victory, when he made his exploicte towarde Darius. Likewise to Hirchanour and Seleucus, and other the successours of Alexandre, prophecied thei many thinges: As also to the Romaines, which had most sure successe. Thei make compte also of. xxiiij. other starres: without, and beside the waie of the zodiaque, xii. towarde the northe, and the residew towarde the southe. Of the whiche, so many as appiere in sight, they iudge to apperteigne to the quicke, and the other to the dead. These troublesome mases haue thei broughte into the worlde more then enoughe, beside the accompte that thei make of their obseruacions, and deuinaciós from their beginninge to Alexandres time: nombringe them thre thousande and fourty yeres (a shamefull lie) excepte thei wil entrepreter their yeres by the Mone, as the Egiptians doe, comptinge euery monethe for a yere.

❡ The. iiii. Chapiter.

J.i.   Of

¶ Of Iewry, and of the life, maners, and Lawes of the Iewes.

Alestina, whiche also is named Iudea, beinge a seueralle prouince of Siria, lieth betwixte Arabia Petrea, and the countrie Coelosiria. So bordering vpon the Egiptian sea on the weſt, and vpon the floude Iordan on the Eaſte, that the one with his waues waſſheth his clieues, and the other sometime with his ſtreame ouerfloweth his banckes.

The Bible, and Iosephus by ensample therof, calleth this londe Cananea : a countrie renoumed for manifolde subſtaunce. Fertile of soyle, well watered with riuers, and ſpringes, and rich with precious balme. Lienge in the nauelle of the world, that it neither might be broyled with heate, ne frosen with colde . By the reason of the which mildenes of aier, it was iudged by the Israelites or Hebrues, (and rightlye so iudged) to be the country that God promised vnto Abraham

ham, Isaac, and Jacob, flowinge in a-
boundaunce of milke and honie. Upon
the hope of enioyenge of this londe, folowed they Moses oute of Egipte fortye
yeres wandering in Campe. And before
thei ware broughte into Cananea by Jo-
sua, his substitute, ouercame with strong
handce, one and thirty kinges.

This is the people that onely of all o-
ther may chalenge the honour of auncien-
tie. This is the people alone ý mighte
haue glorified in the wisedome, and vn-
medled puritie of Language, as beinge
of all other the firste. This is the people
that was mother of lettres, and sciences.
Amonge these remained the knowledge
of the onely and euerliuings God, and
the certeintie of the religion that was
pleasaunte in his eies. Among these was
the knowledge, and foreknowledge of al,
sauinge that Helas, they knewe not the
visitour of their wealthe, and the ende of
their wo, Jesus the sauioure of all that
woulde knowe him, and seeke life in his
deathe. But him whome thei knew not,
when by reason thei should: him shal thei
yet ones knowe in time when the father
woulde.

The Israelites, the Hebrues or the Iewes (for all in effecte soundeth one people) liue aftre the rule of the lawes, whiche Moses their worthy duke, and deuine chiefteine, declared vnto theim. Withoute the whiche also or anye other written, thei liued holily, hundred of yeares before: atteininge to the truthes hidden from other, by a singuler gifte aboue other. That Philosophre of Philosophers, and deuine of deuines, Moses the meruetlous, waienge in his insight, y̆ no multitude assembled, coulde be gouerned to continuaunce without ordres of equitie, and lawes: when with rewardes to the good, and reuenge vpon the euill, he had sufficiently exhorted, and trained his people to the desire of vertue, and y̆ hate of the contrarie: at the last beside the two tables receiued in the mounte Sinah, added ordres of discipline, and ciuile gouernaunce, full of all goodlines and equitie. Whiche Iosephus, the Iewe, (a manne of greate knowledge, and eloquence, as wel in the Hebrewe, his natural tōgue, as in the Grieke, amonge whome he liued in notable fame not a fewe yeres) hath gathered, and framed into one seuerall

all treatiſe. Out of the which, becauſe I
rather fanſie, if I maye with like commoditie, to folowe the founteines of the
firſt Authours, then the brokes of abred-
gers, which often bring with them much
puddle: I haue here tranſlated, and an-
nexed to the ende of this booke, thoſe ordres of the Iewes commune welthe, ſen-
ding the for the reſte to the Bible. And
yet notwithſtanding, loke what I founde
in this Abredger, neither mencioned in
the bible, nor in that treatiſe, the ſame
thus ordrely foloweth.

The heathen writers, and the Chriſtianes, do muche diffre concerninge the
Iewes, and Moyſes their chiefteine.
For Cornelius the ſtylle, in his firſte
booke of his yerely exploictes, called in
Latine Annales, dothe not aſcribe their
departure oute of Egipte to the power
and comaundement of God: but vnto neceſſitie, & conſtrainte, with theſe wordes:

A great ſkuruines, and an ytche ſaieth
he, beinge riſen throughe oute Egipte,
Bocchoris, the king ſekinge remedye in
the Temple of Iupiter Hammon, was
willed by reſponcion to clenſe his kingdome: And to ſende awaye that kinde of

people whom the goddes hated (he meaneth the Iewes) into some other rowtrey. The whiche when he had done, and they (as the poompe of al skuruines, not knowing wher to become) laye cowring vndre hedges, and busshes, in places desert, and many of them dropped away for sorowe and disease : Moyses (whiche also was one of the outerastes saieth he) counseiled them not to sitte ther, awaytinge aftre the helpe of God or of man, whiche thei ware not like to haue: but to folowe him as their capteine, and lodesman, and committe them selues vnto his gouernaunce. And that hervnto thei all agreinge, at wilde aduentures, with oute knowing what thei did, tooke their iorney. In the which thei ware sore troubled, and harde bestadde, for lacke of water. In this distresse, whē thei ware now ready to lye them downe, & die for thirst, Moyses espyenge a great heard of wilde Chamelles comming fro their fiedinge, and going into woddie place ther beside, folowed them . And iudginge the place not to be without watre, for that he sawe it fresshe and grene, digged and founde plenty of watre . Wherwith when thei
had

had releued thē selues, theí passed on.vi.
daies iourney: and so exploíted that the
seuenth daye theí had beaten out all the
enhabitauntes of the contry, where theí
builte their Citie, & their temple. Moyses then to the entent he might satle the
peoples hartes towarde him for euer: deuised them newe ordres, and ceremonies
cleane contrary to all other nacions. For
(saieth Cornelius) Looke what so euer
is holy amonge vs, the same is amonge
them the contrary . And what so euer to
vs is vnlawfulle, that same is compted
lawefull amonge theim. The ymage of
the beaste that shewed them the waye to
the waters, and the ende of their wande-
ringe: did theí set vp in their chambres,
and offre vnto it a rambe, in the despight
of Jupiter Hammō. whom we worship
in the fourme of a Rambe. And becaule
the Egiptians worshippe their goddesse
Apis in the fourme of a cowe, therfore
theí vse to slea also in sacrifice a cowe.
Swines flesshe theí eate none, for that
theí holde opinion that this kynde of
beaste, of it selfe beinge disposed to be
skoruse, mighte be occasion againe to enfecte them of newe . The seuenth daye
theí

thei make holy day. That is to say spende
awaie in ydlenes and rest: for that on the
seuenth daye, they founde reste of they
wandering, and misery. And when they
had caughte a sauour in this holye daye
loytering: it came to passe in processe of
tyme, that thei made a longe holydaye
also of the whole seuenthyere. But other
holde opinion that thei do obserue suche
maner of holye daies, in the honour of
Saturne the god of fasting and famine:
with whose whippe thei are lothe againe
to be punisshed. Their breade is vnleaue
ned. These ceremonies and deuises, by
what meanes so euer they ware brought
in amonge them, thei do stiffely defende.
As thei are naturally giuen, to be stiffe in
beliefe, and depe in loue with their owne
althoughe towarde al other thei be most
hatefull enemies. So that thei neither
will eate ne drincke with them: no nor
lye in the chambre that a straunger of a
nother nacion lyeth in. A people altogether giuen vnto leachery, and yet abstei-
ning from the enbrasinges of the straunger. Emonge them selues thei iudge nothing vnlawfull. Thei deuised to roside
of the foreskinne of their yarde (whiche
                                                    we

we call circumcision)because thei would
haue a notable knowledge betwene thē,
and other nacions. And the firste lesson
thei teache vnto their childzen, is to de-
spise the goddes. The soules of those ỹ die
in tozmentes, oz in warre,thei iudge to be
immoztall. A continuall feare haue thei,&
a,regard of heauen and helle. And where
the Egiptians honour many similitudes
and Images of beastes, and other creatures,whiche thei make them selues: the
Iewes onely doe honour with their spirite and minde,and conceiue in their vn-
dzestandyng, but one onely Godheade.
Iudging all other that wozshippe the I-
mages of creatures, oz of manne: to bee
vngodlie and wisked. These and many
other thinges doth Cozmelius wzite,and
Trogus also in his.rrrbi.booke.

   There ware amonge the Iewes thze
seueralle sectes,differyng in life from the
reast of the people. The Phariseis, the
Sadduceis, and the Esseis. The Phariseis vsed a certeine rough solempnesse of
apparelle, and a very skante fare:deter-
minyng the Tradicions of Moyses, by
certein ozdenaunces and decrees,whiche
thei them selues sette vp.Thei caried vp-

              I.v.   pon

pon their foreheades, and on their lefte
armes, pretie billettes of Paper, facioned for the place, wherein ware written
the tenne preceptes of ye two Tables. And
this did thei for that the lorde saieth: And
these shall thou haue (meanyng the commaundementes) as a remembraunce hãg-
ing before thine eyes, and alwaie ready
at thine hande. These ware called their
Philacteries, of these two woordes Phy-
lexi and Thorat, wherof the former signi-
fieth to Kiepe, and the other, the Lawe.
These menne also hauyng vppon their
skirtes muche broder gardes then other,
stacke them full of Thornes, whiche bea-
tyng and prickyng them on the hieles as
thei wente, might putte them in remembraunce of the cõmaundemẽtes of God.
Thei attributed all thynges vnto God,
and destenie, whiche thei call Emarmeni.
Neuertheles thei graunted, that it laie
muche in the free choise of manne: either
to doe, or not to doe the thinges that are
iust and godlie. but yet destenie to helpe
in al cases. Whiche destenie thei thought
to depende of the influence of the bodies
aboue. Looke what their superiours and
Elders had saied, or answered to any de-
maunde

maunde, thei neuer woulde contrarie it.
Thei beleued that GOD should come
to Iudge the wozlde, and that all soules
ware euerlastyng. And as foz the soules
of the good, thei helde opinion, that thei
passed from one bodie to another, vntill
the date of the generall resurrection. But
the soules of the wicked, to be plongcd in
to euerlasting pzison & dõ geõ. The name
of Pharisei was giue vnto them foz that
thei ware disguised fro ÿ cõmune maner
of other, as ye would saie, Sequestred.

The Sadduceis denied that there was
any destenie, but that God was the be-
holder of all, and that it laie in the choise
of manne, to doe well oz euill. And as foz
soye oz sozowe that the soule should suffre
aftre this life, thei denied. Neither belieued thei any resurrection: because thei
thoughte the soule died with the bodie.
Thei would not beleue that there ware
any spirites, good oz bad. Neither would
thei receiue moze of the Bible, then the
fiue bookes of Moses. Thei ware sterne
men, and vncompaignable: not so muche
as ones kepyng felowshippe one with a-
nother. Foz the whiche sternesse, thei named theim selues Sadduceis, that is to
saie

saie, iusse menne.

The Esseis ware in all poinctes verie like vnto our cloisterers, abhorryng mariage and the companie of women. Not for that thei condempned Mariage, or the procreacion of issue, but for that thei iudged a manne ought to be ware of the intemperauncie of women. And that no woman kept her self true to her husbāde Oh shameful opinion, and muche better to be reported by the dead, then to be credited of the quicke, bee it neuer so true. Thei possessed all thinges in commune. As for checkes or reuilinges, was to thē muske and Honie, and slouenly vndaslinesse, a greate comelinesse. So that thei ware alwaie in a white surcote, all was well. Thei had no certein abiding in any one citie: but Celles ouer all, where so euer thei became. Before the risyng of the Sonne, thei spake nothyng that touched any worldly affaire: but praied the sonne to rise. Aftre whose vprijsse thei laboured vntill eleuen of the clocke. And then, swashyng firste their whole bodie in water: thei satte doune together to meate, in solempne silence euery manne. Swearing thei compted for swearyng. Thei admitted

ted no manne to their sede, vndze a yere
of probacion. And aftre what time thei
had receiued him: yet had thei two yeres
moze to pzoue his maners and condici=
ons. Suche as thei tooke with a faulte,
thei dzaue fro their cõpaignie. Enioyned
by the waie of penaunce, to go a grasing
like a beaſt, vntill his dieng daie. when
tenne ware ſette in a companie together,
no one of them ſpake without the conſẽte
of the other nyne. Thei would not ſpitte
within the pzecincte of the compaignie e=
mong theim, ne yeat on their righte ſids.
Thei kept the Sabboth with ſuche a pze=
ciſeneſſe, that thei would not that daie,
eaſe nature of the belie burden. And whẽ
vpon other daies, nature fozced theim to
that eaſemente, thei caried with theim a
litle ſpade of woodde, wherwith in place
moſte ſecreate, thei vſed to digge a litle
pit, to laie their bealie in. And in the time
of doyng, thei alſo vſed a very greate cir=
cumſpecion, that their clothes laie cloſe
to the grounde rounde aboute theim, foz
offendyng (ſaied thei) of the Maieſtie of
God. Upon whiche reſpecte, thei alſo co=
uered and bewzied it, aſſone as thei had
done that nature required. Thei ware of

verie

verie long life, by the reason of the vni-
fourme diete that thei vsed, alwaie aftre
one rate of fare : whiche was onely the
fruicte of their countrie Palme. Thei occupied no money. If any manne suffered
for wel doyng, or as wrongfully condempned, that thoughte thei the beste kinde of
death. Thei helde opinion that all soules
ware made in the beginnyng, and put in
to bodies from tyme to tyme, as bodies
did niede theim. And for the good soules
beyng ridde of their bodies againe, thei
saied there was a place appoincted be-
yond the weast Oceean, where thei take
repose. But for the euill, thei appoincted
places toward the Eaft, as more stormie
colde, & vnpleasante. Ther ware amonge
them that prophecied thinges. Some of
them gaue themselues to wedlocke: leaft
if thei should be of the oppinion that men
oughte to abfteine vtterly from women,
mankinde should fade, and in processe be
extincte, yeat vsed thei the compaignie of
their wiues nothing at riote.

The lande of Siria (whereof we haue
named Jewrie a parte) is at this daie enhabited of the Grekes, called Gripho-
nes, of the Jacobites, Nestorians, Sar-
racentes

racenes, and of two chziſtian nacions, the
Sirians and Marouines. The Siriãs
vſe to ſaie Maſſe, aſtre the maner of the
Grekes: and foz a ſpace ware ſubiecte to
the churche of Rome.

The Marouines agre in opinion with
the Iacobites. Their lettres and tongue
are al one with the Arabique. Theſe chzi-
ſtianes dwelle at the Mounte Libanus.
The Sarracenes, whiche dwelle aboute
Ieruſalẽ (a people valeaũt in warrs) delighte muche in houſbandzie and tilthe.
But contrary wiſe, thei that enhabite
Siria, in that poincte are nothing wozth
The Marouines are feawe in nombze,
but of all other thei are the hardieſte.

¶ The. v. Chapitre.

¶ Of Media, and the ma-
ners of the Medes.

Edia (a countrie of A-
ſia) as Solinus wzi-
teth, toke the name of
one Medus, the ſonne
of Medea & Egeus,
kyng of Athenes. Of
whõ the people ware
alſo called Medes.
But Ioſephus affirmeth that it was ſo
named

named of Medius, the sone of Iapheth.
This countrie as it is sene in Ptolomie,
hath on the Northe, the sea named Hircanum, on the West Armenia, and Assi-
ria, on the Southe Persie, and on theast
Hircania and Parthia. Sauing that betwixte Parthia and it, there ronneth a
mounteigne, that seperateth their fron-
tiers. The feactes that thei mooste exercise, are shootyng and ridyng. Whereof
thei be righte experte, & almoste (for those
quartres) without matche or felowe. It
hathe bene there a longe continued and
aunciente custome, to honour their kynges like goddes. The rounde cappe, whiche thei cal Tiara: and their long sleued
garmentes, passed from them to the Persians together with the Empire. It was
a peculier maner vsed of the Rynges of
the Medes, to haue many wiues. Which
thyng was aftrewarde also taken vp of
the communes: so that at lengthe it was
thought vnmiete to haue feawer wiues
then seuen. It was also a goodlie thyng
for a woman to haue many husbandes:
and to be without fiue at ones, was compted a miserable state. The Medes entre
leagues and couenauntes, both aftre the
maner

maner of the Grekes, and also with dꝛa
wing bloud vpõ ſome parte of the arme
aboute the ſhouldꝛe, one of another, whi
the theẙ vſe to licke eche of of others bo
dẙ. All that parte of the coũtrey that lieth
towarde the Noꝛthe, is barrein and vn
fruictefulle. Wherefoꝛe theẙ vſe to make
ſtoꝛe of their fruicte, and to dꝛie them, and
ſo to wooꝛke them into a maſſe oꝛ lumpe
foꝛ their foode. Of roſted Almondes theẙ
make their bꝛeade: and their wine of the
rootes of certein herbes. Theẙ eate great
plentie of the fleſhe of wilde beaſtes.

❡ Of Parthia, and the ma
ner of the Parthians.

Certeine nombꝛe of
Outlawes and Ba
niſſhed menne, called
Parthie, gaue name
to this Countrie: Af
tre ſuche tyme as by
train, and ſtealth theẙ
had gotten it. On the
Southe it hath Carmania, on the Noꝛth
Hircanum, on the Weaſt the Meades,

and on the eaffe the country of Arabia.
The countrie is hilly, and full of wod-
des, and of a barreine foyle. And a people which in the time of the Affiriens, and
Medes, ware fcante knowen, and litle
effiemed. In fo moche that when ý highe
gouernaunce of the whole (whiche the
Grekes call the Monarchie) was yelded
into the hädes of the perfians: thei ware
made a butin, as a nombre of rafkalles
without name. Laffe of all thei ware fla-
ues to the Macedonies. But afterward
in proceffe of time, fuche was the valeau-
tenes of this people, and fuch fucceffe had
thei: that thei became lozdes, not ouer
their neighbours onely rounde aboute
them, but alfo helde the Romaines (.the
conquerours of the wozlde) fuche tacke,
that in fondzie warres they gaue them
great ouerthzowes, and notablye endamaged their power. Plinie reherfeth .rtiii
kingdomes of the parthians. Trogus
calleth them Emperours of the eaff part
of the wozlde. Afthoughe they, and the
Romaines holding the weffe, had deuided the whole betwixte them.

Aftre the decaye of the Monarchie of
the Macedonians, this people was ruled

led by kinges. whome generally by the
name of the first king, thei termed Arsa-
ces. Nexte vnto the kinges maiestie, the
communaltie bare the swaye. Oute of
whome they chase bothe their Capteig-
nes for the warres, & their gouernours
for the peace time. Their language is a
speache mixte of the Scithians, & Medes. Their appareil at the firste, was aftre their facion vnlike to all other. But
when thei grewe vnto power, louse and
large, & so thinne: that a man mighte see
thoroughe it, aftre the facion of the Medes. Their maner of weapon, & armour,
was the same that the Scithians vsed.
But their armies ware altogether almoste of slaues and bondemen, contrary
to the maner of other peoples. And for
that no manne hath aucthoritie amonge
them to giue fredome vnto anye of this
bonde ofspring: The nombre of them by
continuaüce, came vnto a greate multitude. These do thei bringe vp, and make
of as deerly, as thei do of their owne chil
dren: teachinge them to ride, to shote, to
throwe the darte, and suche like featies,
with great diligence, and handsomenes.
Eche commune ther, according to his sub

fraunce, findeth a greate nombre of these
to serue the kinge on horsebacke, in all
warres. So that at what time Anthonie
the Romaine made warre vpon the parthians, wher thei mette him with fyftie
thousande horsemen: there ware of the
whole nombre but eyghte hundred fre
borne. They are not skylfull to fighte it
oute at hande stripes, ne yeat in the maner of besieging or assaulting: but all to
gether after the maner of skirmisshe, as
thei spie their aduauntage. Thei vse no
trompet for their warninges or onsettes
but a dromme: neither are thei able to
endure longe in their fighte. For yf they
ware so good in continuaunce, as thei be
violente at a brunte: ther ware no multitude able to susteine their force. For the
moste parte thei breake of, when the skirmishe is euen at the whottest. And within a while aftre thei feigne a flight, wher
with thei beginne againe a new onsette.
So when thou thinkest thy selfe mooste
sure of the honour of the fielde, then arte
thou at the poinct of the hardest hasarde.
Their horsemen vse armour of mayle
entrelaced with fethers: bothe for their
owne defence, & the defence also of their
                                    horses.

horses. In times passed thei occupied no golde ne siluer, but only in their armour. Upon regarde of chaunge in their luste, thei mary echeone many wiues. and yet punishe thei none offece so greuously as adultery. For the auoyding whereof, thei doe not onely forbidde their women by generall restraunte from all feastes, and banckettinges of men: but also from the sighte of them. Some neuerthelesse do wrighte, amonge the whiche Strabo is one, that thei vse to giue their wiues sometime to their friendes, as in ȳ waye of mariage, that thei maye so haue issue. Thei eate none other fleshe but suche as thei kylle at the chace. Thei be euer on horsebacke, whether thei go to the fielde or the banket, to bye, to selle, to comune of aughte with their friende, or to do any thing that is to be done. Yea thei dispatche al commune and priuate affaires, sittinge on horsebacke. And this is to be vnderstonden of the fre borne: for the slaues are alwaies on foote. Their buriall for all menne (sauinge the kinge) is the dogges bealy, and the kytes. But when thei or suche like haue eaten of, the fleshr, thē couer thei the bare bones with earth.

Thei

Thei haue great regarde vnto their god
des, & the worship due vnto them. Thei
are men of a proude nature, basse med-
lers, and sevicious, craftie, deceiptfull,
malaparte, and vnshamefaced: for thei
holde opinion that it becometh the man
aswell to be sterne, as the woman to be
mylde. Thei be euer in some stirre, either
with their neighbours, or elles amonge
them selues. Men of fewe wordes, and
readier to doe, then to saye. And therfore
whether it go with them or against them
thei lappe it vp in scilence. Thei obey not
their superiours for any reuerence, bu,
for feare. Altogether giuen to lechery,
and yet skante in feedinge. No farther
trewe of worde or promesse, then semeth
them expediente for their owne behoue.

¶ The. vii. Chapiter,

¶ Of Persia, and the maners and ordinaunces of the Persians.

Ersia (a countrie of the
easte)was so called of Per-
sius the Sonne of Jupiter
and Danae . Of whome
the chiefe citie of the kinge-
dome also, was named Persepolis. whiche

the in Engliſhe ſoundeth Perſeboroughe
(oʒ as we coʒruptlyterme it) Perſebu-
rie, and the whole nacio Perſiens. This
countrie as Ptolomie wʒiteth in his fiueth booke, hath on the noʒthe, Media:
on the Weſt, Suſiena: on the eaſte, the
two Carmaniaes: and on the ſouthe, an
inſhot of the Sea, called the Boſome of
Parthia. The famous cities therof,
ware Axiama Perſepolis and Dioſpolis.
By the name of Jupiter thei vnderſtode
the whole heauen. Thei chiefely honour
the Sonne, whom thei calle Mitra. Thei
woʒſhip alſo the Mone, the planet Uenus, the fyʒe, the earthe, the water, and
the windes. Thei neither haue aultare
noʒ temple, noʒ ymage, but celebʒate
their deuine ſeruice vndʒe the open heauen vpon ſome highe place foʒ that purpoſe appoincted. In doinge ſacrifice thei
haue no farther reſpecte, but to take a-
waye the life from the beaſte. As hauing
opinion, that foʒaſmuche as the goddes
be ſpirites, thei delighte in nothinge but
the ſpiritual parte, the ſoule. Befoʒe they
ſlea it, thei ſet it aparte by them, with a
coʒone vpon the heade, and heape vppon
it many bittre banninges and curſes.

ſ me of the nacion notwithſtandinge, when thei haue ſlaine the beaſte: vſe to laye parte of the offalle in the fire.

When thei ſacriſie vnto the fire, they ſimbꝛe vp dꝛie ſtickes together, cleane withoute pille oꝛ barcke. And after what time chei haue powꝛed on neates tallowe, and oyle, thei kindle it. Not blowing with blaſte of bloweſſe oꝛ mouthe: but makinge winde as it ware with a ventile, oꝛ trenchour, oꝛ ſuche like thinge. Foꝛ yf any manne either blowe into it, oꝛ caſte in any deade thing, oꝛ any durte, oꝛ puddle, it is deathe to the doer. The Perſians beare ſuche reuerence to their floudes, that thei neither waſſhe, pyſſe, noꝛ thꝛowe deade carcaſſe into them. No not ſo muche as ſpitte into thẽ: But very reuerentlye honour their water after this maner. Comminge to lake, mere, floude, ponde, oꝛ ſpꝛinge: thei trenche out a litle diche, and ther cut thei the thꝛote of the ſacryfice. Being well ware, that no dꝛoppe of bloode ſpꝛinckle into the water by. As thoughe all water ware polluted and vnhalowed ouer all: yf that ſhould happen. That done their Magi (that is to ſay men ſkylſull in ẙ ſecretes of nature)
                                    layeng

layeng the fleſh vppon a heape of Myꝛ¿
tus, oꝛ Laurelle, and tymbꝛyng ſmalle
wandes about, ſette fyꝛe theron & bꝛenne
yt. And pꝛonouncyng certein curſes, they
myngle oyle, mylke, and hony together,
and ſpꝛinkle ī¿ the fyꝛe. But theſe cur¿
ſinges make they not againſt the fyꝛe ne
water. But againſt the earthe, a greate
whyle toguether: holding in their hande
a boūdle of ſmalle myꝛte wandes. Their
kinges reigne by ſucceſſiō of one kinꝛꝛd
oꝛ ſtocke. To whom who ſo obeyeth not,
hath his heade & armes ſtriken of: and ſo
wythout buriall is thꝛowē out foꝛ car¿
reine. Policritus ſheweth that euery king
of the Perſians buyldeth his howſe vpō
a greate hille : and ther hourdeth vp all
the thꝛeaſure, tribute, & tare that he re¿
ceyueth of the people : to be a recoꝛde
after his deathe how good a huſbonde he
hath bene foꝛ ꝥ cōmune wealthe. Suche
of the ſubiectes as dwelle vpon the ſea
roaſt, aꝛe tared to paie money But thoſe
that enhabite toward the mydde loude:
ſuche cōmodities as the quattre bearech
oꝛ hath wher they dwelle. As apothecary
dꝛuggues, woolle, confoures, & ſuche like
and cateille accoꝛdingly. He is not per¿
mitted

any one cause, to putte any man to death. Neither is it lawfull for any other of the Persians to execute any thyng againste any at his house or stock, that maie sieme in any wyse cruelle. Euery one of them marie many wiues; & holde many concubines also bessde, for the encrease of issue.

The king Proclaimeth rewarde vnto him, that within one yere begetteth most children. Fiue yere aftre thei are begotten, thei come not in the fathers sight, by a certein ordenaunce vsed emong theim: but are broughte vp continually emong the women. To the ende that if the childe fortune to dye in the time of his infancie, their fathers grief maie be the lesse. Thei vse not to marie but in one tyme of the yere: toward midde Marche. The bridegrome eateth to his supper, an apple of that countrey, or a litle of the maribone of a Chamel: and so without any farther banquettyng goeth to bedde. From fiue yeres olde, to twentie and fowre, thei learne to ride, to throwe the Darte, to shoote, and chiesly to haue a tongue voide of all vntruthe. For their nourituryng and trainyng in good maners, thei haue appointed theim Masters of greate sobrenes

bꝛenes and bertue, that teache them dit=
ties, aud pꝛetie songes, conteinyng either
the pꝛaiſes of their Goddes, oꝛ of ſome
woꝛthy Pꝛinces. Whiche ſometime thei
ſing, and ſometyme rerite without note:
that ſo thei mighte learne to conſourme
their liues bntotheirs, whoſe pꝛaiſes thei
ſieme them ſelues to allowe. To this leſ=
ſon aſſemble thei almate together, at the
calle of a Trompette And as thei growe
into yeres, an accompt is required of the
how well thei haue boꝛne awate the leſ=
ſons of their childhode. Thei bſe to ronne
the race, & to course, bothe on hoꝛſebacke
and on foote: at the leadyng of ſome no=
bſe mannes ſonne, choſen foꝛ the nones.
The field foꝛ the race, is at leaſt thꝛe mile
and thꝛe quarters longe. And to the ende
that heate oꝛ coldeſhould the leſſe trouble
them, thei bſe to wadꝛ ouer bꝛookes, and
ſwimme ouer riuers, & ſo to rowme and
to hunte the fieldꝛs, and to eate & dꝛinke
in their armour, and wette clothes. The
fruyes that thei eate are akecoꝛnes, wild
Peares, and the fruicte of the Terebin=
thine tree. But their daiely foode aftre
their ronnyng, and other exerciſes of the
bodie: is hard Biſquette, oꝛ a like cruſtie
bꝛeaoe,

bread, Hortechocques, Gromelle sede, a
litle roste flesshe or sodden, whether thei
lust: and faire water their drincke. Their
maner of Huntyng, is with the bowe, or
the Darte on horsebacke. Thei are good
also in the slynge. In the forenoone thei
plante and graffe, digge vp settes, stubbe
vp rootes, make their owne armour, or
fisshe and foule, with the Angle or nette.
Their childzen are decked with garni-
shynges of golde. And their chief iuelle is
the precious stone Piropus, whiche thei
haue in suche price, that it maie come vppon no deade corps. And that honour
giue thei also to the fire, for the reuerence
thei beare there vnto. From twentie, till
fiuetie: thei folowe the warres. As for byeng and sellyng, or any kinde of Lawe
prattle, thei vse not. Thei cary in their
warres, a kinde of shieldes facioned like
a losenge, a quiure with shaftes, & a curti-
sace. On their heades a copintancke, em-
batled aboute like a turrette, and a brest-
plate embossed, of skaled woorke. The
princes and menne of honour did weare
a treble Anaxirides, facioned muche like
a coate armour, and a long coate doune
to the knees, with hangyng slieues acordyng.

dyng. The outside colours, but the lining white. In Somer thei weare purple, and in Wintre Medleis. The abillementes of their heades, are muche like the front-lettes that their Magi doe weare. The comune people are double coated doune to the midde Leggue, and haue about their heade a greate rolle of Sendalle. Their beddes and their drinking vessell, are garnished with gold. Whe thei haue matter of moste importaunce to common of, thei debate and coclude in the middes of their cuppes: thinkyng it muche surer that is so determined, then aftre any other sobrer sorte. Acqueintaunce mietting of equall degre, griete one another with a kisse. But the inferiour mietyng with his bettre, enclineth his bodie foreward with lowe reuerence. Thei bewrie their corpses in the grounde, cearyng them all ouer with waxe. Their Magicens thei leaue vnbewried, for the soules to dis-spetche. The children there, by an orde-naunce no where elles vsed: doe carnal-ly knowe their mothers. Thus haue ye heard what the maners of the Persians ware sometyme.

Herodotus reherseth certeine other, their

their facions not vtterly vnworthe the
tellynge. That thei compted it vilanie to
laughe, or to spitte before the kyng. Thei
thought it fondnes in the Grekes, worthie to be laughed at, to imagine goddes
to be sprong vp of menne. What so euer
was dishoneste to be done, that thoughte
thei not honest to be spoke. To be in debt
was muche dishonour, but of all thinges
moste vile for to lie. Thei vse not to bewrie their deade bodies, vntill thei haue
bene torne with dogges, or with fowles.
And the parentes brought to niedinesse,
vse there to make chenisaunce of theſe
doughters bodies, whiche emong no nacion elles was euer allowed. Howbeit
some holde opinion, that it was also the
proprietie of the Babilonians. The Perſians at this date, beynge subdued of the
Saracenes, and bewitched with Maho-
metes brainsicke wickednesse, are cleane
out of memorie. a people in those daies,
whiche through their greate hardinesse
and force, ware of long tyme Lordes of
the Easte parte of the worlde. But now
tombled cleane from their aunciente re-
nowmie, and bewried in dishonour.

℩ The

❡ The .viij. Chapitre.

❡ Of Ynde, and the vncouthe tra=
des and maners of life of
the people therin.

Nde, a Countrie also
of the Easte, and the
closyng vp of Asia to=
ward that quartre: is
saied to be of suche a
maigne syse, that it
maie be côpared with
the thirde parte of the
whole earth Pomponius writeth, that a=
lône the shore, it is fowrtie daies sailyng
the nighte also comprised therin.

It tooke the name of the floude called
Indus, whiche closeth vp the lande on the
Weste side. Beginnyng at the Southe
sea, it stretcheth to ŷ Sonne risynge: And
Northward to the moût Caucasus. There
are in it many greate peoples: and Tou=
nes and Cities so thicke, that some haue
reported them in nombre fiue thousande.
And to saie truthe, it oughte not to sieme
greatly straunge vnto folkes, though the
coûtrie be reported to haue suche a nom=
bre of Tounes, or to be so populous: con=
sideryng

ſideryng that of all other, the Indiens a-
lone, neuer diſcharged theim ſelues of a-
ny ouerplus of iſſue, as other haue done:
but alwaie kepte their owne offſpryng at
home in their owne countrie. Their principall ſtoudes are Ganges, Indus, and Hy-
panis. But Ganges farre paſſeth in greatnes the other twaine. This lande by the
benefite of the battling breathe of the ge-
tle weaſt winde, reapeth corne twiſe in
the yere. And other Wintre hath it none,
but the bittre blaſtes of Theaſterly windes called Eteſiæ. Thei lacke wine, and
yet ſome men reporte, that in the quartre called Muſica, there groweth a good
wine grape. In the Southe parte there
of, groweth Nardus, Cinnamome, Peper
and Calamus aromaticus: as doeth in Arabia and Aethiope. The wooddſe Ebenum
(whiche ſome ſuppoſe to be our Guaiacum) groweth there, and not elles where
Likewiſe of the Popiniays and the Vni-
cozne. As for precious ſtones, Beralle
Praſnes, Diamantes, iris Carbuncles
and Pearles of all ſortes, be found there
in greate plentie. Thei haue two Som-
mers, ſofte pimpelyng windes, a milde
aier, a rancke ſoile, and abundaunce of
watre.

watre. Diuerse of them therefore liue an
hundred & thirtie yeres. Namely emong
the Musicanes. And emong the Serites,
yet somewhat longer.

All the Indians generally, weare lōg
heare: died either aftre a bright asshe cou
lour, oz elles an Ozenge tawnie. Their
chief iuelles, are of Pearle and pzecious
stones. Their appareille is verie diuers:
and in sewe, one like another. Some go
in Mantles of Wollen, some of Linnen
some naked, some onely bzieched to cou
uer the pziuities, and some wzapped a-
boute with pilles, and lithe barckes of
trees. Thei are all by nature blacke of
hewe: euē so died in their mothers wōbe
acozdyng to the disposiciō of the fathers
nature, whose siede also is blacke: as like
wise in the Aethiopians. Talle men and
strongly made. Thei are very spare sie-
ders, namely when thei are in Campe.
Neither delighte thei in muche pzeasse.
Thei are as I saied, greate deckers and
trimmers of them selues, haters of theft.
Thei liue by lawe, but not wzitten. Thei
haue no knowledge of lettres, but admi-
nister altogether without booke. And foz
ȳ thei are voide of guile, and of very sobze

L.i.   diete:

diete: all thing proſpereth well with the.
Thei drinke no wine, but when thei Sa-
criſie to their goddes. But their drincke
is a bruage that thei make ſometyme of
Rize, ſometyme of Barlie. Their meate
for the mooſte parte is ſoupynges made
alſo of Rize.

In their lawes, bargaines, and couenauntes, their ſimplicitie and true meanyng well appeareth: for that thei neuer
are muche contencious aboute the. Thei
haue no Lawes concernyng pledges or
thynges committed to another mannes
kiepyng. No witneſſynges, no handwri-
tynges, no ſealynges, ne ſuche like tokes
of trecherie and vntruſt: but without all
theſe, thei truſte and be truſted, thei belieue and are belieued, yea, thei oftenty-
mes leaue their houſes wide open without keper. Whiche truely are all greate
ſignes of a iuſte and vprighte dealyng e-
mong them. But this peraduenture can
not ſeatle well with euery mannes fan-
taſie: that thei ſhould liue eche manne a-
parte by hymſelf, and euery body to dine
and to ſuppe when he luſt, and not all at
anhowre determined. For in dede for the
felowſhippe and ciuilitie, the contrary is
                                            more

moze allowable Thei commede and occupie muche as a commune exercise, to
rubbe their bodies : specially with skrapers made foz the nones. Aftre whiche,
thei smoche them selues again with Ebenum, wherof I spake afoze.

In their Toumbes, and Bewzialles,
very plaine and nothyng costlie : But in
trimming and arraieng of their bodies,
to, to, gaude-glozious . Foz there aboute
thei neither spare gold, ne pzecious stone
ne any kinde of silke that thei haue. Thei
delighte muche in garmentes of white
Sarcenet. And foz that thei sette muche
by beautie , thei cary aboute with them
phanelles to defende them fro the sonne,
and leaue nothyng vndone, that maketh
foz the bettre grace of their faces . Thei
sette asmuche by truthe alone , as by all
other vertues together.

Age hath there no pzerogatiue, except
thei winne it with their wisedome , and
knowledge . Thei haue many wiues,
whiche thei vse to buye of their parentes
foz a yoke of Oxen. Some to serue them
as their vndzelynges, and some foz pleasure , and issue. Whiche maie neuerthelesse vse buttoke banquetyng abzode (foz

any lawe oz custome there is to restreine them) excepte their housebandes by sine force, can compelle them to kepe close.

No one emong the Indians either sacrifieth cozoned, ne offreth odours, ne liquours. Thei wounde not their Sacrifice in no maner of wise: but smoze hym by stopping the bzeath. Least thei should offre any mangled thing vnto God, but that that ware in euery parte whole. He that is conuicte of false witnessyng, hath his fingres cutte of by the toppe ioinctes. He that hath taken a limme from any manne, suffreth not onely the like losse, but loseth also his hande. But if any man haue taken from an artiricer, his hande, oz his eye, it lieth vpon his heade.

The kyng hath a garde of bought women: who take chardge of his bodie, and haue the trimmyng and ozderyng thereof. The residue of the armie, remainyng without the gates. If the Kyng foztune to be dzoncken, it is not onely lawfull foz any one of these women to slea hym: but she shall also as in the waie of rewarde, be coupled in mariage to the nexte king. Whiche (as is saied) is one of his sonnes, that afoze enioied the Croune. It is not

lawfull

lawful for the king to slepe by daie tymes
and yet in the night tyme to auoide tre=
cherie, he is forced euery houre to chaūge
his chambre. When he is not in campe,
he ofte tymes cometh abroade: bothe to
giue sentence, and to heare matters de=
pendyng in question. And if it be time of
daie to trimme his bodie; he bothe hea=
reth the pleaes & is rubbed in the meane
season with the skrapers afoze mencio=
ned, by thre of his women. He cometh
furthe also to Sacrifices, and to hunting:
Where he is accompaignied with a ra=
ble of women, in as good ordre as ours
ware wonte to be vpon Hocke mondaie.
His waie is ranged with ropes, and his
garde of menne abideth without. But if
it fortune any to steale in, to the women
(whiche is contrary to their ordre & due=
tie)he loseth his heade for it. There go a=
foze hym Tabours and Belles. When
he hunteth in places fensed aboute, two
oz thre armed women stande prease, foz
his aide, and defence. But when he hun=
teth in open place, he is caried vpon an
Eliphante: & euen so sittyng on his backe
shooteth, oz throweth the darte at his
game, Some of his women ride vpon

Horses, some vpon Elephantes. As likewise in the warres, where thei fight with all kinde of weapons skilfully.

Suche menne also as haue gathered thinges into writynges, recorde: that the Indians worshippe as their goddes the father of raine Jupiter: Ganges their floude, and the familiar spirites of their countrie. And when their kyng wash eh his heade, thei make solempne feast, and sende his highnes greate giftes, eche ma enuyenge other, who maye shewe hym self moste riche, and magnificent.

The commune wealthe of the Indians, was sometyme deuided into leuen states or degrees. The Sages (whiche other calle Philosophers) ware of the first ordre, or state: the whiche although thei ware in nombre feawer then any of the rest: yet ware thei in honour and dignitie aboute the kyng, farre aboue all other. These menne (priuiledged from all busines) neither be troubled with office, ne be at any mannes commaundemente: But receiue of the communes suche thinges as serue for the Sacrifices of their goddes, and are requisite for bewrialles. As though thei ware bothe well acqueinted,

and

and beloued in heauē, and knewe muche of the trade in helle. For this cause haue thei bothe giftes and honour largely giuen thē. And in very diede thei do muche good among the people. For in the begin̄ning of ẙ yere, assemblyng together, thei foreshewe of raine, of drouthe, of winde and of sickenesse : and of suche like thynges as maie to profeight be foreknowen For aswell the kynge as the people, ones vnderstādyng their foresawes, and knowyng the certeintie of their iudgementes by former experience : shone the euilles, and are preste to attende vpon that, that is good. But if any of their said Sages shall fortune to erre in his foresight: other punishement hath he none, thenfor euer aftre to holde his peace.

The seconde ordre is of housebande menne, whiche beyng more in nombre then any of the other states, and exempte fro the warres, and all other labour : bestowe their tyme onely in housebandrie. No enemie spoileth thē, none troubleth them: but refraineth fro doing them any hurte or hinderaunce, vpon respect of the profighte that redoundeth to the whole, throughe their trauailles. So that thei,

hauyng libertie without all feare to followe their busines, are instrumétes and
meanes of a blessed plenteousnesse. Thei
with their wiues and childzen, dwell alwaie in the countrie, without resoztyng
to the tounes oz citie. Thei paie rente to
the Kyng (foz all the whole Countrie is
subiecte to their kyng) neither is it lawefull foz any of the communes to occupie
and possesse any grounde, without paie-
ynge rente. And the housebande men beside this rente, yelde vnto the Kynges
maiestie, a fiueth of their fruictes yerely.

The thirde ozdze standeth all by bzie-
ders and feeders, of all soztes, whiche like
wise neither enhabite toune ne village:
but with tentes, in the wilde fieldes. And
these with huntyng and foulyng in sondzie wise, so kiepe vndze the beastes and
hurtefull foules: that wheare other wise
the housebande menne should in siede
tyme, and towarde harueste, be muche a-
zioyed and hyndered by the fowles, and
theim selues alwaie by the beastes, the
countrie is quiete frō al suche annoyáce.

In the fowzthe ozdze are Artificers,
and handitraftesmen. Whiche are deuided, some into Smithes, some into Armourers,

mourers, some for one purpose, some for another, as is expediente. These doe not onely liue rente free, but also haue a certaine of graine allowed them at the kinges allowaunce.

In the fiueth ordre are the menne of warre, a greate uombre daiely exercised in armies, bothe on Horsebacke, on Elephantes, and on foote. And all their Elephantes, and horses miete for their warres, are found of the kinges allowaunce.

The sixteth ordre is of Surueiours or Maisters of reporte, whiche haue the ouersighte of all thynges that are done in the realme, and the charge to bryng reaporte vnto the kyng.

In the seuenth place, are thei that be Presidentes, and heades of the commune cousailles, very fewe in nombre, but worthy men for their nobilitie and wisedome. Out of these are chosen counsailours for the kynges Courtes, and officers to administrethe commune wealch, and to determine controuersies: yea, cap ❦ ines for the warres, and Princes of the realme.

The whole state of Ynde beyng deuided into these ordres or degrees: it is also ordeined, that a man shall not marie out

of the ordre, wherin his callyng lieth, ne
chaunge his trade. For neither maie the
souldiour occupie housebandrie thoughe
he woulde: ne the artificers entremedle
with the doctrine of the Sages.

There are also amonge the Indians,
persons of honour appointed to be as
it ware Tutours of straungers, to see
that no wronge be done them, to put or-
die for their kepyng, and Phisicke, if any
falle sicke. As also (if it fortune any of thē
to die) for the bewriēg of theim, and to
deliuer their goodes, and money to their
nexte friendes.

All causes are broughte afore the iudges, who heare the parties, and punysshe
the offenders diligently. Ther is no sla-
uery amonge them. Yea, thei haue a certaine ordināunce, that none shalbe slaue
or bonde amonge them, but all fre, and
of equalle aucthoritie and honour. For
thei holde opinion that who so accusto-
meth his selfe neither to be Lorde ouer
other, ne ŧ wrōge any bodie: ŷ man hath
prepared him selfe sauftie and ease what
so euer shall happen hym by any aduenture. And a fonde thing ware it to make
the lawes indifferente for all, and not to
make

make the ſtates of the men indifferente

But becauſe ther are in Inde manye ſondꝛie contries, diuerſe bothe in people and tongue (as in ſo large a thing muſte nedes happen) ye ſhall vnderſtonde that thei do not all alike vſe ſuche trade as I haue deſcribed, but in ſome places ſome-what woꝛſe.

Of thoſe that lie towarde the Eaſte, ſome occupie bꝛieding, and ſome do not. Other dwellinge in the merſhe, and fen-nes vpon the riuers ſide: occupie fiſſhing, and liue by the ſame all rawe. And the bettre to woꝛcke their feate, thei make them ſelues boates: of ſuche canes as growe ther, of a wonderfull biggenes. So, that ſo muche of the cane as is be-twixte ioyncte and ioyncte, is a luſte pro-poꝛcion of timbꝛe foꝛ one of their boates.

Theſe of all the other Indians, are ap-pareilled in matte, made of a certayne ſofte kinde of mere ruſhes. Which when thei haue gathered out of the ſtoude, and ſliced oute in maner of lace: they bꝛayde together muche like oure ſiggeſtad e, oꝛ ſuche like kinde of mattinge, & make them ſelues ierkins therof.

Thoſe that bꝛ yet by Eaſte of them, are
bꝛieders

bꜩeders of cataille: and liue altogether with rawe fleſhe, and haue to name Padians. Whoſe condicions are ſayde to be ſuche.

As often as it foꜩtuneth any of their citezeins to be ſicke, yf it be a manne: his niereſt friendes, and thoſe that are moſte aboute him, kylle him by and by. leaſte (ſaye thei) his fleſhe ſhould ware woꜩſe. Pea, thoughe he woulde diſſemble the matter, and denie him ſelf to be ſicke, it boteth not. Foꜩ withoute pardon, they kille him, and make a feaſte with him. If it be a woman, looke how the menne did by the manne, ſo do the women by a woman. Likewiſe do thei with bothe ſoꜩtes, when thei ware croked foꜩ age, oꜩ become impotente: where thꜩoughe, what by the one meanes and the other, none of them die foꜩ age.

Ther is another ſoꜩte of the Indians that kille no liuinge thing, ne plante, noꜩ ſowe, noꜩ builde houſe: but liue with herbes, and a certeine ſede whiche groweth there of the owne accoꜩde, muche like vnto gromelle. whiche thei gather with the cuppe oꜩ ſhelle that it groweth in, and ſo ſeeth it, and eate it. If any of theſe falle

ſicke,

ficke, he wandereth forthe into some deserte place, and ther laieth him downe:
no manne taking hede either to his lieng
oz to his dienge.

All these Indians that I nowe haue
spoken of, in quenching of natures heate,
vse their women as secretly as beastes
do their females.

These Indians haue a kinde of sages,
that the Griekes calle Gimnosophistæ,
whiche as the worde Sophista soundeth
now, might merily be interpreted brie-
thelesse bablers. But as Sophista did sig-
nefie then, naked Sages: oz to giue one
Grieke worde for a nother, naked Phi-
losophres. These (as Petrarche writeth)
haunte the outemoste bozders, and shadowie partes of that countrie, wandering
naked acozdinge to their name, vp and
downe, heather and theather, studienge,
and searching the natures of thinges, the
course of the heauens, and the secretes of
knowledge. Thei continued sometime al
the whole daye from the sonne risinge, till
his downe goinge: beholdinge the same
with stedfaste eye, neuer tourning away
the heade (althoughe it be ther moste fer-
uently hote) searthing and spienge aftre
certaine

certaine secretes in the body thereof.

At another time thei passe the day likewyse, standing one while on one legge,
another while on another in ý broilinge.
sande of that contrie. Frosse nor snowe,
nor firie heate greued not them.

Amonge these, is ther a people called
Brachmanes, whiche (as Didimus their
king wrate vnto Alexandre when he wēt
aboute to subdue them) liue a pure and
simple life, led with no likerous lustes of
other mennes vanities. This people lō-
geth for no more then nature requyreth
naturallye. Thei are content with suche
foode as commeth to hande, desiryng no
suche as other menne tourne the worlde
almost vpside downe to haue, leauing no
elemēt vnransaked to gette a gowbin for
their glotenous gorge : but suche as the
earth vnploughed, or vndoluē, yeldeth of
her self . And because thei aqueinte not
their table with surfet, in dede thei know
not so many kindes of sickenesses, ne so
many names of diseases as we doe : but
thei bettre knowe what sounde healthe
meaneth, and staied continuaunce of the
same . then euer we are like.

Thei haue no niede to craue one anus
ther

thers helpe and reliefe , wher no manne
maketh clayme by (thine) and by (myne)
but euery manne taketh what he lusteth
and lusteth no moze then he niedeth.
Enuie cannot dwell ther, ne none of her
impes , wher all be equalle, aud none a-
boue other. and all alike pooze, maketh
all alike riche . Thei haue no officers of
Justice among them, becaule thei do nothing that ought to be punisshed . Ther
can no lawe appiere, becaule none offëce
appeareth.

The whole people hath one onely lawe,
to do nothinge against lawe that nature
pzescribeth. To cherisshe labour, to barré
out ydlenes, and banisshe colle couetyse .
That lechery licke not away the vigour
of their spirites, and strength: noz lacke
thzowe menne into desperate doompes.
That euery manne hath enoughe, wher
no manne couettes moze. That neuer có-
tent, is of all other the moste cruell rest-
les plague. Foz whome she catcheth , she
thzoweth a foote beneth beggery, whilest
thei canne finde none ende of their scrat-
tinge, but the moze thei haue, the sellier
gnaweth their longing .

The warme by the Sonne, the deawe

is their moiſture, ẙ riuer is their drinke, the faire groũde their bedde. Care breaketh not their ſleape, Compaſſing of vanities wearieth not their minde. Pride hath no ſtroke ouer them, among whom ther is no diuerſite. Neither is their any kinde of bonde knowen amonge them: but the bondage of the body to the minde whiche thei onely allowe to be iuſt.

For the building of their houſes, they ſende not ouer ſea for ſtone, thei burne no Caliõ to make lime to tempre their mortre, thei bake no brickes, nor digge no ſande. But either make them caues in the earthe, or take ſuche as thei finde ready made in the ſides of the mounteines and hilles. Ther dwel thei without feare of rage or ruine, of weather or of winde. He thincketh him ſelf ſaufſter fenced frõ ſhowres with his caue, then with a fewe tiles: and yet hath by it a double commoditie. A houſe while he liueth, ẙ a graue ready made when he dyeth. Ther is no glitteríng apparell, no rattelinge in ſylkes, no ruſtling in beluettes, but a litle breche of brawded ruſſhes, or rather a couering of honeſte ſhamefaſtneſſe. The women are not ſette oute to allure,

N＇

ne pinched in to please, ne garnisshed to
gase at. No heare died, no lockes outela-
ed, no face painted, no skinne slicked, no
countrefeicte countenaunce, nor mynsing
of passe. No poticary practile, no ynke-
horne termes, nor pithlesse pratlig. Finally no colours of hipocrisie, no meanes to
set oute more beautie then nature hathe
giue them. Thei ioyne not in engēdrure
for likerous luste, but for the loue of yt
selfe and succession. Thei kepe no warres, but mainteine peace: not with force,
but with peaceable behauour and maners. The father and the mother folowe
not the childe to $\tilde{y}$ bewrialle. Thei builde
no toumbes for the deade: more like vn-
to chirches then graues. Thei bewry not
vp their asshes in pottes dasshed full of
pearle and precious stone. For why they
estieme in these, neither the honour of the
quicke, ne the pleasure of the deade: but
rather the trouble and paine of bothe.
Pestilence or other diseases (as I haue
sayd) the Abrahmanes are not annoyed
with, for thei enferte not the ayer with
any filthye doinges. But nature alwaye
with them, keapeth accorde with the season: and euery elemente his tourne, with
oute

oute ſtoppe oʒ barre. Their Phiſicque is
abſtinence, which is able not only to cure
the maladie already crepte in: but alſo to
holde oute ſuche as otherwiſe mighte entre. Thei couette no ſightes, noʒ ſhewes
of miſrule: no diſguiſinges noʒ entrelu-
des. But when thei be diſpoſed to haue
the pleaſure of the ſtage, thei entre into
the regeſtre of their ſtoʒies, & what thei
ſinde theremoſte ſit to be laughed at, that
do thei lamente & bewaile. Thei delighte
not as many do, to heare olde wiues tales, and fantaſies of Robin hoode: but in
ſtudious conſideracion of the wondʒeful
woʒkemanſhip of the woʒld,& the perfect
diſpoſinge of thinges in ſuche oʒdʒe of
courſe and degree. Thei croſſe no ſeale
foʒ merchaundiſe, ne learne no colours
of Rethoʒicque. Thei haue one kinde of
plaine eloquence commune to them all:
tongue,& harte agrein ye in truth. Thei
haue neither moote halles, ne vniuerſi-
ties, whoſe diſagreable doctrine moʒe
leaning to apiſſhe arte, then natural reaſon and experience, neuer bʒingeth anye
ſtaye, oʒ certeintie of thinges. One part
of this people iudgeth manes perfeteſte
bleſſednes to ſtande in honeſtie. And a
nother

mother in pleasure . Not in the tickelinges of the taste, or pamperinges of the bealy, more bittre then pleasaūce as thou maye vse them: but to lacke nothing that perfecte nature desireth, ne nothing to do that perfecte nature misliketh . Thei thincke it no honour to God, to slea for him an innocēte beast: yea thei say he accepteth not the sacrifice of men polluted with bloode, but rather loueth a worship voide of all bloodsheade . That is to saye the humble entreatie of woorde, because that propriety only (to be entreated with woordes) is coūmune to God and to manne. With this therefore saye they he is pleased, because we somewhat resemble him self therin. And this was the life of ý vnchristened Brahmanes, wher with we christianes are so farre out of loue, that we are afraied leaste any man should beleue it to be true .

The Indians called Catheis, haue eche man many wiues. And assone as anyone husbande fortuneth to die, his whole nōber of wiues assemble before the chiefest iudges of the citie, and there eche for her self, sheweth and alledgeth her welle deseruinges towarde her housebande: how

verely

derely she loued him, howe muche she
tendered & honoured him. And she that
is by them iudged to haue borne her self
beste in that behaulfe, and to haue bene
dierest to her husbonde: she in the beste
maner and moste gorgeous that she can
deuise, triumphing and reioysinge, getteth her vp vpon the funeralle pyle, wher
her housebandes corps lieth ready to be
brence, and ther kissinge and enbrasinge
the deade body, is burned together with
her housebāde. So gladde is she to haue
the victorie in the contencion of wiuely
chastitie, and honeste behauiour toward
her husbande. And the other that lyue,
thincke them selues dishonoured: and
escape not without spotte of reproche as
longe as thei liue. Their childrē in their
infancie, are not nourisshed vp at the libertie and will of the parentes: but cer-
teinether are appointed to viewe the children: whiche yf thei spie vntowardnes in
the infante, deformitie, or lacke of lym-
mes, commaunde it to be slayne.

Thei ioyne not mariages for nobilitie
of birthe, or aboundaunce of substaunce,
but for beaultie. and rather vpō regarde
of frute, then of luste.

Certaine

Certaine also amonge the Yndians haue this custome, that yf thei be of suche pouertie that thei be not able to marye oute their doughters: euen in the floure of her age thei bringe her, or them, furthe into the marcate with trompet & drōme, or suche other their noyses of warre: And their, aftre the multitude is comen toge-ther, the maiden first vncoucreth her self wholie vp to the harde shoulders, on the backe haulfe, to be sene starke naked, and aftre that likewise on the bealy. Yf the multitude finde no faulte, but allowe her as worthye to please for her bodye, then marieth she to some one ther, whome she beste liketh.

Megasthenes writeth that vpon diuerse mounteines in Ynde, are people with dogges heades, and lōge clawes, cladde in hydes of beastes, speakinge with no voyce like vnto manne, but barking on-lye, muche like vnto dogges, with mou-thes roughe like a grater.

Thei that dwelle aboute the heade of Ganges, haue no nede of anye kinde of meate: for thei liue by the sauour of their frutes. And yf thei fortune to iorney, so that thei thincke to fayle of the sauour

M.iii.   when

when thei would haue it, they cary with theim to smell to, at times as thei fainte. But if it fortune those to smelle any horrible stincke, it is as present deathe vnto theim, as poyson to vs. It is recorded in writyng, that certaine of those ware in Alexandres campe.

We rede also that there are in Inde men with one eye and no mo. And certein so notably eared that thei hange downe to their hieles, with suche a largenesse that thei may lye in either of them as vpon a pallet: and so harde, that thei maye rende vp trees with them. Some other also hauing but one legge, but vpon the same such a foote, that when the sonne is hote, and he lacketh shadowe, lyenge downe vpon his backe, and holdinge vp his fote, he largely shadoweth his whole bodie.

It is redde that in Clesia certein women haue but ones childe in all their life time: and the children assone as thei are borne, immediatly to become horeheded. Againe, that there is another nacion, much lóger liued then we are, whiche in their youth are horeheared: and in their age, their heare wareth blacke. They
affirme

affirme also that ther is another sorte of women that conceiue at fyue yeres olde, and liue not aboue the age of.viii.yeres. Ther are also that lacke neckes, & haue their eyes in their shoulders. Ther are also beside these, certeine saluages with dogges heades, & shacke heared on their bodies, that make a very terrible charringe with their mouthes.

But in these and suche like tales of the Indians, and their countrie: for that a manne had nede of a redie beliefe that should take theim for truthes, one had not niede to bee so large: consideringe specially that menne nowe a daies, will skante beleue the reporte of other mens writinges, in the thinges that almost lye vndre their noses.

Ther is a place betwixt Gedrosia and the floude Indus which is called Cathaius of the Cathaiens that enhabyte it. This people ware an offspring of $\mathcal{y}$ Scithiâs, muche altered from their naturall condicions, and wonted maners, if that that Aitone the Arminiane writeth of them in his storie, be true.

Thei passe (saieth he) all other men in quicke smelling. And thei saye of them

selues

M.iiij.

selues, that though all other menne haue
two instrumentes of sight, yet do none se
with both two in dede, but thei: all other
men in comparison either to haue no sight,
or elles as it ware but with one eye.
Their wittinesse is greate, but their boa
stinge greater. The whole nacion of the̅
is perswaded, that thei muche passe all other men in knowledge, and the subtilties of sciences. Thei are all of colour shining white, smalle eyed, beardelesse by
nature. Their lettres are aftre the facio̅
of the Romaine, all in squares. Thei are
diuerselypledde with fonde supersticions,
some aftre one sorte, and some aftre another. But thei are all voyde of the true
knowledge which is in Jesus Christe.
Some worship the sonne, some y̆ moone.
Other, ymages of poten metalle, manie
of them an ore. And thus to sondry suche
other monsters, hath this people in sondry wyse deuided it selfe in supersticion.
Thei haue no maner of written lawes,
nor knowe not what we meane whe̅ we
speake of faithfulnesse or trustinesse. And
wher (as I said afore) thei haue in al hādi
worckes a passing subtiltie of witte, yet
in the knowledge of heauenly thinges,
                              thei

thei are altogether to learne: that is to
saie, thei are btterly ignozaūt. A coward-
ly people and bery fearcful of death. Pet
erercise thei a maner of warre, but that
thei handle rather by witte, and pollicie,
then by strength and hardinesse. In their
sighte thei bse a kinds of shaftes, and certaine other weapons of slight, bnknowen
to other countries.

Their money is a piece of square paper, with their Rynges Image bpon it.
And because it cannot be durable: ozdze
is taken, that when it is soiled oz dusked
muche, with passyng from man to man,
thei shall bzing it to the cosignyng house,
and make erchaunge foz newe. All their
btensiles and necessaries of house, are
of golde, siluer, and other metalles. Dile
is so deintie emong theim, that the kyng
onely bseth it, as it ware foz a pzecious
ointement. Thus haue we treated of the
Pndians, and now to their bozderers,
the Scithians.

¶ The .ir. Chapitre.

¶ Of Scithia and their
Berne maners.

M.b.　　Scithia

Cithia (a countrie li-
eng by Moꝛth) is ſaid
of Herodotus, to take
the name of Scitha
Hercules ſonne. Oꝛ
as Beroſus Judgeth,
of an other Scitha,
boꝛne ofoure greate
graundame Araxe, Noahes wife, that
dwelt firſt in that countrie. This people
in the beginnyng, pente within narowe
boundes, ſo in pꝛoceſſe by litle and litle,
thꝛough their valeauntnes and foꝛce enlarged their limites:that thei became loꝛ-
des of many coūtries aboute,and grewe
into a great gouernaunce and renoume.
Thei neſtled firſt vpon the floude Araxis
ſo fewe in nombꝛe and ſo baſe : that no
manne thought theim woꝛthie the trou-
blyng oꝛ talkyng of. But gettyng vnto
them a certein king,hardie,of great courage,and notable experience in the war-
res:thei enlarged their land ſo,that thei
made it ſtretche on the one parte (whiche
is altogether Hille, and Mounteigne)
vnto Caucaſus,and ouer al the plain vnto the Oꝛcean,ꝙ vnto the greate marſhe
of Meotis,and Tanais the floude.From
whence

whére the countrie of Scithia now stret
cheth all along toward the East. And be
cause the mounteigne Imaus, ronnyng
along as the countrie coasteth, deuides it
in the middes into two haulues: the one
haulfe is called Scithia within Imaus,
and the other without (as ye would saie)
on this side the Mounte, and beyonde.
There neuer medled any power with
theim, that was able to conquere theim:
oz muche to endamage theim. Thei fozced Darius, the Kyng of the Persians,
with greate dishonour to flie their countrie. Thei slue Cirus with all his armie.
Thei made an ende of Alexandze with al
his power. The Romaines sente theim
thzeates thei would warre with theim,
but thei pzoued in fine but wozdes. Thei
are a people not tameable with any toile
bittre warriours, and of greate strength
of bodie. At the first very rawe, and with
out any ozdinarie trade of life: neither
knowyng what tillage meant, ne yet hauyng any houses oz cotages to dwell in.
But wandzyng vp and doune the wilde
fieldes and dziuyng their catteille afoze
theim, their wiues and their childzen ridyng in wagons by them. Thei obserued

iustice

suffice, without constraint of lawe. Thei compted none offece moze heinous, then thefte. As folke that had nothyng vndze locke noz keye, barre, noz bolte: but altogether in the open fielde. Thei nether occupied golde ne siluer. Their chief foode was milke and Hony. Against colde and other stozmes, thei wzapped their bodies in felles, and hides of beastes, and Mice skinnes. Thei knewe not what Wollen meante, ne any facion of garmente.

This maner of life was in many of the Scithians, but not in all. A greate nombze of theim, as thei muche differed in distaunce of place frō other, so differed thei also from other in maners: and vsed a certeine trade of liuyng emong them selues, wherof we aftreward will entreate, when we haue saied somewhat moze of their facions in generall.

¶ Many of the Scithians delight in mā slaughter. And the firste man that he taketh in fight, his bloud dzincketh he: and offreth vnto his Kynge the heades of all thoseȝ he ther sleaeth. Foz when he hath so done, he is admitted to be partaker of the butine what so euer it be, whereof he sheuld be otherwise partles. He cutteth

of

of the heade aftre this sorte. Firste, with his knife he maketh in it a gashe rounde aboute like a circle, vndre the eares: then taketh he it by the heare of the croune, & striketh it of. That done, he fleaeth it, and taweth the skinne betwixte his handes, vntill it become very souple and soft and kiepeth it for a hande kercher. This wille he hange vpō the reine of his horse, and glorieth not a litle in it. And he that hath moste of suche hādkerchers, is compted the valeauntest manne. There are many also that sowe together these skinnes of menne, as other doe the skinnes of beastes, and weare theim for their clothyng. Some of them flea the righthand of their enemies beyng slaine, so that the nailes also remain vpon the fingres, and make couers of theim for their quiuers.

Many of thē flea the whole bodie, and stretche out the skinne vpō certaine stickes fitted for the nones, and so sprede thē vpon their Horse. Of the Skulles of the heades thus slaine, thei make masures to drincke in: coueryng them on the outside with rawe Neates leather, and gilding them on the inside, if he be of habilitie. And when any gheste of estimacion commeth

meth vnto theim, thei offre thē to dzincke in as many as thei haue, and declare foz a greate bzaggue of their valeauntnesse, that so many thei haue slaine with their owne hande.

Ons euery yere, all the chiefe heades of the Scithians, kepe a solempne dzinckyng. At the whiche the maner is, out of one of these Skulles, as out of a wassailing boule, to giue all those the wine that haue slaine an enemie. But he that hath done no suche notable acte, tasteth not therof, but sitteth aparte in a cozner without honour: which is iudged among thē a greate repzoche. But thei that haue achieued many slaughters, thei dzancke of two Gobletes together, which thei haue foz that purpose.

The goddes whom thei wozshippe and doe Sacrifice vnto, are these: Firste and chiefly vnto Vesta, then to Jupiter, and the goddesse of the grounde: foz that thei take her to be Jupiters wife. Nexte vnto Appollo and Venus, Mars and Hercules. Yet erecte thei no Chapelle, Altare, noz Image to any of these: but onely to Mars: to whom thei offre of euery hundzed przisoners that thei take, one foz a sacrifice.

trifice. To the other thei offre bothe hoꝛ-
ses and other beastes, but spetially hoꝛ-
ses. Swine thei so litle estieme, that thei
neither offre them to any of their goddes
ne vouchesaufe to kiepe theim in their
Countrie. Looke whom the kyng punis-
sheth with death, his childꝛen he also commaundeth to be slain, as many as be males, but the women are pardoned.

VVith whom the Scithians couenaūt
oꝛ make League: after this maner thei
doe it. Thei fille an earthen panne with
wine, and of the parties that shall strike
the League oꝛ couenaunte, thei dꝛawe a
quantitie of bloude, whiche thei mingle
therwith. Then diepe thei into the panne
their Curtilasse, their shaftes, their axe,
and their darte. That done thei wisshe vnto them selues many terrible curses and
mischiefes, if thei holde not the league oꝛ
couenaunte. And then dꝛincke thei the
wine. And not thei onely that strike the
couenaūtes, but also those that are moste
honourable in their compaignie.

The bewꝛiall of their kynges is after
this maner: where the Kyng dieth, those
that are of his bloude, rounde his heare,
cutte of one of his eares, slice his armes
rounde

rounde aboute, all to begasthe his foreheade and his nose, & shoote him through
the lifte hande, in thre or fowre places.
Then laie thei the corps in a Carte, and
cary it to the Gerrites, where the Sepul-
thres of all their Rynges are. And thei
dwell vpō the floude Borissthenes, about
the place wher it becometh first saileable.
This people when thei haue receiued it,
trenche out a square plotte in the ground
very wide and large. And then rippe the
bealy of the corps, and bowelle it cleane:
clensyng it and drieng it from all filthe,
and fille it vp with Siler Montanum,
Franckencense, Smallache siede, and A-
nise siede, beaten together in a Mortre.
And when thei haue sowed it vp againe
close, thei ceare the whole bodie, and conueighe the same in a Carte, to the nexte
people vndre the gouernaūce of the Sci-
thiās, whiche with honour receiue it, and
conueigh it vnto the nexte of their dominion: and so from one to another, vntill it
haue passed rounde aboute, to as many
peoples, as are of their dominion, and be
comen againe to the place of bewriall e-
mong the Gerrites. whether it is accom-
painied with a certain of all the peoples,

to

to whom it hath comen, as thei gathered
encreace from place to place. Thei, aftre
what tyme thei haue laied the corps, cophine and all, vpon a bedde of state, amid
the square afoze mencioned: sticke doune
their iauelines and speares aboute him,
and with stickes laied ouer from one to
another, frame as it ware a Cielyng,
whiche thei couer with a funeralle palle.
Then in the reste of the voide space, that
yet remaines in the Cophine made foz
the nones: thei bewzie one of his dierest
lemmans, a waityng manne, a Cooke, a
Hozsekeper, a Lacquie, a Butler, and a
Hozse. Whiche thei al first strangle, and
thzuste in, together with a pozcion of all
soztes of plate, and of euery suche thyng
as apperteined to his housholde, oz body.
And when the yere comes about, then do
thei thus. Thei take of those that ware
nerest aboute the Kyng (now there are
none aboute the king, but thei be Scithians free bozne, and suche as his self doth
commaunde: foz he maie be serued with
no bought slaue) of those take thei fiuetie
and as many of his best hozses. And whē
thei haue strangeled bothe the men and
the hozses, they bowell the Hozses, stuffe

their

their bealies againe with Chaffe, and
sowe theim vp close, and sette the menne
vppon their backes. Then make thei a
voulte ouer rounde about the borore of the
greate square, and so dispose these Horse
menne enuiron the same, that thei sieme
a farre of, a troupe of liuyng horsemen
gardyng the kyng.

The communes haue also a maner of
bewrialle aftre a like sorte. When one of
theim dieth, his nexte neighbours and
kindsfolke laie hym in a Carte, and cary
hym aboute to euery of his frindes: whiche at the receipte of hym make a feaste,
aswell to the kindsmen, as to all the res-
dewe that accompaignie the corps. And
when thei haue thus caried hym aboute
by the space of fowretene daies, he is bewried. All the braine of his heade beyng
first piked out, and the skulle rinsed with
water cleane. Aboute the bodie thei sette
vp three sparres of woodde slopyng, and
restyng one vpon another at the toppes.
Rounde about these sparres, thei straine
rappyng wollen, packyng theim as close
as thei can. And within betwixt the sparres, as it ware in the middest ouer the
deade, thei set a traie or shallowe trough,
                                     where

where in to thei caste a kinde of stones,
that glistereth by fire light.

The menne among the Scithians, do
not vse to washe thē selues. But the women vse to powze water vpon their own
bodies,and to rubbe themselues against
some roughe stone:and then with a piece
of a Lipzesse,Ceadze,oz Encence tree,to
grate their whole bodie,vntill it be some
what bollen oz swollen. And then enoint
thei bothe that and their face, with certaine medicines foz the nones : whereby
thei become the nexte daie a of very good
smell,and (when the medicine is washed
awaie)slicke and smothe.

Their commune othe, and the othe of
charge in matiers of controuersie, oz
iudgemente,is by the kynges clothe of e-
state:by the whiche if a man shalbe tried
to haue fozswozne hymself (as their en-
rhauntours haue a maner to trie with sa
lowe roddes whether thei haue oz not)by
and by without respighte, he loseth his
heade,and all his goodes.whiche tourne
to the vse of them that haue pzoued hym
periured.

The Massagetes,a people of Scithia
in Asie,beyond the sea called Caspiū mare
in

in apparesile and liuyng, muche like to
the Scithians, and therefore of some so
called: vse to fighte bothe on horsebacke
and on fote, with suche actiuitie and force,
that thei are almoste inuincible in bothe.
Their weapons are bowe and arrowes,
Launces and Armynge swordes. Their
beltes aboute their waste, the ornament
of their heades, and their pollerone, are
garnished with golde. Their Horses are
barbed on the bresi, with barbes of gold.
Their reines, bridles, and trappour are
all of golde. The heades of their Launces are of Brasse, and their Quiures armed with Brasse. As for Siluer and I-
ron thei occupie none. Eche manne marieth one wife, and yet are the wiues of
them all, commune one to another. whiche thyng is not vsed emong any of the
other Scithians. When so euer any man
lusteth for the compaignie of his woma,
he hangeth vp his quiuer vpon the carte
wherein his wife is caryed by hym, and
there openly without shame coupleth.

When any one of this people wareth
very aged, his friendes, acquaintaunce,
and kindesfolke assembled togrther, make
a bealie Sacrifice of hym: sleayng as many

ny shiepe besides, as will serue for the ful
nesse of the nombre. And when thei haue
dressed theim, eate parte and parte like,
the one with the other. And this kinde of
departynge is compted emong theim, of
all other moste blessed. If any fortune to
pine awaie of sickenesse, hym eate thei
not: but put in a hole, and throwe earthe
vpõ him. Sory for the losse, that he came
not to the feaste.

Thei neither sowe nor mowe, but liue
by flesshe of suche beastes as thei haue,
and suche fishe as Araxe the floude doeth
plēteously minister vnto them: and with
drinckynge of Milke, wherof thei make
no spare. Thei knowe no goddes but the
Sonne: In whose honour thei offre vp
Horses in Sacrifice, as beyng in swifte-
nesse moste like vnto the Sonne.

The Seretines are a debonaire people, and suche louers of quietnesse, that
thei shōne to entremedle with any other
people. Merchauntes passe their outmost
floude toward them, but thei maie come
no nigher. Along the banques there, thei
sette out suche thynges, as thei are disposed to selle. Not the Merchauntes, but
the indwellers of the Countrie. For thei

selle to other, and buie of none. And thei sette them in ordre as thei iudge them in prite. The buyer cometh, and as he iudgeth theim by his eye to be worthe, without further trade or felowesthippe betwirte theim, so laieth he doune. And if thei receiue it, he departeth with ý ware. Emong them is there neither whore nor thiefe, nor adulteresse broughte to iudgemente. Neither was it euer hearde, that there was a manne slaine emong theim. For the feare of their Lawes woorketh more strongly with theim, then the influences of the Starres. Thei dwelle as it ware in the beginnyng, or entryng of the worlde. And for that thei liue aftre a chaste sorte: thei are neither skourged with Blastynges, ne Haile, ne Pestilence, ne suche other euilles. No manne toucheth a woman there, aftre she hath conceiued, ne yet in the tyme of her flowres. Thei eate none uncleane beastes, ne knowe what Sacrifisyng meaneth. Euery man there is his owne Judge, acordyng to Justice. Therefore are thei not chastised with suche corrections as happen unto other for synne, but bothe continue long in life, and die without grief,

The

The Tauroschithiās (so called for that thei dwell aboute the mounteigne Taurus) offre as many as fortune to make Shipwracke vpon their shore:) to the virgine, whose name ye shall after heare. And if it fortune any Greke or Grekes, to be driuen thether, him doe thei Sacrifice after this maner.

Aftre what tyme thei haue made prayer after their maner, thei strike of his heade with an hachet. And (as some saie) tomble doune the carkesse into the Sea, (for this Virgine hath a Chapelle vpon the toppe of a high clieue, hangyng ouer the Sea, where this feate is doone) and naile vp the heade vpon a Gibet. In this pointe of nailyng vp the heade, all the writers agre, but in tomblyng doune the body, not so. for some affirme that the body is bewried. The Virgine Deuille, to whom thei Sacrifice: is saied to be Iphigenia Agamēnons doughter. Their ennemies as many as thei take, thus thei handle. Euery manne cutteth of his prisoners head, and carieth it home: and fasteneth it vpon the ende of a long pole, & setteth it vp: some vpon their house toppe some vpō their chimneis as high as thei

can. And no merueile though thei set the
so that thei might well see rounde about
theim: for thei sate: thei are the wardens
and kepers of al their whole house. Thei
liue by spoile, and by warre.

The Agathirsians are menne verie
neate & fine, & greate wearers of golde
in their appareill. Thei occupie their women in commune, so that thei seme all of
one kindred, and one householde: neuer
striuyng nor grudgyng one with another, muche like in body vnto the Thra-
cians.

The Neuriens vse the maners of the
Sithians. This people the somer before
that Darius set farthe, ware constrained for the greate multitude of Serpen-
tes y ware bredde in their quartres, to
chaunge their dwellyng place. Thei ve-
rily doe belieue, and wille sweare it: that
euery yere ones for a certaine daies, thei
become Woulues, and retourne againe
into their former shape and sate.

The Antropophagites (so called for that
thei liue by mannes fleshe) of all menne,
are the worste codicioned, without lawe,
or officer, apparesiled like the Scithiens:
but in language like vnto no bodye but
                                        them

them selues.

The Melanchleni do all weare blacke, as their name dothe signifie. And of these also are eaters of mannes fleshe: so manie as folowe the trade of the Scithians.

The Budines are a great nacion, and a populous, graye eyed, & redde headed al. Their heade citie is Gelone, wherof thei are also called Gelonites. Thei kepe euery thirde yere a reuelle in the honour of Bacchus: whereat thei make reuelle in dede, yea, reuell route. Thei ware sometime Griekes, whiche put of fro their countrie, seatled them selues there. And by processe, losing the propzietie of their owne tongue, became in laguage haulfe Grekes, and haulfe Scithians. Yet are the Gelonites bothe in language and liuinge, different from the Budines. For the Budines being natiue of the place, are bzeders of Cattelle: The Gelonites, occupienge tilthe: liue by cozne, and haue their frute yardes. Neyther lyke in colour ne countenaunce to the other. All their quartres are verye full, and thicke of trees. It hathe also many meres and greate. In and about the
M.v.　　whiche

whichethei take Otters, and Beauers, & many other beastes: of whose skinnes they make them pilches, and Ierkins.

The Lirceis liue by woodmanshippe, and huntinge, and aftre this maner. Their countrie beinge also very thicke of trees, thei vse to climbe suche as siemeth them beste: and there awaite their game. At the foote of euery mannes tree steth a dogge, and a horse well taughte to couche flatte on the bealy, as lowe as ran bee. When the beaste cometh within daungier, he shoteth. And, yf he hitte, he streighte commeth downe, taketh his horse backe, & foloweth with his houde.

The Argippians dwell vndre the foote of the highe mountaines. Men whiche fro their birthe are balde, bothe the males and the females. Their noses tourne vp like a shoinge horne, and their chinnes be great out of measure. The sounde of their voice vnlike to all other: ther apparell aftre the sorte of the Scithians. Thei haue small regarde to breding: by the reason wherof thei haue smalle store of cattaile. Thei lie vndre trees, which in the wintre theicouer ouer with a white kinde of felte, and in the somer take the
same

fame awaye, and lie vndze the open tree.
Ther is no manne that wil harme them
foz that thei are compted holy halowed:
neither haue thei anye kinde of armour,
oz weapõ of warre. These men haue the
arbitrement of their neigbours controuersies
rounde aboute And as thei determine
so are thei ended. Who so fliteth vnto
them, is saufe as in sanctuary.

The Issedonnes haue this propzetie.
When so euer any mannes father ther,
dieth: all his kinsfolke bzinge euery man
one beast oz other to the house of ȳ sonne
that kepeth the funeral. Which whẽ thei
haue killed and minsed: they minse also
the body of the deade. And bothe the fleshes
beinge mingled together, thei fall to
the banket. Then take thei the dead man
nes heade, ꝭ pike the bzaine oute cleane,
and all other moistures and ragges, and
when thei haue guilte it, thei vse it foz a
repzesentaciõ of the partie departed. Solempnissinge
euery yere furthe, the memoziall,
with newe ceremonies, and mo.
This dothe the sonne foz the father, and
the father foz the sonne, as the Grekes
kepe their birthe daies.

These are also sayde to be verye tusse
dealers

dealers, ¬ their wiues to be as valeaunte
and hardie as the husbādes. Suche haue
the maners of the Scithians bene. But
afterwarde being subdued by the Tartares, and wearing by proceſſe into their
maners and ordinaunces: thei nowe liue
all after one ſorte, and vndꝛe one name.

¶ The .x. Chapiter.
¶ Of Tartarie, and the maners
and power of the Tar-
tarians .

Artaria, otherwyſe
called Mongal : As
Vincentuis wꝛyteth,
is in that parte of
the earthe where the
Eaſte and the noꝛthe
ioyne together . It
had vpō the eaſte, the
londe of the Katheorines and Solangores,
on the South, the Saracenes: on the weſte
the Naymaniens, ¬ on the noꝛthe is enclo-
ſed with the ocean. It hath the name of
the floude Tartar that ronneth by it . A
country very hilly, and full of mountaines. And wher it is champe in, myngled
with ſāde and grauelle, Barreine, except

it

it be in places where it is moysted with floudes, which are very fewe. And therfore it is muche waaste, and thinly enhabited. Ther is not in it one Citie, ne one village beside Cracuris. And wood in the moste parte of the country so skante, that the enhabitautes are faine to make their fyre, and dresse their meate with the drie donge of neate and horses. The ayer intemperate and wonderfulle. Thondre, and lightening in somer so terrible, that sondry do presently die for very feare. Nowe is it broiling hote, and by and by bittre colde, and plenty of snowe. Suche stronge windes sometime, that it staieth horse and man, and bloweth of the rider: teareth vp trees by the rootes, and doeth muche harme . In wintre it neuer raineth ther, and in Somer very often . But so slendrely, that the earthe is skante wette with al. And yet is ther great store of Cattaile: as Camelles, neate. &c. And horses and mares, in suche plentie, as I beleue no parte of the earth hath againe. It was first enhabited of foure peoples. Of the Ieccha mongalles that is to saye, the greate mongalles. The Sumongalles, that is to say the watre mongalles, whiche the called them selues Tartares, of the floude Tartar whose neighbours thei are.

The thirde people ware called Merchates, and the fourthe Metrites. There was no difference betwixte them eyther in body or láguage, but al aftre one sorte and facion. Their behauour was in the beginning very brute, and farre oute of ordre, without lawe or discipline, or any good facion. Thei liued amonge the Scithians, and kept herdes of cattalle in very base state and condition: and ware tributaries to all their neighbours. But within a while aftre, thei deuided them selues as it ware into wardes, to euery of the which was appointed a captaine: in whose deuises and consentes cósisted thordre of the whole. Yet ware thei tributaries to the Naimánes (their next neighbours) untyll Canguissa by a certaine prophecie was chosen their kynge. He assone as he had receiued the gouernaunce, abolished all worshippe of deuilles, and commaunded by commune decree that all the whole nacion should honour the highe godeuerlasting: by whose prouidence he would seme to haue receiued

ned

ued the kingdome . It was further decreed that as manye as ware of age to
beare armour, should be preste, and ready with the kyng at a certeyne daye.
The multitude that serued for their warres, was thus destributed. Their capitaines ouer ten (which by a terme borowed
of the Frenche, we calle Diseners, are at
the commaundemente of the Centurians.
And the Centuriane obeied the Millena-
rie, that had charge of a thousande. And
he againe was subiecte to the grande
Coronelle that had charge ouer ten thousande: aboue the whiche nombre thei
mounted no degree of captaines.

This done, to proue the obedience of his
subiectes, he commaunded seuen sonnes
of the Princes or Dukes whiche before
had gouerned the people: to be slaine by
the handes of their owne fathers, and mothers. Whiche thinge althoughe it ware
muche againste their hartes, and an horrible diede, yet did thei it. Partely vppon
the feare of the residew of the people: and
partly vpon conscience of their obediece.
For why, the people thoughte when thei
sawe him begyn aftre this sorte: thei had
had a god amongest them. So that in dis-
obeyng

soueynge of his commaundemente, thei thought thei should not haue disobeied a king but God him selfe.

Canguista takinge stomake with this power, firste subdued those Scithians that bordred vpon him, and made them tributaries. And where other afore had bene tributaries also vnto them: now receiued he in that one peoples righte, tribute of many. Then settinge vpon those that ware further of, he had suche prosperous successe that from Scithia to the sonne risinge, and fro thence to the middle earthe sea, and beyonde: he broughte all together vndre his subiection . So that he moughte nowe worthely wryte him selfe highe Gouernour, and Emperour of the Easte.

The Tartares are very deformed, litle of bodie for the moste parte, hauyng great stiepe eyes: and yet so heary on the eye liddes, that there sheweth but litle in open sight. Platter faced and beardlesse, sauyng vpon the vpper lippe, and a litle aboute the poincte of the chinne thei haue a feawe heares as it ware pricked in with Bodkins. Thei be communely all, slendre in the waste. Thei shaue the hindre

haulfe

haulfe of the heade, rounde aboute by the
croune, from one eare to another : com-
passyng towarde the nape of the necke
after suche a facion, that the polle behind
sheweth muche like the face of a bearded
manne . On the other parte, thei suffre
their heare to growe at lengthe like our
women: whiche thei deuide into two tres-
ses, oz braudes, and bzyng aboute to fasten behinde their eares. And this maner
of shauyng, do thei vse also that dwelle a-
mong theim, of what nacion so euer thei
be. Thei theim selues are very light and
nimble: good on Hozse, but naughte on
foote. All from the moste to the leaste, as
well the women as the menne : doe ride
either vpon Geldynges, oz Kien, where
so euer thei become . Foz stoned Hozses
thei occupie none, ne yet Gelding that is
a striker, and lighte of his heles . Their
bzidelles are trimmed with muche gold,
siluer, and precious stones. And it is compted a ioly thyng emong theim : to haue
a great sozt of siluer sounded belles, gyn-
glyng aboute their hozse neckes . Their
speache is very chourlishe and loude .
  Their singyng is like the bawlynge of
Woulues. When thei dzincke, thei shake

the heade: and drincke thei do very often
euen vnto drockennesse,wherin thei glorie muche. Their dwellyng is neither in
tounes ne Bouroughes. But in the fieldes abrode,aftre the maner of thaunciet
Scithians in tentes.And the ratherso,for
that thei are all moste generally catteil-
maistres. In the wintre timethei are wôt
to drawe to the plaines, & in the Somer
season,to the mounteignes & hillie places
for the better pasture. Thei make their
Tentes, or elles rounde cotages of wick-
res, or of Felte vndersette with smothe
poles. In the middes thei make a round
windowe that giueth thē lighte,& letteth
out the smoke. In the middes of the Tēt,
is their fire,aboute the whiche their wife
and their childrē doe sitte. The menne
delight muche in dartyng,shootyng,and
wrastelyng. Thei are merueilous good
hunters, to the whiche thei go armed at
all pieces. And assone as thei espie the
beaste,thei come cossing together rounde
aboute and enclose her. And when euery
manne hath throwen his darte, or shotte
his arrowe: whilest the beast is troubled
& amased with the stripes, thei steppe in
to her,& slea her.Thei neither vse breade

ne bakyng:table clothe ne napkin.

Thei belieue that there is one GOD that made all thynges, bodily & ghostly, sene or vnsene, and hym thei honour: but not with any maner of Sacrifice or ceremonie. Thei make theim selues litle pupettes of silke or of felte, or of thrumme, like vnto menne: whiche thei sette vp vpon eche side of their Tentes, and do thē muche reuerence, beseching them to take hede to their catteille. To these thei offre the first milke of all their milche catteill, of what kinde so euer thei be. And before thei begin either to eate or drinke aught, thei sette a portion thereof before theim. Looke what beaste thei kille to be eaten, thei reserue the harte all nighte in some couered cuppe, and the nexte mornpnge seath it and eate it.

Thei worshippe also and Sacrifice to to the Sonne, Moone, and elementes fowre. To Cham also their Lorde and Kyng, thei do very deuoute honour and Sacrifice: supposyng him to be the sonne of god, and to haue no piere in the whole worlde: neither can thei abide to heare any other manne name hym.

This people so despiseth al other men,

and thincke theim selues so farre to sur-
mount them in wisedome and goodnes:
that thei abhorre to speake to theim, or to
compaignie with theim. Thei calle the
Pope and all christen menne, Doggues
and Idolatres: beecause thei honour stones and blocques. And thei theim selues
(beyng giuen to deuelishe supersticions)
are markers of dreames, & haue dreame
readers emong theim: as well to enter-
preate their sweuens, as to aske knoweledge of Idolles. In whom thei are perswaded that God speaketh: and therfore
acordyng to their answeres, frame them
selues to do. Thei marke many seasons,
and specially haue regarde to the chaun-
ges of the Moone. Yet make thei for no
season, ne chaunge, any singuler holidaie
or obseruaunce: but ilike for them all indifferently. Thei are of so gredte a couei-
tousenesse, and desire, that if any of them
se aughte, that he coueiteth to haue, and
cannot obtein with the good wille of the
owner: if it apperteigne to no Tartarre,
he will haue it by force. And thei thincke
(through a certein ordenaunce that their
Kyng made) thei offende not therin. For
suche a commaundemente had thei of

Languista

Tanguissa, and Cham, their firste Kynges: That if it fortune any Tartarre, or Tartarres seruaunt, to finde in his waie, horse, man, or womā, without the kinges ettres or his saulfcōduite: he should take it, him, her, or them as his owne for euer.

To suche as lacke money thei lende, but for shamefull gaines: that is to saie, two shillynges of the pounde for euery Monethe. And if it fortune ye to faile to make paiemente at the daie: ye shall also be forced to paie the enterest, acording to the rate of the Usurie. That is to saie, of euery tenth penie, one.

Thei do so polle and oppresse their tributaries, with subsidies, tares and tallages, as neuer did people but thei, that euer manne redde of. It is beyonde belief to saie. Thei euer coueite, and as Lordes of all, do rape, and rende from other, and neuer recompence aught. No, the begger that liueth on almose, getteth not an aguelette of hym. Yet haue thei this one praise worthie propretie, that if he fortune to finde them at meate: thei neither shutte the doore against hym, ne thruste him out, if he be disposed to eate. but charitably bidde them, and parte with them

suche

suche as thei haue. But thei fiede the vn-
cienlieft in the woylde, as I haue saied,
without tableclothe, napkinne, oy towell
to couer the boyde, oy to wipe at meate, oy
aftre. Foy thei neither washe hande, face,
ne body, ne any garmēte that thei weare,
Thei nether eate byead, noy make byead,
noy sallottes noy potage, noy any kinde of
Pultz. But no maner of flesshe cometh
to them amisse. Dogges, Cattes, Hoyses
and rattes. Pea, sometime to shewe their
crueltie, and to satisfie their vengeaunce,
the bodies of suche their enemies, as thei
haue taken, thei vse to roste by a greate
fire: and when thei bee assembled a good
nombye together, thei teare theim of the
spittes like Woulues, with their tieche,
and deuoure thē. And aftreward dyincke
vp the bloude, whiche thei reserue afoye
hande foy the nones. Otherwise thei vse
to dyincke Milke. Thei haue no wine of
the coūtrie it self, but suche as is byought
into thē thei dyincke very gredilie. Thei
vse to Lowse one anothers heade, and e-
uer as thei take a Lowce to eate her, sai-
eng: thus wille I doe to our enemies. It
is compted a greate offence emong them
to suffre dyincke, oy a piece of meate to be
losse

losse. Thei neuer therfore giue the bone to the Dogge, till thei haue eaten out the marrowe. Thei neuer eate beaste (suche vile niggardes thei are) as long as the same is sounde & in good likyng: but whē it fortuneth to be hurte, sicke, or febled by age, then bewrie they it in their bealies. Thei are greate sparers, & contente with smalle chaunge, and litle foode. Thei drincke in the mornyng, a goblet full of Milke or twaine, whiche serueth theim sometyme for their whole daies foode.

The men and the women moste communely are appareilled ylike. The men weare vpon their heades shallowe copin tackes, cōmyng out behinde with a taile of a handefull and a haulfe long, and as muche in breadth: whiche thei fasten vndre their chinnes, for falling or blowing of, with a couple of strynges of ribbande lace, as we doe our nighte cappes. Their maried women weare on their heades, fine wickre Basquettes of a foote and a haulf long: round, and flatte on the toppe like a barrelle. Whiche are either garni shed with chāugeable silkes, or the gaiest parte of the Pecockes feathers, and sette with golde and stones of sondrie sortes.

As for the residue of their bodie, thei wear acording to their abilitie, bothe men and women, Skarlet or Veluet, or other silkes. Thei weare coates of a straunge fasion, open on the left side, whiche thei put on acordingly, and fasten with fowre or fiue Buttons. Their Somer wiedes are all comunely blacke: and those that thei weare in winttre and foule weather, white: and neuer lower then the knee. Wearing furres (wherin thei muche delight) thei weare not the furre inwarde, as we communely doe: but contrariwise the heare outwarde, that thei maie enioie the pleasure of the shewe.

It is harde to discerne by the appareue the malde, fro the wife, or the woman fro the manne: so like arated doe the menne and the wome͂ go. Thei weare brieches, the one and the other. When thei shal go to the skirmische, or to battaille, some couer their armes (whiche at all other tymes are naked) with plates of iron, buckeled together alonge, in many pietes, that thei may the easelier sturre their armes. Some doe thesame with many foldes of Leather: wherwith thei also arme their head. Thei cannot handle a target:

nor but fewe of theim a launce or a long
sweard. Thei haue curtilasses of iij. quar
ters longe: not double edged but backed.
Thei fighte all with a quarter blowe, &
neither right downe, ne foyning. Thei be
very redy on horsebacke, and very skilful
archers. He is compted moste valeaūte,
that best obserueth the commaundement
and the obedience dewe to his capitaine.
Thei haue no wages for their souldie,
yet are thei prest, and ready in all affay-
res, and all commaundementes. In battayle, and otherwise wher oughte is to be
done, very politike and experte. The princes and capitaines entre not the battle,
but standing aloofe, crye vnto their men,
and harten them on: lookinge diligently
aboute on euery side what is nedefull to
be done. Sometime to make the armye
sieme the greater, and the more terrible
to the ennemy: thei set vp on horsebacke
their wiues and their children, yea and
men made of cloutes. It is no vilany a-
monge them to flye: if any thinge maye
eyther be saued or wonne by it. When
thei will shoote, thei vnarme their righte
arme, and then let thei flye with suche violence, that it pearceth all kinde of ar-

D.v.   mour

mour. Thei giue the onset flockinge in plumpes, and likewise in plompes they flie. And in the flighte thei so shoote backewarde behinde them, that thei slea many of their ennemies pursuinge the chase. And when thei perceiue their ennemies dispersed by pursuinge the chase, or not to fighte any thing wholse together: soudeinly retourninge, thei beginne a newe onset with a hayle of shotte, neither sparing horse ne mā. So that oftetimes thei ouercome when thei are thoughte to be vāquisshed. when thei come to enuade any quartre or countrie, thei deuide their armie, and sette vpon it on euery parte: so that the enhabitours can neither haue laisure to assemble and resiste, ne waye to escape. Thus are thei alway sure of the victory, whiche thei knytte vp with moste proude crueltie. Neither sparinge manne woman ne childe, olde ne younge sauing the artificer onely, whome thei reserue for their own vses. And this slaughter make thei aftre this maner. When thei haue all taken them, thei distribute them to their Centurians: who committe them againe to the slaues: to euery one fewer or moe acordinge to the

multitude

multitude. And when the slanes haue all
slayne them as bouchers kylle hogges:
then for a terrour to al other ther about:
ofeuery thousãde of ÿ dead thei take one,
and hange him vp by the hieles vpon a
stake, amydde these deade bodies: and so
ordre his heade as though it appiered by
his faction or maner of hanginge, that he
yet bothe harkened the complainte of his
felowes, and lessoned them againe. Many of the Tartarres when the bodies lie
fresshe blieding on the grounde, laye
them downe alonge, and sucke of ÿ bloud
a full gloute.

Thei kepe faithe to no manne, howe de-
pely so euer thei binde them selues thervnto. Thei deale yet wourse with those
that thei ouercome with force. The maidens and younge women thei deflowre,
and defile as thei come to hande, neither
do thei iudge it any dishonestie. The be-
autifuller sorte thei leade away with thẽ:
and in extreame misery, constraine them
to be their slaues all their lyfe longe.
Of all other thei are moste vnbrideled in
leachery. For althoughe thei marye as
many wiues as thei luste, and are able
to kepe: no degre prohibited, but mother,
doughter,

doughter, and sister: yet are thei as racke
bouguers with mankinde, and with beastes, as the Saracenes are, and no punish
mente for it amonge them. The woman
that thei marie, thei neuer take as wife,
ne receiue any dowrie withher, vntill she
haue borne a childe. So that if she be bar-
ren he maye caste her vp, and mary another.

This is a notable meruaile, that though
amonge theim manye women haue but
one manne: yet thei neuer lightely falle
out, ne brawle one with another for him.
And yet are the menne parcialle in theyr
loue: shewing muche more fauour to one
then another, and goynge fro the bedde
of the one, streighte to the bedde of an o-
ther. The women haue their seuerall tē-
tes and householdes: And yet liue verye
chastely, and true to their housebandes.
For bothe the manne and the woman taken in adultery, suffre death by the lawe.

Those that are not occupied for y̆ warres, driue the catteile a felde, and there
keps them. Thei hunte, and exercise them
selues in wrastlinge, other thing doe thei
not. The care of prouision for meate and
drincke, appareille and householde, they
betake

betake to the women. This people hath
many superstitious toyes . It is a hey-
nous matier with them , to touche ỹ fier,
oz take fleſſhe out of a potte with a knife.
Thei hewe oz choppe no maner of thing
by the fire , leaſſe by any maner of meanes,thei might foztune to hurte the thing
which alway thei haue in reuerence, and
iudge to be the clenſer, and purifier of al
thinges . To laye them downe to reſte
vppon the whippe that thei ſtirre theyz
hozſe with (foz ſpurres they vſe none) oz
to touche their ſhaftes therewith, in no
wyſe thei wylle not . Thei neither kille
younge birdes, ne take them in the neſte
oz otherwaies. Thei beate not the hozſe
with the bzidle. Thei bzeake not one bone
with another. Thei are ware, not to ſpill
any ſpone meate , oz dzincke, ſpecially
milke. No manne piſſeth within the com-
paſſe of their ſoiourning place. And if a-
ny one of ſelf willed ſtubbozneſſe ſhould
do it, he ware ſure withoute all mercy to
die foz it. But if neceſſitie conſtraine thē
to do it (as it often happeneth) then the
tente of hym that did it , with all that is
in it, muſte be clenſed and purified aftre
this maner . They make two fires, thze

ſtrides

strides one from another.   And by eche
fire thei pitche downe a Iaueline. Upon
them is tied a lyne stretching fro the one
to the other, and couered ouer with buc-
kerame. Betwene these. ii. Iauelins, as
throughe a gate, muste all thinges passe
that are to be purified. Two women (to
whome this office belongeth) stande, on
either side one , sprinckelinge on watre,
and mumblinge certaine verses .   No
straungier, of what dignitie so euer he be ,
or of howe greate importaunce so euer
the cause of his comming be: is admitted
to the kinges sighte before he be purified
He that treadeth vppon the thressholde
of the tente wherin their kinge, or, anye
of his chiefteines lyeth, dieth for it in the
place. If any manne bite a gobet , greater then he is able to swallowe, so that he
be constrained to put it out of his mouth
againe : thei by and by make a hole vndre the tent, and ther drawe him out, and
cruelly slea him . Many other thinges
ther are which thei compte for faultes be
ponde all forgiuenesse. But to slea a mā,
to enuade a nother mannes country, cō-
trary to all righte and reason, to bereue
them of their goodes and possessions , to
breake

breake the preceptes of God, thei estteme
as nothinge. Thei haue a beliefe that aftre this life thei shal liue for euer in another worlde (but what maner of worlde
thei cannot telle) & ther receiue rewarde
for their well doinges. When any of thē
falleth sicke, & lieth at the pointe of death,
thei sticke vp a Iaueline with a piece of
blacke clothe at the dore of the tēte wher
he lieth, that none come in as they passe
by. For no manne when he seeth this,
dare entre thether vncalled.

Aftre what time the sicke is deade, his
whole house gather together, and prine-
ly conueighe the corps into some place
withoute the tente, chosen for þ purpose.
Ther cut they out a trenche, broade and
diepe enoughe to sette vp another lyttle
tent in: so that the toppe of the tent maye
be well within the groundes. In that thei
prepare a table with a banket: at the
whiche thei sette the deade bodye in his
beste appareille . And so together, as it
ware with one hāde, couer all with earth
againe. Thei bewry with him also some
beaste of bourden, and a horse ready sad-
led and appointed to ride. The gentlemē
by their life time, appointe out a slaue
whome

(whome thei marke with their brande)
to be specially bewried with him when
he dieth. And this do thei vpon perswasion of a life in a nother worlde, wher thei
woulde be loth to lacke these necessaries.
Then doe the deades friendes take another horse, and slea him . And when they
haue eaten the flesshe, thei stuffe the hide
full of haye, and sowe it againe together
and sette it vp ouer the graue vpon foure
poles, in remembraunce of the deade.
The bones do the two ordenarie women
burne, for the clensinge and purifienge of
the soule. But the gentlemen, and thei of
higher degree, handle the hide aftre another maner. Thei cut it out into very fine
thonges, to asmuche lengthe as thei can,
and measure cute asmuche grounde a-
boute the Sepulchre as the thonge wille
stretche vnto. for so muche groūd thincke
thei shall the deade haue in a nother
worlde . At the thirtieth daye thei ende
their mourning.

Certaine of the Tartarres, professing
the name of Christe, yet farre from his
righteousnes: when their parentes ware
aged, to haste their death, cramme thē with
gobins of fatte, Whē thei die thei burne
them

them to pouldze, whiche thei referue as a
pzecious Iewelle, to ſtrawe vppon their
meate euery daie. But to declare with
what ſolempnitie and ioiſulneſthei ſette
vp their newe Rynge, aſtre the death of
tholde: becauſe it ware to longe a thyng,
bothe foz the reader & wziter to ſet out at
length, I will ſhewe you in bzief theffecte

Abzode in the fieldes, in a faire plaine
ozdenary foz the purpoſe: all the Dukes,
Erles, Barons, Lozdes, and the reſte of
the nobilite, together with the people of
the whole kyngdome, do aſſemble. Then
take thei hym, to whõ the croune is due,
either by ſucceſſion, oz by cleation. And
when thei haue ſet hym vp in a thzone of
Golde: thei all fall doune on their knees,
and together with one voice crie out a
loude, aſtre this maner. We require the,
yea, we will and commaunde the, to take
the rule & gouernaunce of vs. He anſwe-
reth, if ye will haue me doe ſo, then muſt
ye of neceſſitie be redy to do whatſoeuer
I commaunde yᵉ. To come when I calle
ye, to go whether ſo euer I ſende ye, to
ſtea whom ſo euer I commaũde ye, without ſtaieng oz ſtackering. and to put the
whole kingdome and rule in my handes,

P.i.   when

when thei haue aunſwered, we are content: Saieth he againe, from hencefurthe
then the ſpeache of my mouth, ſhalbe my
ſwearde. To this the people yealde with
greate ſhoutes, and reioiſynges. In the
meane while the princes and the nobles,
taking the king out of his chrone, ſpread
abrode on the grounde a piece of felte: v-
pon the whiche, thei cauſe hym in ſimple
ſorte to ſitte doune, and thus ſaie to hym.
Looke vp, and remembre GOD aboute
the. And now looke doune alſo, and be-
hold this felt vndre the. If thou gouerne
welle, thou ſhalte haue all euen as thou
wouldeſt wiſſhe it. But if contrarywiſe,
thou ſhalt ſo be broughte doune againe,
and ſo nighe be bereued of all: that thou
ſhalte not haue ſo muche, as this poore
felte left the, whervpon thou ſitteſt. This
ones ſaied, thei ſette in to hym, of all his
wiues the diereſt derlyng. And liftyng
vp the felte alofte, haile hym by the name
of Emperour, & her by the name of Em-
preſſe. Then come there preſetes ſtreight
from al countries, and peoples of his dominion: and all the Threaſoures that the
kyng, his predeceſſour left, are broughte
him. Of the whiche he giueth giftes to al

the

the princes and high estates : commaun-
dyng the reste to be kepte for himself, and
so dissolueth the Parlament as it ware.

In his hande and power is then altogether, no manne can: or though he can,
he dare not saie this is myne, or this is
his . No man maie dwelle in any parte
of the lande, but in that wherevnto he is
appoincted. The Emperour hymself ap-
poincteth the Dukes: the Dukes, the
Millenaries: the Millenaries, the Cen-
turianes: and thei the Disniers: and the
Disniers the residewe. The seale that he
vseth hath this superscripcion. GOD in
heauen, and Chutchuth Cham in earth,
the force of God , and Emperour of all
menne . He hath fiue armies of greate
multitude and force: and fiue chiefteines,
by whom he subdueth all that stande a-
gainst hym . He hymself neuer speaketh
to any foreine ambassadours, nor admit-
teth thē to his presence, as is abouesaied:
exepte bothe thei and their giftes (without the whiche specially thei maie not
come) bee purified by the ordenarie women. The Kyng aunswereth by another
mannes mouthe . And the persone by
whom he aunswereth, be he neuer so ho-

nourable

ourable, for the tyme that he becometh
the kynges mouthe, kneleth on his knees
and giueth so diligent eare, that he swar-
ueth not from the Kyng in one woorde.
For it is not lawefull for any manne, to
chaunge the kynges woordes: ne for any
man in any wise, to replie againſt suche
sentēce as he giueth. He neuer dzincketh
in open pzesence, but some body firſt sing
to hym, oz plaie vpon some inſtrumente
of Muſicque.

The gentlemen and menne of honour
when thei ride, haue a phannell bozne a-
foze them, on a Iauelines ende, to kiepe
awaie the Sonne. And as it is saied, the
womē likewise. These ware the maners
and facions of the Tartarres, for a two
hundzed yeres paſte.

The Geozgiās, whom the Tartarres
aboute the same tyme did subdue: ware
chziſtians, aftre the fourme of the Greke
Churche. Thei ware neighbours to the
Perſians. Their dominiōs ſtretched out
a great length, from Paleſtine in Iewzie
to the mounteignes called Caſpij. Thei
had eightene Biſhopzies: and one Ca-
tholicque: that is to saie, one generall biſhoppe, whiche was to them, as our Metropolitane

tropolitane to vs. At the firste thei ware
subiecte to the Patriarche of Antioche.
Menne of greate courage and hardinesse. Thei all shaued their crounes: the
Laietie square, the Clercques rounde.
Their women (certeine of theim) had the
ordre of Knighthode, and ware trained
to the warres. The Georgianes when
thei ware sette, ordered, and raunged in
the fielde, and ware at pointe to ioyne the
batteill: vsed to drincke of a gourdfull of
strong wine, aboute the bigguenes of a
mannes fiste. And to sette vpon their ennemies: muche amended in courage.

Their Clercques, whiche we calle the
Spiritualtie, mighte vse bothe Simonie
and vsurie at their wille. There was continuall hatred betwixte Tharmenians
and them. For the Armenians ware also
christians, before the Tartarres had subdued the Georgianes and thē. But thei
differed in many thinges, from the beliefe
and facions of the true Churche. Thei
knewe no Christemas daie, no vigilles,
nor the fowre quartre fastes, whiche we
call Embryng daies. Thei fasted not on
Easter euē, because (saie thei) that Christ
rose that daie aboute euen tide. Vpon e-

uery

very Saturdaie, betwixte Eaſter and
Whitſontide, thei did eate fleſſhe. Thei
ware greate faſters, and beganne their
Lẽte thre wekes aſoze vs: and ſo ſtreightly faſted it, that vpon the Wedenſdaie
and Fridaie, thei neither eate any kinde
of fiſſhe, ne aughte wherin was wine, oz
oile. Belieuing that he, that dzancke wine
on theſe twoo daies: ſynned moze then if
he had bene at the ſtewes with a whoze.
On the Monedaie thei abſteined from
all maner of meate. On Tewſdaie and
Thurſdaie, thei did eate but one meale.
Wedenſdaie and Fridaie, nothyng at al.
Saturdaie and Sondaie, thei eate fleſhe
and made luſtie chiere. Thzoughe their
whole Lente, no manne ſaid Maſſe but
on Saturdaies and Sondaies. Noz yet
on the Fridaies thzoughout the whole
yere: foz thei thoughtthen, that thei bzake
their faſt. Thei admittedto the houſeale,
aſwell childzen of two monethes olde, as
all other indifferently. When thei went
to Maſſe, thei vſed to put no watre in the
wine. Thei abſteined from Hares fleſhe
Beares fleſhe, Crowes, and ſuche other
as the Grekes did, and Jewes do. Their
Chalices ware of Glaſſe, and of Tree.

Some

Some said Masse without either albe oz
vestement, oz any maner suche oznamēt.
Some onely with thoznamētes of Deacon oz Subdeacon. Thei ware all busie
vsurers, and Simonites: bothe spirituall
and Tēpozalt, as the Geozgianes ware.
Their pziestes studied Sothesaieng and
Nigromancie. Their Spiritualtie vsed
Junckettyng oftener then the Laiette.

Thei maried, but aftre the death of the
wife, it was not lawefull foz the housebande to marie againe, noz foz the wife,
aftre the death of the housebande. If the
wife ware a whoze, the Bisshoppe gaue
hym leaue to put her awaie, and marie
another. As foz the fire of Purgatozie
thei knewe nothing of it. Thei denied also verie stiflye, that there ware two natures in Chziste. The Geozgianes saied
that thei swarued from the truthe of
Chzistes Religion, in thirtie poinctes oz
articles.

¶The.xi.Chapitre.

¶Of Turcquie, and of the maners,
Lawes, and Oʒdenaunces
of the Turcques.

P. iiii.   The

HE lande, whiche
now is called Turc-
quie: hath on Theaste
Armenia the more, &
ronneth endelong to
the Sea of the Cili-
cians: hauyng on the
Northe, the Sea na-
med Euxinus. There are in it many coû-
tries conteined. As Lichaonia, whose
heade citie is Iconium. Cappadocia with
her heade citie, named Cesarea. Isauria,
whiche hath for the chief citie Seleucia. Li-
cta, whiche now is called Briquia, Ionia:
now called Quisquom, in the whiche
standeth Ephesus. Paphlagonia, and in
it Germanopolis. And Leuech: that hath
for the heade Citie Trapezus. All this
countrie that now is called Turcquie, is
not enhabited by one seuerall nacion, but
there be in it Turcques, Grekes, Armenians, Saracenes, Iacobites, Nestorians, Iewes and christians. Whiche liue
for the moste parte, acording to the Tradicions and Ordenaunces, that Mahomet the countrefeict Prophete, gaue vnto the Saracenes (a people of Arabie) the
yere of our Lorde and Sauiour Iesus
Christe.

Chriſte .vi. hundꝛed and. xxix. A manne
whome I can not telle whether I maye
calle an Arabiane oꝛ a Perſiã. Foꝛ ther
be aucthoꝛities of wꝛiters on either behaulfe. His father was an idolaſtre after
the maner of the heathen. His mother an
Iſmalite leaning to the lawe of the Jewes. And whileſt in his childehode, his
mother taught him aftre one ſoꝛte, ⁊ his
father aftre another: thei pꝛinted in hym
ſuche a doubtfull belief, ỹ when he came
to age he cleaued to neither. But as a
manne of ſubtyle and guilefull witte, aftre what time he had bene longe conuer-
ſaunte amongeſt menne of the Chꝛiſtian
religion: he dꝛaue a dꝛiſte, deuiſed out of
both lawes (the olde and the newe) how
he mighte notably enfecte the woꝛlde.

He ſaid the Jewes did wickedly to
denie Chꝛiſte to be boꝛne of the virgine
Mary, ſeinge the pꝛophetes (mẽ of great
holineſſe, ⁊ enſpired with the holy ghoſt)
had foꝛeſhewed the ſame , ⁊ warned mẽ
of many yeres paſſed to looke foꝛ him.
Contrariwyſe he ſaid to the Chꝛiſtians
thei ware very fonde to beleue that Je-
ſus, ſo dierly beloued of God, and boꝛne
of a virgine, wﻻuld ſuffre thoſe vilanies

and

and tormentes of the Jewes.

Martinus Segonius nouomõtanus, in his booke of the Sepulchre of Christe our king, writeth that the Turkes, and Saracenes by an auncient opinion receiued from Machomet: do laughe Christian menne to skorne, that seke thether with so greate reuerence. Sayeng that Christ ŷ prophet of all prophetes endewed with the spirite of God, and voyde of all earth ly corruption: had ther no sepulchre in very diede, for that hé being a spirituall body cõceiued by the breathe of ŷ holy ghoſt coulde not suffre, but should come againe to be iudge of the Gentiles. This saieth Segonius, and many other thinges sounding to like effecte: whiche the Mahometeines are wõte to throwe out againſt the christians, bothe foolisſhely and wickedly. When this countrefeitte prophet had ſauſed his secte with these wicked opinions: he gaue them his lawe, and sorte of religion. Againſt the whiche leſſe any man of righte iudgemente should afterwarde write or dispute (as againſt a peſtilent and filthie perswaſion) he wrote a lawe in his Alcorane that it ſhoulde be deathe to as many as ſhould reason or dispute

dispute vppon it. Wherby he euidentlie
declared,that ther was nothing godly oz
goodly therin. For why should he elles
haue so raked it vp in the asshes, and for
bidden it to be examined: so that the people coulde neuer come to knowledge
what maner of thinge it is that thei be
leue in. In the giuing of his lawe,he vsed
muche the counselle & helpe of the môche
Sergius:of the wicked secte of the Ne-
stozianes.And to the ende it might please
the moze vniuersally:he patched it vp together with peces of all maner of sectes.
He thoughte it good to sette out Chziste
with the beste,affirminge that he was a
manne excelling in all holinesse and vertue. yea he extolled him to a moze heigth
then was appliable to the nature of mâ,
calling him the woozde, the spirite, the
soule of GOD,bozne out of a virgines
wombe,whome he also with many wondzefull pzaises magnified.He confirmed
with his consente,the miracles, and stoz-
ry of the gospel,as farre as it varieth not
from his Alcozane.

The Godspelles said he ware cozrupte
by the disciples of the Apostles.And ther
foze it behoued his Alcozane to be made,
for

for to correcte and amende them. Thus
fawning into fauour with the christiās,
he would haue bene christened of Sergius. Then to procure,⸮ moue other also to fauonor his procedinges: he denied
with the Sabellians the Trinitie. With
þ Manicheis he made two goddes. With
Eunomius,he denied that the father and
the sonne ware equal. With Macedoni-
us he said that the holy ghosse was a creature,or substaunce created. With the
Nicholaites he allowed the hauinge of
many wiues at ones. He allowed also
the olde testament. Althoughe sayd he,it
ware in certain places faultie. And these
fondenesses did he beswiete with a wonderfull lure of the thinges that menne in
this lyfe moosse desire. Lettinge louse to
as many as helde of him,the bridle of al
lechery and luste. And for that cause doth
this cōtagious euil sprede it self so wide
into innumerable contries. So þ if a mā
at this day compare the nombre of them
that are by him seduced,with the other
that remaine in the doctrine of faithe: he
shal easeli perceiue the great oddes,ware
it but herin. That wher Europe alone,
(and not al that by a great deale)stādeth
iii

in the belief of Chziste: almosfe all Asie, and Aphzique, yea and a greate pere of Europe standeth in the Turkisshe belief of Mahomete.

The Saracenes that firste receiued the bzainesicke wickednesse of this countre-feicte pzophete, dwelte in that parte of A-rabia, that is called Petrea: wher it entre-communeth with Iewzy on the one side, and with Egipt on the other. So named of Sarracum, a place nere vnto the Naba-theis, oz rather as thei woulde haue it them selues, of Sara, Abzahams wife. Wherupon thei yet sticke faste in this o-pinion, y thei onely of al mē are the law-full heires of goddes beheste. Thei gaue them selues to tilthe, and cattle, and to the warres. But the greater parte to the warres. And therfoze at what time they ware hired of Heraclius in the warres againste the persians: when he had got-ten the victozy, and thei perceiued them selues to be defrauded by him: kindled with the angre of the villanye thei had had done vnto them, by the counsell and perswasion of Mahomet (who tooke vp-pon him to be their captaine) thei forsoke Heraclius. And going into Siria, en-uaded

uaded Damasco. Wher when thei had
encreased them selues bothe in nombre,
and purueiaunce necessary for them, thei
entred into Egipte. And subdued firste
that: then Persis, then Antioche, & then
Jerusalem. Thus their power and fame
daily so encreased, and grewe: that men
muche feared, that any thing afterwarde
shoulde be able to resiste them . In the
meane season, the Turkes: a ferce and a
cruell people, of the nation of the Scithiens, driuen out by their neighbours fro
the mountaines called Caspij, came
downe by the passage of the moute Caucasus, firste into Asia the lesse, then into
Armenia, Media, and Persis. And by
stronge hande wanne all as they came.
Against these the Saracenes went forth
as to defende the bordres of their gouernaunce. But forasmuche as this newe-
come power was to harde for them, the
Saracenes within a while felle into such
despaire of their state: that vppon condicion that the other would receiue Maho-
metes belief: thei ware content thei shold
reigne felowlike together with them, in
Persis. Wherto when thei had agreed,
it was harde to saye whether of the peoples

ples had receiued the greater dammage.
The Saracenes, in yelding to them the
haulf right of their kingdome: oz the o-
ther, whiche foz coueteousnes therof yelded them selues to so rancke, and wicked
a poyson of all vertue and godlynes.

One bonde of belief then so coupled and
ioyned them: that foz a space it made to
them no matter whether ye called them
all by one name, Saracenes, oz Turkes.
But nowe as ye se, the name of the Turkes hath gotten the bettre hande, & the
other is out of remembzaunce. This people vseth moe kindes of hozseme the one.
Thei haue Thimarceni, that is to saye
Pencioners, aboute a foure skoze thousande. These haue giuen vnto them by
the kinge, houses, billages, and Castles
euery one as he deserueth, in the steade of
his wages oz pencion. And thei attende
vppon the Sensacho, oz capitaine of that
quarter, wher their possessions lye. At
this daye the Turkes are deuided into
two armies: the one foz Asie, and the o-
ther foz Europe. And either hath a chief
teine, at whose leading thei are. These
cheifteimes in their tongue be called
Bassay. Ther are also another sozte much
lyke

lyke to our aduenturers, that serue with
oute wages, called Aconizie. And these
euer are spoiling afoze when the campe
is yet behynde. The fiueth parte of their
butine is due vnto ye king. And these are
aboute a fourty thousande. Their thirde
sozte of hozsemen is deuided into Charip
pos Spahiglauos, & Soluphtaros. The
beste, and wozthiest of those, ace ye Cha-
rippte: of an honourable ozdze of knight
hode, as it ware foz the kinges body.
And those be euer about him, to the nombze of eyghte hundzed, all Scithians and
Persians, and elles of none other kinde
of menne. These, when nede is, being in
the sighte of the kinge: fight notably, and
do wondzefull feates on hozsebacke.
Spahy, and Soluphtary be those whiche
haue bene at the kinges bzinging vp fra
their childehode, to serue his filthy abho
minacion. And when thei are come to
mannes state, thei marye at the kynges
pleasure: And be enriched bothe with the
dowery of their wife, and a stipende.
These foz the moste parte serue foz em-
bassadours, deputies, lieutensuntes and
suche other dignities, and are nexte vnto
the kinge on bothe sides of him, when he

goeth

goeth any whether as a garde. They are
in nombre a thousande and thre hudred.

Among the footemen are thre sortes,
Janizarie, these be chosen all the Empire
ouer, of .vij. yeres of age, or there aboute,
by certein that haue Commission for the
purpose: And are for a space enstructed in
the feactes of warre, in commune schooles. And then aftrewarde are thei chosen
into souldie, and haue giuen them a shorter garmente, and a white cappe, with a
tarse tonrned vpwarde. Their weapon
is a Targette, a Curtilas, and a Bowe.
Their office is to fortifie the Campe, and
to assaulte cities. Thei are in nombre a-
boue twentie thousande.

The seconde sorte are called Asappi, and
are all footemen of light harnnesse, weaponed with swearde, target, and a kinde
of long Iauelines, wherwith thei slea the
horses of their enemies, in the skirmishe
and battaile. These, to be knowen fro the
Ianizaries, weare redde cappes. These
are appointed in nombre, accordyng as
the case shall require. But thei are euer
at the leaste fouretie thousande. When
the warres are finished, for the whiche
thei ware hired: these are no longer in

wages

wages. Tharmie roialle hath about two hundred housande armed menne, beside a greate rable offootemen aduenturers, that take no wages, and suche other as be called out of Garrisons. And amonge these, Pioners and Cookes, Carpenters Armourers, and suche other as thei must niedes haue to make the waye, wher the place is combresome: to dresse victualles, to amende harnesse, to make bredges ouer floudes, to trenche aboute their ennemies, to plante battries, make Ladders, and suche other thinges necessarie for the stege. Ther foloweth the armie also, sondrye sortes of money Masters: some for lone, some for erchaunge, some to buy thinges. And sondrie sortes of occupiers, such as be thought nedeful in such cases.

But there is nothing in all that nacion more to be merueiled at, then their spiedinesse in doeyng of thinges: their constantnes in perilles, and their obedience and precise obseruinge of all commaundemetes. For the least fault, of goeth the heade. Thei passe ouer raginge floudes, mounteignes and rockes: roughes and plaines, thicke and thinne, if thei be commaunded. Not hauing respecte to theyr

life,

lyfe, but to their rulers. No men maie
awaie with moze watche, no men with
moze hongre. Among them is no muti-
nyng, no vpzoures, no sturres. In theyz
fyght thei vse no cries, noz shoutes, but a
certeine fiercenes of bzayeng. Thei kepe
suche pzecise sciléce in the night, thzough
out their campe: that thei wil rather suffre such as they haue taken pzisoners, to
run their waie, then to make any sturre.
Of all the peoples at this daie, thei onely doe warre, acozding to the ozdze of armes. So that no manne niedeth to meruaile howe it cometh that no people this
two hundzed yeare and aboue, haue had
like successe vnto them. Pea, it may truely be sayd, that excepte it be by some plague oz murreyn, oz discozde among them
selues, they can not be subdued. The ap-
parail that the souldiers do vse, is most
comely and honeste. In their sadles and
bzidles, there is neither curiositie, ne yet
superfluitie. No man emong them wea-
reth his Armour, but when niede is to
fight. They carry their harnesse behynde
theim, at their backes. They vse neither
banner, stannderde, ne flaggue : but certein Jauelins that haue streamynge out

fro the toppe, diuers coloured thzicoes,
by the whiche euery bande knoweth his
capiteine. Thei vse a dzõme and a fiphe,
to assemble their Bandes, and to sturre
them to the batteile. When the batteile
is done, all the armie is pzesented to the
Regesfour (whiche is some one of the
nobles) bothe that it maye bee knowen
who is slain, and what nombze: and that
newe may be entred in their places. In
all assemblies and mietinges, feaste, oz
other: thei pzaie foz their souldiours, and
menne of warre. But specially aboue all
other, foz those that haue suffred death foz
the commune quarelle of their countrie:
calling them happie, foztunate, and blessed, that thei yelded not vp their liues at
home, amidde the lamentacions and be-
wailpnges, of their wiues and chldzen,
but losse them abzode, amonge the shoutes of their enemies, & the ratling of the
Harneis, and Launces. The victozies of
their forefathers and eldzes, thei put into
Balade, and sing theim with greate honour and pzaises: foz that thei thinke the
courages of the souldiours and menne
of warre, be muche quickened, and kindled thereby.

Their

Their dwelling houses are commun-
ly of timbre and claie, very fewe of stone:
for of them are the noble mennes houses
their temples, and Batthes. And yet are
there amonge the communes, men able
of them self alone, to set furthe an whole
armie, furnisshed at all pointes. But because thei are naturally giuen to sparing
and to abhorre all sumptuousenesse, em-
brasing a lowe and simple state: thei wel
beare this voluntarie pouertie, and rude
homelinesse. For this cause also, doe thei
not set by any kinde of Painters Imagerie. As for the other imagerie of coruē
grauen, or molten worke, thei do so hate
and abhorre: that thei call us Christians
for delighting so muche in them, verie
Idolatours and Image worshippers.
And do not onely so calle vs, but wil ear-
nestly argue, that we are so in dede. Thei
vse no Seales to their Lettres, of what
sorte so euer thei be, the kynges or other.
But they credite the matier, assone as
thei haue red the superscripcion, or heard
the name of the sender. Thei occupie no
belles, nor suffre not the christianes that
dwelle amōg them to do. Thei game not
for money, or ēny valewe elles. And if it

D.iii.   fortune

fortune that any manne be founde to do,
in many sundrie wise thei reuile him, and
baite him with shames and reproche.

No man among them, of what degree
or dignitie so euer he be: requireth for me
chaire, stoole, or other kinde of seate to
sitte vpon. But foldinge bothe him selfe
and his clothes, aftre a mooste comely
sorte: rucketh downe vpon the grounde,
not muche vnlike to the sitting of our gē-
tlewomen ofte times here in Englande.
The table wherupon thei eate, is for the
mooste parte of a Bullockes hide, or a
Hartes skinne. Not dressed, but in the
heare, facioned rounde, beyng a fowre or
fiue spanne ouer, and so set rounde about
on the bordre, or verge, with ringlettes
of iron: that putting a couple of stringes
throughe the ringes, it maye be drawen
together, and shutte and opened like a
purse. House, or Churche, or any other
place wher they entende to sitte, no man
entreth with his shoes on. For it is compted a very dishonest and an vnmanerly
facion, to sitte shoed. wherfore they vse a
maner of slippe shooes, that may lightly
be putte of and on. The place where thei
sitts, either at home, or at Churche, is in
some

some place matted, and in some place o-
uerspzed with course woollen Carpette,
And some places also, either foz the lowe
nes, moistenes, oz vncleanelinesse therof
are plancked with boozde.

The garmentes aswell of the menne,
as the women, are large and longe, and
open afoze: that thei may the moze hone
stlie and couertly hide all, when nature
craueth to be eased. And in doeyng those
niedes, thei take greate hiede, that their
face be not into the Southe, as it is whē
thei pzaye. As also that thei discouer no
pzinie parte, that any man myghte foztune to see. The menne make water sitting, aswell as the women. Foz if a man
amonges them, ware sene to make water standing: he should be iudged of all, a
foole, oz an heritique.

From wine (as from a pzouoker of al
sinne and vnclennesse) thei absteine by
their lawe. And yet eate they the Grapes, & dzincke muste. Thei also fozbeare
to eate any thinge, that commeth of the
Hogge: oz any thinge elles that dieth of
sickenesse, oz by aduenture vnslain. But
any other thinges, being mannes meate,
thei refuse not to eate. Thei wozshippe

the Fridaie, laieng all labour and businesse aparte, with as greate solempnitie and deuocion, as we doe the Sondaie, or as the Iewes doe the Sabboth date. In euery citie there is one principall or head Churche. In the whiche vppon the Fridaie at aftre Noone, thei all assemble together. And aftre solēpne praiers, heare a sermone. Thei acknowledge one God, to whom thei make no like, nor equalle: and Mahomet to be his trustie and welbeloued Prophete. All the Saracenes are bound to praie fiue times on the daie, with their faces toward the South. And before thei so do, to the ende thei maie be cleane from all filthe of bodie: to washe them selues toppe and taile, heade, eares, eyes, nose, mouthe, armes, handes, bealy, collions, legges and fiete. Specially, if he haue bene late at the soile with a woman or strouped on his taile to vnburden his bealie. Except he haue some lette of iournie, or sickenesse. But if he lacke watre to doe this withall (as that sieldome or neuer can happen, for that thei haue in all cities, bathes ordenarie for the purpose) thei supplie the defaulte with the moulde of fresshe cleane earthe, wherewith thei

rubbe

rubbe ouer their whole bodies. Who so
is polluted in any maner wise: suffreth no
man before this clensing, to speake with
hym, or to see him, if it be possible. Euery
yere for the space of ffue wickes continually together, thei faste al daie as presice-
ly as is possible, bothe fró meate, drincke
and women. But aftre the sonne is ones
doune, till the next daie he riseth, thei neither spare eatyng ne drinckyng, ne pres-
syng of pappes. In thende of their lente,
and againe the sirtieth daie aftre : Thei
kiepe their passeouer or Easter, in remé-
braunce of the Rambe shewed vnto A-
braham, to be Sacrificed in the steade of
his sonne, and of a certaine nighte in the
whiche thei doe beleue that the Alcorane
was giuen them from heauen.

Euery yere ones, the Saracenes also
are bound of duetie to visite the house of
God, in the citie of Merha : bothe to ac-
knowlege their homage, and to yelde vnto Mahomete his yerely honour at his
Sepulchre there. The Saracenes compelle no man to forsake his opinion or belief: ne yet labour so to perswade any coūtrie to do. Although their Alcorane commaunde theim to treade doune and de=

strote

ſtroye all menne of the contrary belieue
yea them & their prophetes. But through
this ſufferaūce, ther are to be ſounde enhabiting in Turkie, peoples of all opinions, and beleue: euery man vſinge ſuche
kinde of woꝛſhippe to his God, as to his
religion apperteineth. Their pꝛieſtes do
not muche diffre from the commune people, noꝛ yet their churches from their
dwelling houſes. Yf thei knowe the Al-
coꝛane, and the pꝛaiours and ceremonies
of their lawe, it ſuffiſeth. Thei are neither giuen to contēplacion ne yet ſchole
ſtudy. Foꝛ why thei are not ocupied with
any churche ſeruice oꝛ cure of ſoules. Sacramentes haue thei none, noꝛ reliques,
noꝛ halowinges of foūtes, Aulters, and
other neceſſaries. But pꝛouidinge foꝛ
their wiues their childꝛen, and houſehol-
des, thei occupie their time in huſbōdꝛie
marchaundiſe, hunninge, oꝛ ſome other
meane to get the penie, and mainteyne
their liuing, euen as the tempoꝛall men
doe. Ther is nothing foꝛbidden them,
nothing is foꝛ them vnlawfull. Thei be
neither burdoned with tillage, ne bondage. Thei be muche honoured of al mē,
foꝛ that thei are ſkilfull in the ceremoni-

 es

ts of the lawe, teache them to other, and
be the gouernours of the churches.

They haue many schooles and large,
In the which great nombres are taught
the lawes there giuen by kinges, for the
ciuile gouernaunce and defence of the
Realme. Of the whiche some are afterwarde sette fourth to be men of the churche, and some to be temporalle officers.
Their spiritualtie is deuided into many
and sondry sortes of religions. Of the
whiche some liue in the wooddes & wyl-
dernes shonnyng all companye. Some
kiepe open hospitalitie in cities, and yet
liue by almose them selues. These if they
lacke meate to refreshe the niedy straunger and pelligrine, yet at the least waie
they giue him herbour and lodgyng. O-
ther, roumyng the cities vp and downe
and caryeng alway in bottles faire watre and fresshe, if any man be disposed to
drinke, vnasked they willingly proffre it
him, and refuse not to take, if he for their
gentlenesse offre aught vnto them agayn
Otherwise they craue nothyng, but in al
their woordes gesture, behauour, & diedes : shewe theim selues aungelles raither then menne. And euery one of these
                                        haty

hath one knowledge oz other, of differēce
from the reaste. The Saracenes oz Tur
kes are very pzecise executours of Jus
tice. who so committeth bloudshed: hath
in like sozt e his owne shedde againe. Ta
ken in adultery, both parties are streight
without mercy stoned to deathe . Thei
haue also a punisshement foz foznicatiõ,
whiche is to the manne taken with the
diede, foure scoze ierkes oz lasshes with
a skourge. A thief foz the first and the se
conde time, escapeth with so many stri
pes. But at the thirde time, hath his hãde
cut of, and at the fourthe his foote . He
that endamageth any manne: as the losse
oz hinderaunce shalbe valewed, so muste
he of foze recompence. In claiming of
goodes, oz possessions, the claimer muste
pzoue by witnesse that the thing claimed
is his: and the denier shalbe tried by his
othe . witnesses thei admitte none , but
persones of knowen honestie, e suche as
mighte be belieued withoute an othe .
Thei haue also certaine spiefaultes oz
dinarilye appoincted (muche like to our
Sompnours) that spie in euery shiere foz
suche as be necligent, and let slippe suche
ozaisons, and seruice as thei be boũde to

Those

Those if thei fortune to finde them : do
thei punishe aftre this maner. Thei hãge
a borde about their neckes, with a great
many of fore tailes, and togginge them
vp and downe the stretes: all ouer the citie, thei neuer lette them go vntyll they
haue compounded by the purse. And in
this also nothing vnlike to our Sompno
urs. It is lawfull for no manne, beinge
come to mannes state, to liue vnmaried.
It is compted amonge them as lawfull
to haue. iiii. wiues, as it is amonge vs to
haue one. Marie whatsoeuer is aboue
this nombre (as thei may if thei liste, and
be able to kepe them, no degree excepted,
but mother and sister, marie a hundred)
thei are not iudged so lawfulle. The children that thei haue bothe by the one, and
the other haue equalle portion in the fathers enheritaunce. Sauing that. ii. women children are compted in portiõ but
for one man childe. Thei haue not. ii. of
their wiues together in one house, ne yet
in one citie. For the busines, ꝯ disquietin-
ges that might happen therby, but euery
wife in a seuerall towne. The houseban
des haue libertye to put thẽ away thrise,
and thrise to take them againe. But yet
                                        when

when he hath ones putte her awaie, if a= ny manne haue taken her, and she lust to abide with hym, she maie.

Their women are moste honestlie ap= pareiled. And vpon their heades doe vse a certeine attire, not muche vnlike the veluet bonette of olde Englande: wherof the one lappe so hangeth vppon whiche side semeth her good: that when she is di= sposed to go out of the doozes, oz to come amongest menne within the house, she maie hide therwith by and by her whole face, sauyng her eyes.

The Saracenes woman, neuer dare shewe her self wher ther is a company of menne. To go to the marchate to occupy byeng oz sellyng in any wise : is not syt= tyng foz their womē. In the head church they haue a place farre a part fro ý men: so close that no manne canne looke into them. Into the which not withstandyng it is not laufull foz euery mans wyfe to entre : but foz the nobilitie onely. Ne yet foz them neyther, but on friday, at the onely houre of noone praier : whiche as I haue afozesayd, is kept amonge them high and holy.

To see a man and a woman talke to
g ether.

ther ther, in the open ſtrete oz abzode: is
ſo ſtraũge, and ſo vnwonte a thing, that
in a whole pere it ſkãte happeneth ones.
Foz a man to ſitte with his wyfe in open
ſighte, oz to ride with any wemã behinde
him: amongeſt them ware a wondze.
Maried couples neuer dally together in
the ſighte of other, noz chide oz falle out.
But the menne beare alwaies towarde
the women a manly diſcrete ſobzenes,
and the women, towarde them a demure
womanlie reuerence. Greate menne,
that cannot alwaie haue their wiues in
their owne eye, appoincte redgelinges,
oz guelte menne to awaite vppon them.
Whiche waite them in diede ſo narrow-
lye, that it ware impoſſible foz any man
beſide the houſebande to ſpeake with the
wyfe vnſene: oz the wyfe by any ſtealthe
to falſe her trouth and honeſtie. Finally
the Saracenes do ſo full and whole beleue their Mahomete & his lawes: that
thei doubte no whitte, but the kepers of
them ſhall haue euerlaſting bleſſedneſſe.
That is to ſaye, after their opinion, a
paradiſe of pleaſure, a gardein platter of
delighte, full of ſwiete rindles of Chzi-
ſtalline watre. In whoſe botomes y̆ grz-

uelle

uelle, popleth like glisteryng golde. The
ayre alwaie so attempre and pure, that
nothyng can be more swiete, more pleasaunte nor healthsome. The grounde couered and garnisshed with natures Ta-
pesserie, neither lacking any colour that
pleasaunte is to the eye, or sauour that
maie delight the nose. Birdes syngyng
with suche armonie, as neuer mortalle
eare heard. Briefly flowyng in all pleasure that any harte can after thincke.
Disshes for the mouthe, of all deinties.
All maner of Silkes, Neluettes, Purples, Skarlettes, and other precious apparelle. Godly younge damoselles, with
graie rowlyng eyes, and skinne as white
as Whales bone, softe as the Silke, and
breathed like the Rose, and all at their
becke. Uesselles of siluer and golde, Angelles for their Butlers that shall bryng
theim Milke in Goblettes of golde, and
redde wine in siluer. But contrariewise,
thei threaten vnto the breakers of them,
helle, and euerlastyng destruction. This
thei also beleue, that be a manne wrap-
ped in neuer so many synnes, yet if at his
death, he beleue vpon God, and Macho-
mete, he shalbe saued,

The

¶The.xij.Chapitre.

¶Of the Chꝛistians, of their firste
commyng vp, their Ceremo=
nies, and oꝛdenaunces.

Chꝛiste Iesu, the eter=
nalle and verie sonne
of thalmightie father,
the seconde persone in
the holie inseparable,
equalle, and euerla=
styng Trinitie : Of a
sette purpose, and spi=
ritualle secrete, not reuealed from the be
ginnyng of tyme, ⁊ aboue mannes capa=
sitie: was by the meane of the holy ghost,
conceiued and boꝛne manne. In Iewꝛie,
of a Virgine, of the stocke of Dauid, a
thousande fiue hundꝛed, and twentie ye=
res gone. To sette vs miserable, and vn=
happie menne on foote againe, whiche
ware in Adam and Eue, by the sinne of
disobedience ouerthꝛowen. And to bꝛyng
vs againe, vnto our heauenlie natiue
countrie, from the whiche we haue by so
many ages, foꝛ that pꝛesumpcion bene
banished. Finally, to repaire and supplie
in heauen againe oꝛvs, the ruine and fal

It appereth by this place that this was wꝛitten.xxxv yeres gone.

R.j.   of

of those spirites, whiche a space afoze oure
creacion, ware thurste doune fro thence.
Foz the whiche purpose, we chiefly ware
made . This Iesus, from thirtie yeres
of age, vntill thirtie and fowze (in the
whiche, thzoughe the maliciousnes of the
Iewes , he suffred on the galowe tree)
traueillyng all Iewzie ouer: first moued
and exhozted the Iewes, and then other
peoples, from the olde Lawe of Moses,
and their wicked Image wozshippe, to
his newe ozdenaunce and trade . And as
many as would folowe, and doe aftre
hym, he called theim his scholers oz disciples. Out of the whiche, he gaue vnto. xii.
that he had specially chose, Comission aftre his death (when he had appered to the
on liue again, as he had fozewarned the
ȳ he would) to go as Legates, oz Embas-
satours into ȳ whole wozld, ꝛ to preache
vnto all creatures, what so euer thei had
sene oz learned of him. Simon Petre (to
whom longe afoze he had surrendzed the
gouernaunce and chiefteinshippe of his
Churche, as in reuercion aftre him) whe
aftre the comyng of the holy ghoste some
wente into one coste, and some into another, euery manne his waie, as thei ware
                                    allotted

allotted and commaunded: came firſt vnto Antioche. And there ſetting vp the firſt and chief chaire of the Churche, kepte a counſaille with the other Apoſtles, whiche often tymes came to hym. In this Counſaille among other thinges it was decreed, that aſmany as ſhould receiue, and cleaue vnto the doctrine, and righte perſwaſion of Chriſtes godlines: ſhould fro thence furthe be called Chriſtianes. This Seate of ſuperioritie, beyng aftrewarde tranſlated to Rome: bothe he and his Succeſſours, tooke it for their chief charge and buſineſſe, to put the rude and rawe ſecte of their Chriſte, and the folowers of theſame, in ſome good ordre and trade of gouernaunce. Bothe aftre the maner of Moſes Lawe (whiche Chriſte came not to breake, but to conſummate and finiſhe) and the ſtate of the Romain gouernaunce the Greke, and Egiptian: and alſo by paterne of the Ceremonies, obſeruaunces, lawes, and ordenaunces Eccleſiaſticalle and Temporalle, of many other peoples: But ſpecially aftre the doctrine, of Chriſte Ieſu, and the woorkyng of the holy ghoſte, to bryng them in to frame and facion. When theſ ware en

tred in the mattier: As thei sawe that men
not emong the Hebrues alone, but emōg
other peoples also, ware deuided into
Ecclesiasticalle and Temporalle, Spiritualtie and Laïetie: and eche of theim in
moste goodly wise, into their dignities
and degrees (The Romaine Emperour then being gouernour of the whole
worlde alone, to haue Consulles, Fathers or Senatours: at whose becke all
thinges ware deuised and doone: And in
the residewe of the earthe to bee many
Kynges, many Dukes, Erles, Presidentes, and Deputies of countries, and their
Lieutenauntes: Mareschalles of the
fielde, and highe Conestables for the cōmunes, Pretours or Prouostes, Stan-
derdbearers roialle, Centurians, and
Disners, Serieauntes, Conestables,
Collectours, Surueiours, Porters, Scri-
bes, Listers, and many other persones
without office, bothe menne and women.
And in the Temples of their Goddes, a
Sacrificer roialle, whiche is to saie in
effecte, a highe Prieste of the dignitie of
a kyng. Archeflamines, flamines of honour, and other flamines inferiour and
laste in degree their Priestes. And by
like

like ordre emong the Hebrues: an highe
Bisshoppe, and inferiour Priestes, Leuites, Nazareis, candle quenchers, com-
maunders of Spirites, Churche Wardeines, and Syngers, whiche wee calle
Chauntours aftre the Frenche. And a-
mõg the Grekes: Capiteines, or heades
ouer a thousande, ouer an hundred, ouer
fiuetie, ouer tène, and ouer fiue. And that
there ware yet beside these, bothe emong
the Hebrues, and the Romaines, many
couentes, or compaignies of menne and
women Religious. As Sadduceis, Esseis, and Phariseis emong the Hebrues:
Salios, Diales, and Uestalles, emong
the Romaines: The moste holy Apostles
did all consente, that Petre, and thei that
should folowe him in the seate of Rome,
should for euermore be called Papa. As
who would saie, father of fathers, the v-
niuersalle, Apostolicalle, moste holy, and
moste highe bisshoppe. And that he should
at Rome be Presidente ouer the vniuersalle Churche, as the Emperour there,
was ruler of the vniuersall worlde. And
to matche the Consulles (whiche ware
euer twaine) thei appoincted fowre head
Fathers, in the Greke named, Patriar-

R.iij. ches,

ches, one at Constantinople, another at
Antioche, a thirde at Alexandrie, and the
fowrthe at Hierusalem . In the place
of the Senatours , thei tooke the Cardi-
nalles. To matche their kynges, whiche
had three Dukes at commaundemente,
thei deuised Primates: To whom ware
subiecte thre Archebishoppes. So that the
Archebishoppe or Metropolitane , standeth in the place of a Duke . For as the
Duke had certein Erles or Barones at
his commaundemente: so haue the Arch-
bisshoppes, other inferiour Bisshoppes
at theirs . whiche also by reason muste
countreuaile an Erle. The Bisshoppes
coadiutour or Suffragane, came into the
Presidentes place. The ordenarie into the
Deputies, then did the Officialle matche
with the Mareshalle. And with the high
conestable for the comunes, the Bishoppes Chauncelour . And for the Pretour
or Prouoste, thei sette vp an Archedeacō
In stede of the Centuriane, was a Deane
appoincted. And for the Disnere, the Persone or Uicare. For the Aduocates, crept
in the Parisshe Prieste, Soule Prieste,
Chaunterie Prieste , Morowe Masse
Prieste , and suche other . The Deacon
                    standeth

ſtandeth for the Suruiour. The Sub⸗
deacon, for the Serieaunte. For the two
Conſtables, came in the two Commaun⸗
ders of Spirites, called Exorciſtæ in the
Greke. The Colleƈours office, was mat⸗
ched with the Churche wardeines. The
Porter became the Serteine. The Chaū⸗
tour, Scribe, and Liſſer, kiepe ſtille their
name. The Acholite, whiche we calle Be⸗
net and Cholet, occupieth the roume of
Candlebearer.

All theſe by one commune name, thei
called Clerj, of the Greke woorde Cleros,
that is to ſaie, a Lotte. For that thei ware
firſte from among the people, ſo allotted
vnto God. Thereof cometh our terme
Clerque, and his coſine Clergie. Neuer⸗
theleſſe, this name Clergie, was not ſo
commune vnto all: but that it ſemed
moſte proprely to reſte in the ſeuen de⸗
grees, that the Pope of Rome vſed for
his Miniſtres, when he ſaied Maſſe in
perſone him ſelf. That is to ſaie, the Bi⸗
ſhoppe, the Prieſt, the Deacon, ⁊ ſubdea⸗
con, ỹ Acholite, and the Chaū tour. Unto
euery of theſe gaue thei in ỹ church their
ſeueralle dignities offictes, ⁊ appareile.

To the Biſhoppe was giuen authori⸗
tie

tie,to ordeine and make other Clerckes.

That is to
saie, to make
Nonnes,

To*enueile virgines,& to hallow them.
To consecrate their likes,and their superiours also.To laie handes vpon thē. To
confirme and Bisshoppe childrē. To hallowe Churches. To put Priestes from
their Priesthode: and to degrade theim,
when thei deserue it. To kepe Conuocacions and Sinodes. To make holy oile:
to hallowe the ornamentes and vesselles
of the churche. And to do also other thinges, that the inferiour Priestes doe.To
enstructe those that be newly come to the
faithe. To Christiane, to make the Sacramente of the Altare, and to giue it to
other.To absolue the repētaunte of their
sinnes, and to settre the stubberne more
streighte.To shewe furthe the Gospelle.
To enioyne all Priestes to shaue their
heades in the croune, like a circle of, iiii.
fingres brode,aftre the maner of ÿ Naza-
reis.To kepe their heare shorte,to weare
no bearde. And to liue chaaste for euer.

Their liuyng onely to rise of the firste
fruictes,tenthes,and offringes:and vttre-
ly to be voide of all temporalle and Laie-
mennes cares and businesse. To be honestlie appareiled, and accordyngly to vse
their

their passe and conuersacion , Onely to
serue God and the churche. Diligētly to
plye the reading of holy scripture, ꝯ they
them selues mighte perfectly knowe all
thinges perteining to Christian religiō,
wherin thei are boūd to enstructe other.
The companies or couētes of religious,
aswel men as women: are Benedictines,
Preachers, Franciscanes , Augustines,
Barnardines , Anthonines, Johānites,
Cistertnots, and innumerable other. whi
che al haue their habite, and maner of liuing by them selfe: acordinge to the rule
that echeone priuately prescibed to them
selues. And liued for the moste parte a so-
litary life, professing, chastitie, pouretie,
and perpetuall obedience. And for their
solitarines the Greke called them Mona
uachi. Some of these haue for their heades Abbotes, some Priours: whiche are
either subiecte to the Pope onely, or to
the bishoppes. Al these vsed coules, much
aftre one facio, but in colour diuers, sab-
stained fro fleshe. The bisshoppes when
thei say masse, haue. vb holy garmentes,
aftre ꝯ maner of Moyses lawe, for ꝯ per-
fectiō of thē. His boatewes, his Amice an
Albe, a Girdle a Stole, a Maniple, a Tu
nicle

ele of biolette in graine fringed, his gloues, ringe, and chesible or vestimente, a Sudarie, a cope, a mitte and a ✳ crosse staffe. And a chaire at the Aultares ende, wherin he sitteth. Of the whiche .vi. are commune to euery inferiour priestke: the Amice, the Albe, the girdle, the stole, the Maniple, and the vestiment. But ouer, and aboue all these the Pope, by the gifte of Constantine the greate, hath libertie to weare al the ornamentes Imperialle. That is to saye a kirtle of skarlet, a robe of Purple, a sceptre, and a close corone. With the whiche afrer he hath rauisshed him selfe in the vestrie, vppon solempne feastes, when he entedeth to do masse: he commeth forth to the aultare, hauing on the right side a priestke, on the lefte side a Deacon, a Subdeacon going before him with a booke faste shutte, two candle bearers, and an encensour with the censoure in his hande smoking. When he is come to the griessinges, the stayers, or foote of the aultare: putting of his mitre, he maketh open ✳ confession of his sinnes together with his company.

That done he goeth vp to the aultare, openeth the booke, lienge vpon the lefte

corner

The latine calleth it a shepe hooke.

That is, he saieth confiteor.

co2ner of the same, kysseth it, and so p2o-
cedeth in the Solempnisacio of y̆ Maſſe.
The ſubdeacon readeth the epiſtle, and
the Deacon the godſpelle. P2ieſtes of al
degrees, are charged to p2ayſe God ſeuen tiunes a dale, and to p2aye with o2de
narie o2aiſons. Towarde the eueninge,
euenſonge: and compline mo2e late. Ma-
tines in the mo2ninge, and incontinente
p2ime, and how2es, in o2d2e of tyme, as
thei ſtande in * o2d2e of name. And this
humbly befo2e the aultare, if he maye
conueniently, with his face towarde the
Caſte. The pater noſtre and the Crede
ſaid thei, onely at the beginnyng of their
ſeruice, as the commune people do nowe
a daies alſo. Saincte Jerome, at the b2-
gent requeſt of Pope Damaſus, parted
out the Pſalmes aco2ding to the daies
of the wieke. And appoincted fo2 euery
houre apo2tio of p2op2e pſalmes. Fo2 the
nighte houres on the holy daye. ix. and on
the wo2ckingdaye. xii. Fo2 laudes in the
mo2ning. v. fo2 euenſonge as many, and
fo2 eche other houre but th2e. He alſo o2-
deined the Epiſtles, Godſpelles, and o-
ther ſeruice, vſed to be red out of the olde
o2 newe teſtament, in maner altogether,
                              ſauing

Hora pri-
ma, tertia,
ſexta nona.

sauing ŷ note. The Anthemes (which Am
bzose, wysshoppe of millayne wzate, and
endited) Damasus put ozdze that the
quiere should sing side aftre side, ⁊ added
to euery psalmes eude. Gloria patri, &c.
The lessons and Himpnes that go befoze eche one of the howzes did ŷ coūcel-
les of Thoulouse and Agathone auctho-
rise. The ozisons, the grailes, the trac-
tes, the Alleluya, th offertozie, the Com-
munions in the Masse, the Anthemes,
Uersicles, repitions, and other thinges, either songe oz redde by nyghte
oz by daye, to the beautifieng, and pzay-
sing of God: did Gregozy, Gelasius, Am
bzose, and many other holy fathers, deuise, and put furthe. not at one time but
at sondzy. The Masse (so terme thei the
sacrifice) was firste vsed to be done in
suche simple sozte, as yet is accustomed,
vppon good friday, ⁊ Easter euen, with
certeine lessōs befoze it. But then Pope
Celestinus put to the office of the Masse.
Thelesphozus, Gloria in excelsis: But Hi
larius of pictauia made the Et in terra. Si
machus ozdeined it to be songue. The
Salutaciōs, which by ŷ terme of Domi-
nus vobiscum, be made seuen tymes in a
                                    Masse

Masse, ware taken out of the booke of
Ruthe, by Clemente, and Anaclete, and
put in, in their places. Gelasius made vp
all the reste to the Offertory, in the same
ordre thei be vsed. Excepte the Sequen-
ces and the Crede: wherof Nicolas put
in the firste, ϟ Damasus the nexte: acordinge to the Sinode of Constantinople.
The bidding of the beades, with the col-
lacion that was wonte to be made in the
pulpite on Sondaies, and halydaies: raither grewe to a custome by the example
of Nehemias, and Esdras, then was by
any aucthorised. In this collation at the
firste comming vp therof, when so many
as ware presete at the Masse did receiue
the communion, acording as was ordeyned by a decree: thei that ware at any discorde ware exhorted to concorde, ϟ agre-
mente. And that thei should receiue the
sacrament of the aulter cleane from the
fylthe of sinne, vppon the whiche consideracion at this daye it endeth with confiteor, or an open confession. There ware
thei wonte to teache the instrumentes of
the olde lawe, and the newe. The ten cō-
maundementes. The xii. articles of our
beleue. The seuen sacramentes, holy folkes

kes liues, and Martirdomies, holy dayes, doctrines, and disciplines: vertues,
and vices, and what soeuer are necessary
beside forthe, for a christiane to knowe.
Gregory lincked on the offertorie. Leo
the prefaces. Gelasius the greate Canõ,
& the lesse. The Sanctus blessed Sixtus.
And Gregory ý Pater noster out of the
Gospell of sainte Mathewe. Martialle
the scholer of blessed Peter, deuised that
Bysshoppes should gyue their benediction at the Agnus. And as for other infeour priestes, Innocentius commaũded
them to giue ý pare, that is to saye peace.
Sergius tacked on the Agnus, and Gregory the poste communion. The closing
vp of all with Ite missa est, Benedicamus,
Deo gratias: was Leoes inuencion.

The .xii. articles of our beleue, whiche
the blessed Apostles would euery manne
not onely to confesse with mouthe, but
to beleue also in harte, are these.

Firste that ther is one God in Trinitie, the father almighty maker of heauen
and earthe. The seconde, Jesus Christe
his onely sonne our Lorde. The thirde
the same beinge conceiued of the holye
ghoste, to haue bene borne of ý Virgine
                              Marie

Marie. The fourthe, to haue suffred vndre Ponce pilate, to haue bene crucified,
deade, bewried, and to haue descended in
to helle. The fiueth, to haue risen agayne
the thirde daye fro the deade. The sixteth
to haue ascended vp into the heauēs, and
to sitte on the right hande of God the father almighty. The seuenth, that he shall
come fro thence like a triūpher, to iudge
the quicke and the deade. The eight, that
ther is an holy ghoste. The nineth, ÿ ther
is an holy churche vniuersalle, the communion of the godly and good. The tenthe, forgiuenesse of sinnes. The eleueth,
the rising againe of the fleshe. The twelueth, aftre our departing, life in another
worlde euerlasting.

The tenne commaunde mentes, whiche god wrate with his owne fingre, and
gaue vnto the Israelites by Moises,
whiche thapostles willed vs also to kiepe
The firste, thou shalte haue none other
Goddes but me. The seconde, thou shalte
nor make the any graue Image, or like-
nesse of any thing that is in heauē aboue,
in the earthe benethe, or in the water vnder the earthe, thou shalt not bowe doune
to them, nor worshippe them. The third,
thou

thou shalt not take the name of thy lorde
God in baine. The fowrthe, remembre
that thou kepe holie thy Sabboth daie,
The fiueth, honour thy father & mother
The sixteth, thou shalte doe no murdre.
The seuenth, thou shalte not commit adulterie. The eight, thou shalte not steale.
The nineth, thou shalt beare no false wit
nesse against thy neighbour. The tenthe,
thou shalte not bespre thy neyghbours
house, his wife, his seruaunte, his maide,
his Ore, nor his Asse, nor any thing that
is thy neighbours.

The seuen Sacramentes of the churche, whiche are conteined in the fiue laste
Articles of our beleue, and commaunded
vs by the holie fathers to be beleued.

The firste, diepyng into the water, called Baptisyng aftre the Greke. This, by
canonicalle decree, in time paste was not
wonte to be giuen (excepte greate necessitie soner required it) but to those that
had bene scholers a space afore, to learne
the thinges appertinēt to christendome.
Yea, and that aftre thei had bene excea-
dingly welle enstructed in the faithe: and
proufe taken of their profityng, by seuen
examinacions, whiche ware made vpon
seuen

seuen seueralle daies in the Lente, and so
ware thei Baptised vpon Easter euen,
and Whitesondaie euen. Upon whiche
daies, thei ware accustomed to hallowe
the christening watre, in euery Paroche
But because this specially of all other, is
chiefly necessarie vnto euerlasting salua-
tion: leaste any bodie should die without
it, thei decreed that assone as the childe
was borne, godfathers should be sought
for it, as it ware for witnesses or sureties
whiche should bryng the childe vnto the
Churche doore, and there to stande without. And then the Priest should enquire,
before the childe be dieped in the Fonte,
whether it haue renounced Sathan and
all his pompe and pride. If it beleue cer-
teinely and wholie, all the Articles of the
Christiane faithe. And the Godfathers
answeryng, yea: for it, the Prieste brea-
thyng thrise vpon his face, exorciseth it,
and cathechiseth it. Aftre that, doeth he seuen thinges to the childe in ordre. Firste,
he putteth into the mouth hallowed salt.
Secondely, he mingleth earthe and his
spattle toguether, and smereth the eyes,
eares, & nosethrilles of the childe. Third-
ly, giuyng it suche name as it shall euer

aftre

aftre bee called by: he marketh it on the
breast and backe with holie oile, aftre the
facion of a crosse. Fourthly, he diepeth it
thrise in the water, or besprinckleth it
with watre thrise, in maner of a crosse, in
the name of the holie Trinitie, the father
the sonne, and holie ghost. In the whiche
name also, all thother Sacramentes are
ministred. Fiuethly, wetting his thumbe
in the holie ointement, he maketh therewith a Crosse on the childes foreheade.
Sixthly, he putteth a white garment vppon it. Seuenthly, he taketh it in the hāde
a Candle brennyng. The Iewes before
thei be Christened (by the determinacion
of the counsaile holden at Agathone, are
cathechised, that is to saie, are scholers ao
the enstruction of our beleue, nine monethes. And are boūd to fast fourtie daies:
to dispossesse them selues of all that euer
thei haue, and to make free their bonde
men. And looke whiche of their children
thei haue Circumcised, acording to Moses lawe: hym are thei bounde to banishe
their companie. No merueile therfore if
thei come so vnwillingly to christēdome.

Bishopping, whiche the Latines calle
Confirmacion, a confirming, a ratifieng
establishing

establishyng, authorisyng, or allowyng
of that went before : is the second Sacramente. And is giue of the Bishoppe onely, before the Aultare in the Churche, to
suche as are of growē yeres, and fastyng
(if it maie be) aftre this maner. As many
as shalbe Confirmed, come all together
with euery one a godfather. And the Bishoppe aftre he hath saied one oraison o-
uer thē all, wetyng his thumbe in the holie oile, maketh a crosse vpō eche of their
foreheades : In the name of the father,
sonne, and holie ghoste. And giueth hym
a blowe on the lefte chieke, for a remembraunce of the Sacrament, that he come
not for it againe. The godfathers, to the
ende the enoilyng should not droppe a-
waie, or by negligence bee wiped awaie,
clappe on a faire filette on the foreheade.
Whiche thei iudge to be vnlawfully takē
awaie, before the seuenth daie. The holie
fathers estemed this Sacrament so high
ly, that if the name giuen to the childe at
his Christendome, siemed not good : the
Bisshoppe at the giuyng hereof mighte
chaunge it.

The thirde Sacramente is holie Ordres, whiche in the firste Churche, was

giuen likewise of the Bishoppe, onely in
the monethe of December. But now at
sixe seuerall tymes of the yere:that is to
saie, the fowre Saturdaies in the embre
wekes (whiche ware purposely ordeined
therefore) vpon the Saturdaie, whiche
the Churche menne calle Sitientes, be=
cause the office of the Masse for that daie
appointed,beginneth with that woorde,
and vpon Easter euen.This Sacrament
was giuen onely to menne : and but to
those neither,whose demeanour and life,
dispositiō of bodie,and qualitie of minde,
ware sufficiently tried and knowē. Aftre
the opinion of some,there ware seuen or=
dres,or degrees,wherby the holy fathers
would vs to beleue that there ware fiue
speciall influences , as it ware printed in
the soule of the receiuer,wherby eche one
for eche ordre,was to be compted an hal=
lowed manne. Aftre the mindes of other
there ware nine. That is to saie, Musi=
cens(whiche encludeth singing and plai=
eng)Doore kiepers,Reders, Exorcistes
Acholites,Subdeacon,Deacon,Priefte
and Bishop. And for all this,it is cōpted
but one Sacramente, by the reason that
all these tende to one ende,that is to saie,

to consecrate the Lordes bodie. To euery one of these, did the Counsaile of Toledo in Spaine, appointe their seuerall liueries, and offices in the Churche. The Doorekepers had the office of our Common Sexteine, to ope the churche dores, to take hede to the churche, and to shutte the dores. And had therfore a keie giuen vnto theim, when thei ware admitted to this ordre. The Reader, in signe and token of libertie to reade the Bible, and holie stories, had a greate booke giuen him. The Exorcistes, serued to commaunde euill spirites out of menne, and in token therof, had a lesse booke giuen them. The Acholite, had the bearyng and the orderyng of the Tapers, Candelstickes, and Cruettes at the Altare: and therfore had a Candlesticke, a Taper, and two emptie Cruozettes deliuered hym. The Subdeacon, mighte take the offring, and handle the Chalice, and the Patine, carie theim to the Altare, and fro the Altare, and giue the Deacon Wine and water, out of the Cruettes. And therfore the Bisshoppe deliuereth hym an emptie Chalice with a Patine, and the Archedeacon one Cruet full of wine, and another full of watre,

S.iij.　　and

and a Towelle. To the Deacons, is the
Preachyng of Goddes Gospelle to the
people comitted, and to helpe the priest
in al holy ministracion. He hath the Gospelle booke deliuered hym, and a towell
hanged vppon his one shouldre, like a
yoke. The Prieste hath power to consecrate the Lordes bodie, to praie for sin-
ners, and to reconcile thē againe to God
by Penaūce entoined them. He hath deliuered hym a Chalice with Wine, the
Patine, with a singyng cake, a stole vpō
bothe shouldres, and a Chesible. What
Ornamentes the Bisshoppe hath giuen
vnto hym, ye haue heard afore. He maie
not be made Bisshoppe, but on the Sondaie about the. iii. houre aftre Prime, be
twene thoffice of the Masse and the Gospelle: at the whiche tyme twoo Bisshoppes, and a Metropolitane, laie their handes vpon his heade and a booke. The Bishoppes in the firste Churche, did litle or
nothyng diffrs from other Priestes, and
ware ruled by the commune Counsailes
of the Churche, before that dissecion and
deuision entred emong the people, cau-
sing theim in sondrie sortes, to cleaue vnto sondrie names, euery sorte as thei fortuned

runed to be conuerted and Chziffened of
a fonozie perfone. As whom Paule Bap-
tifed, thei would be called Paulines.
whom Appollo, Appollonians. whom
Cephas, Cephites, and so of other. To
auoide therefoze these bzeaches of con-
cozde, and foz an vnifozmitie, the holy fathers ware dziuen to decree and ftablifh
that as many as fhould afreward be ba-
ptifed, fhould be called Chziftianes of
Chziffe. And that ouer euery Countie oz
Shiere, there fhould be sette one Pzieffe
oz moe, acozdyng to the greatneffe of the
fame, fuche as ware beft tried. whiche
fhould haue to name, Ouersears in En-
glifhe: in Greke, Episcopj. whom we cal
Bifhopes, by chaungyng of. P. into. B.
and leauing out the. E. foz fhoztnes, acozdyng to the nature of our tongue. These
mighte not then gouerne their Clergie,
and other their Diocefans, at their owne
pleafure, as thei did befoze: but acozding
to the decrees of the Churche of Rome,
and the holie Counsailes of the fathers
affembled. Then began thei firffe (by the
fuffraunce and helpe of deuoute pzinces)
to deuide all Chziffendome into Diocef-
fes, and the Diocesse into Conuocacions

oz Chaptres, and those againe into Pa-
roches, and to set that goodly ozdze, that
yet continueth, aswell emong the clergie
as the laietie. That the parishe should o-
beie their lawfull Persone, the Persone
the Deane: the Deane, the Bishoppe: the
Bishoppe, the Archebishoppe. The Arch-
bishoppe, the Primate oz Patriarche:
the Primate oz Patriarche, the Legate:
the Legate, the Pope: the Pope the generalle Counsaile: the generalle Counsaile, God alone.

For the fourthe Sacramente it is holden, that euery pzieste rightly pziessed, a-
cozdyng to the keies of the Churche, hauing an entente to consecrate, and obser-
uyng e the fourme of the woozdes: hathe
power, of wheaten bzeade to make the
very bodie of Chzisse, and of Wine to
make his very bloude.

Chzisse our Lozde hym selfe, the daye
befoze he suffred, kepte it solemply with
his disciples, and consecrated, and ozdeined it continually to be celebzated, and
eaten in the remembzaunce of him selfe.
And about this mattier a man had nede
of a great faythe. Firsse to beleue the
bzeade to be chaunged into the body, and
the

the wine into the bloude of Chꝛiſte . A-
gaine thoughe this be done euery daye
that yet Chꝛiſt foꝛ all that ſhould growe
neuer a whitte the bigger foꝛ ẏ making,
noꝛ the leſſe foꝛ the eatinge . Thirdely
that the Sacrament being deuyded into
many partes, Chꝛiſt ſhould yet remaine
whole in euery cromme . Fourthly that
thoughe the wicked eate it, yet ſhould not
it be defiled . Fiuethly that it bꝛingeth
to as many euyll as receiue it, death: and
to the good euerlaſting life. Sixthly that
it tourneth not into the nature of the eater to his nouriſhemente as other meate
dothe: but turneth the eater contrariwiſe
into the nature of it ſelfe. And yet being
eaten, that it is rapte into heauen, vn-
hurte oꝛ vntouched. Seuenthly that in ſo
ſmalle a ſyſe of bꝛeade and wine, the infinite, and incompꝛehenſible Chꝛiſte,
God and manne ſhoulde be compꝛehen-
ded. Then, that one, and the ſelf ſame bodye of Chꝛiſte, at one very inſtaunte,
ſhoulde be in many places, and of many
menne receiued at ones, and in ſondꝛye
parcelles. Ninethly ẏ thoughe the bꝛead
it ſelfe be chaunged into the very fleſſhe
of Chꝛiſte, and the wine into his bloude,

that yet to all the ſences thei remaine
breade and wine, and neither fleſſhe ne
blond. Further that all theſe cōmodities
cōteined in theſe verſes folowing ſhould
happen vnto thoſe that worthely eate it.

It putteth in mynde and kindleth, encreaſeth hope, and ſtrengtheneth.
Mainteineth, clenſeth, reſtoreth, giues
life, and vniteth.
Stabliſſheth beliefe, abates the foode of
ſinne, and all vnclennes quencheth.

Finally, to be very profitable for the
ſaluaciō aſwell of thoſe liuyng as deade,
for whō it is ſpecially offred by the prieſt
in the Maſſe. And therefore to haue to
name Euchariſtia communio.

In the beginning of the Chriſtiane
faithe (and yet amonge certeine ſchiſma-
tiques as thei ſaye) one whole lofe was
conſecrated, of ſuche bigguenesſe, as whē
the Prieſt had broken it in a platter into
ſmalle pieces, it mighte ſuffiſe the whole
multitude that ware at the maſſe to participate of. For in time paſſe the Chriſti-
ancs came every day to communicate by
a ſpeciall commaundemente, and ordenaunce. Aftrewarde but ones in a wieke
and that on the Sonday. But whan it
begann

began to be skant well kepte vppon the
Sonday neither: then was it commaunded that euery manne should receiue it
thrise in the yere, or ones at the leaste, at
euery Easter. And that euery christian
manne, when he stode in any daungier
of death, beynge whole of minde, should
receiue it as a wayfaring viande, to staye
him by the waye: with as good preparation of bodye and soule, as he possibly
mighte.

Matrimonie (whiche is the lawefull
coupling of the manne and the woman)
broughte in by the lawe of nature, the
lawe of God, the lawe of all peoples, and
the lawe ciuile, is the siueth Sacrament.
The holy fathers woulde haue but one
mariage at ones, & that not in secrete but
with ope solemnitie eyther in ye churche,
or in the churche porche, and so that the
priest be called to the matter. Who shold
firste examine the man, and then the wo-
manne, whether thei bothe consent to be
maried together. Yf thei be agreed (whiche is chiefely in this case requisite) he
taking them bothe by the right handes:
coupleth them together in the name of
the holy and vnseperable trinitie, the father,

ther, the sonne, and the holy ghoste. And
commaundeth, and exhorteth them that
thei alwaye remembring this their coupling of their owne free wille & consent:
as longe as thei liue, neuer forsake one a
nother, but loue & honour one another,
be debonaire and buxome one to another, giuing them selues to procreacion,
and not to lecherous luste. And that thei
honestly and diligently bringe vp, suche
childzen as God sendeth them of theyr
bodies. Aftre that he affiaunceth thē both
with one ringe. And sprinckling holy wa
ter vpon them, reacheth them a stole, and
leadeth them into the churche, where (yf
thei ware not blessed afoze) he blesseth
them kneeling befoze the altare. The wo
man hath on a redde fillet oz frontelette,
and ouer that a white veile, withoute the
whiche it is not lawfulle foz her fro that
daye forewarde, to go oute of doozes a-
bzode, oz to sitte by any manne. Twelue
thinges ther be, whiche the holy fathers
woulde haue to barre persons from con-
tracting of matrimonie, and to disseuer
them againe, yf thei be contracted . Errour of person, that is to saye, mistaking
one foz another. A betrowthing vpon a
condicion

condicion, Consanguinitie or kindred, An opē crime Diuersitie of sects, Force, or constrainte. Holy ordres, a Bōde or former contracte, Commune or open honestie, Affinitie, and Dishabilitie of engēdrure.

The sixteth Sacramente is penaunce or repentaunce, giuen of Christe as it ware for a wracke boorde, wherby men are preserued fro drowninge. Eche christian oughte vndoubtedly to beleue that this consisteth in foure poinctes. To saie, in Repētaūce of our sinnes, Canonicalle cōfession, Absolucion, and Satisfaction, or amendes. Firste let him sorowe, not with a lighte forthinckinge, but with a mosse earnesse and bittre repentaunce in the botome of his conscience: for the puritie and innocencie that he had gotten eyther by baptisme or the benefite of former repentaunce, and nowe hathe eftsones losse, and forgone throughe sinne. And let him hope with this repentaunce, to be reconciled to the fauour of God againe And let him humbly, and truly with his owne mouthe, confesse to a wise prieste, in the steade of God : all those offences wherwith he knoweth him selfe to haue losse his innocencie and clennesse, and to

haue

haue prouoked the wrathe of GOD a-
gainste him selfe. And let him assuredly
beleue that the same prieste, hath power
giuen him of Christe (as beinge his vi-
care, or deputie on earthe) to absolue him
of all his sinnes. Finally for satisfaction
or amendes making for the faulte : lette
him not with grudginge, but chierfully,
and gladly doe, what so euer he shalbe cō-
maūded. Beleuig with vndoubted faith,
that he is absolued, and quyte of all, assone as the priest in dewe forme of wordes, hath pronounced the absolucion.

The seuenth, and the laste Sacramēt
is the laste enoynting, by an oyle that is
made to this vse, by the bisshope in euery
diocesse, by an yerely custome vpō maū-
dy thursdaie, like as the chrismatory oyle
is. And this by the precepte of sainte Ia-
mes the Apostle, and by the ordinaunce
of Felix the fourthe Pope after Sainte
Peter: was giuen only to them that laie
in dyeng, being of full age, and requy-
ring it. Thei vse to enoynte with a prescripte fourme of wordes, and with often inuocation of sainctes: those partes
of the bodie, wher our fiue wittes or sen-
ses: the hearing, seyng, smelling, tasting
and

and touching, beare moste stroke, & with
whiche man is iudged chiefely to sinne.
That is, the eares, the eyes, the nosethril
les, the mouthe, the handes, and the fete.
Wherby the holy fathers would vs to be
leue, that there was not onely purchased
cleane forgiuenesse of all smaller offences, or venialle sinnes: but also either pre
sente recouerie, or a riper and gentler
deathe. All the feastes and holydaies,
throughout the yere, whiche the churche
hath commaunded to be obserued & kept:
beginne at the Aduente, or approche of
Christe our Lorde. Whiche Peter the
Apostle instituted to be obserued in De-
cembre, with fasting and praier, thre wie
kes and a haulfe before Christemas, whē
we close vp the last. viii. daies of that mo
neth, with great ioye and feaste. Thei deuided the yere into two & fiuetie wekes,
and xii. seueral monthes. The monethes
cōmonly into. xxx. daies. The firste daye
of Ianuary the churche recordeth howe
Christe was circumcised acordinge to
Moyses lawe. The. iii. daye aftre, howe
he was worshipped of the thre Sages,
with thre sondry presentes: and howe beinge baptissed of Iohn in Iordaine the
floude,

floude, he laide the foundacion of the
newe Lawe. The seconde of Febzuarie,
how his mother vnspotted, obeyeng the
maner of her cõtry: bzought him into the
temple, and suffred her self to be purified
oz clensed, whiche we calle churching of
childe. In memozie wherof the churche
vseth that daye, solempne pzocession, and
halowing of candles. The fiue and twen
tieth of Marche, howe ý aungel bzought
woozde to the virgin Marie, that Chzist
shoulde be bozne of her, being conceyued
in her wombe, by the ouershadowing of
the holy ghoste. At the whiche time they
willed vs to faste the fourtie daies that
he fasted him selfe, being with vs vppon
earth, and to renewe the remembzaunce
of his passion, and deathe, whiche he willingly susteined to deliuer vs frõ ý yoke
and bondage of the deuell. The laste day
of that faste, which oftentimes falleth in
Apzille, to celebzate the highest feaste in
al the yere: in remembzaunce howe he
ouercame deathe, descended into helle,
vanquisshed the deuell, and retourned a-
gaine on liue, and appeared in glozious
wyse vnto his scholers, oz disciples.
In Maye, howe all those his scholers lo-
king

king vpõ him,he by his owne vertue and
mighte,ſtied vp into the heauens. At the
whiche time, by thordenaunce of ſainte
Mamerte,biſhoppe of Vienne : there be
made ganginges with the leſſe Letanies
from one Churche to another, all Chriſ-
ſtendome ouer. In June,and ſomtime in
Maie,how the holy ghoſte, promiſed to
the diſciples,giuen from aboue, appered
to them like glowing tongues:and gaue
them to vnderſtande, ç to ſpeake the ton-
ges of al naciõs. Theight date folowing,
Trinitie Sondaie. The ſiueth date aftre
that, how Chriſte in his laſte ſupper, for
a continualle remembraunce of himſelf,
inſtituted the moſte holſome Sacramête
of his bodie and bloud,vnder the fourme
of breade and wine,leauyng it to be ſene
and eaten of his. The ſiuetenth of July,
how the bleſſed Apoſtles, acordyng as
thei ware cõmaunded, the twelueth yere
aftre the Aſcencion of their Maſter into
heauen: wente their waies into the vni-
uerſalle worlde,to Preache vnto all people. The departyng of Chriſtes mother
out of this life, the ſiuetenth date of Au-
guſte. And her Natiuitie,theight of Se-
prembre. And thone and twentie of No-

uembre,

uembre, how she from thre yeres of age
(at the whiche tyme she was presented to
the temple)vntill she was mariage able,
remained there seruing God stil a peace
And theight of December, how she was
of her parentes begotten, that longe a-
fore had bene barreine. The second daie
of Julie, how Elisabethe passyng the
Mounteines, visited her kineswoman.

There ware also certeine holie daies
appoincted to the . rii. Apostles. To certeine Martyres, Confessours, and Uir-
gines.As the sowre and twentieth of fe-
bruarie to sainct Matthie. To sainct
Marke the Euangeliste, the . rrb . of A-
prille. Upon the whiche daie, Gregorie
ordeined the greate Letanies to be songe
The firste of Maie is hallowed for Phi-
lippe and James the more . The. rrir.of
June,for Petre and Paule:৳ the . rriiii.
of the same,for the Natiuitie of .S. Jhon
Baptiste. The.rrb. of July, for James
the lesse . for Bartholomewe the sowre
৳ twentie of Augusti.For Mathewe, the
one and twentie of Septembre. And the
eight and twentie of Octobre, for Simõ
and Jude.The last of Nouembre, for .S
Andrewe. The one and twentie of De-
cembre,

rembze, foz sainct Thomas. And the .vii.
and twentie of the same moneth foz Jhõ
the Euãgeliste. The daie befoze, foz Ste-
phin the first Martire. And the daie aftre
foz the Innocentes. The tenth of August
foz sainct Laurence. And the thze & twentie of Apzille, foz sainct Geozge . Of all
the Confessours, there are no moe that
haue holidaies appoincted, but S. Mar-
tine and saincte Nicholas . The firste, on
the eleuenth of Nouembze: and the other
the sixteth of Decembze . Katherine the
virgine, the fiue and twentie of Nouembze, and Marie Magdalene the twentie
and two of July. There is also vndze the
name of sainct Michael alone, the. xxix.
of Septembze : a holy daie foz all blessed
Angelles. And one other in commune foz
all the sainctes, and chosen of GOD, the
firste of Nouembze.

Thei would also that euery seuenthe
daie, should be hallowed of the Chzistia-
nes, by the name of Sondaie, as the Jewes doe their Sabboth: restyng from all
wozldly woozke , and beyng onely occupied with pzaising of GOD, and the deuine Seruice in the Churche. To learne
by the Pziestes pzeachyng, the Gospelle

L.ii.   and

and the commaundementes of our faith.
And by what meanes so euer we thinke
in our conscience we haue prouoked the
wrathe of God against vs all the wieke
afoze: that, this daie to amende, to sette
cliere, and aske pardone foz. In time past
euery Thursdaie also was kepte as the
Sondaie. But because we mighte sieme
therein, somewhat to grātesie the Hea-
then(whiche that daie kepte solempne holie daie, to Jupiter their Idolle) it was
laied doune againe. Moze ouer the clerkes and the people, vsed bothe Thursdaie
and Sondaie befoze Masse, to go round
aboute the Churche a Pzocession, and
the Pzieste, to spzinckle the people with
holy watre. Agapitus instituted the one,
and the other. The Thursdaie, in remembzaunce of Chzistes Ascencion, and the
Sondaie, of his glozious Resurrection:
whiche we celebzate fro Sondaie to Sō-
daie continually, ones euery eight daies.
The night afoze euery ozdenary holidaie
oz feastefull daie: the whole clergie, and
the people, ware bounde to kiepe Uigile
in euery churche. That is to saie, to wake
all nighte, in deuine seruice and pzaier.
But vpon consideracion of many slaun-

derous

derous crimes and offences, that ware
by diuers naughtie and malicious persones committed, by the oportunitie of the
darke:this maner was taken awaie, and
ordeined that the daie before the feaste,
should be fasted, whiche yet kiepeth stille
the name of Uigile. The fathers decreed
that the churche in the whole yere should
renue the memorie of fiue thynges.

Fro the Sondaie called Septuagessi-
ma (because there are seuentie daies, betwiene that and the octaues of Easter)
thei would vs to renue the memorie of
Christes Fasting, Passion, Death & Be-
wriaile. The miserable falle also of our
first parentes, and those extreme errours
of mankinde, by the whiche thei ware
ledde awaie fro the knowledge and worshippe of one verie GOD:to the wicked
supersticion and honour of Idolles and
d'uelles. And further, the greuous and
intollerable bondage that the people of
Israell suffred vndre the Pharao of E-
gipte. Upon whiche consideracion, the
bookes of Genesis and Erodus be redde
in the seruice of the churche. Whiche sheweth then in all her demeanour, and ap-
pareilyng, heauinesse and sorowe.

From the octaues of Easter, to the octaues of Whitsontide, Christes Resurrection, and Ascencion, with the comming of the holy Ghoste. And together with that, the redempcion, reconciliatió, and at onement of mankinde with God the father, throughe Iesus Christe: and the restoryng againe of the children of Israell, to the lande of beheste. Wherein was prefigured our reconciliacion and redempcion aforesaied. For that cause is all the seruice out of the newe Testamét, and al thinges done with ioye & gladnes.

From the octaues of Whitsontide, till Aduente, xy. wiekes space, and more, thei would haue to bee celebrated the cóuersacion of Christe here in the worlde, with his miracles and woorkes of wondre. And ouer and beside that, the longe pilgrimage that mankinde, by longe reuolucion maketh, from one generacion to another, from the tyme of our redempcion, saluacion and sauyng, vntill the laste date of time. Wherfore duryng this while, vpon consideracion of the diuerse happe and hasarde, wherwith the Churche is tossed, like a Shippe in the troubled Seas, she neither greatly reioiseth,

ne

ne soroweth, but redeth greate chaunge
of bookes, out of the olde and newe Te-
stamente: to the ende she maie walke the
warelier, and the better wiinde her self
out of the stormes, that are ready to as-
saile her.

From Aduente to Christemas, to remembre the tyme from Moses, to the
commyng of Messias. In the whiche
mankinde certefied of saluacion, bothe
by the lawe and the Prophetes, awaited
with moste earneste desires for his comming, and the kingdōe that he shold haue
Wherefore thei ordeined that the Pro-
phecies should be redde, and fasting exercised. That the churche the better enstructed, and abled by these, mighte the wor-
thelier receiue the Birthe daie of Christ
her Lorde (whiche euer falleth the fo-
werth wieke aftre) and from thens holde
on with feaste, and continuall gladnesse,
vntill Septuagesima. Reioising that he
was now come: whiche should bee the
saulutour of the worlde. Their oratories
Temples, or places of praier (whiche we
calle Churches) might not be built without the good will of the Bisshopps of the
Diocese. And when the Timbre was re-

L.iiij.   oy

by to be framed, and the foundacion digged: it behoued them to sende for the Bishoppe, to hallowe the firste corner stone
of the foundaciõ, and to make the signe of
the crosse therbpon, and to laie it, and directe it iuste Easte and Weste. And then
might the Masons sette bpon the reste,
but not afore. This Churche did thei vse
to builde, aftre the facion of a crosse, and
not vnlike the shape of a manne. The
Chauncelle (in the whiche is conteined
the highe Altare and the Quiere) directe
full into the East, reprelenteth the heade.
And therfore ought to be made somwhat
rounde, and muche shorter then the body
of the churche. And yet bpon respecte that
the head is the place for the eyes, it ought
to be of more lighte, and to bee separate
with a particion, in the steade of a necke,
from the body of the Churche. This particion the Latine calleth Cancelli: and out
of that cometh our terme, Chauncelle.
On eche side of this chauncelle peraduenture (for so sitteth it beste) should stand a
Turret, as it ware for two eares. And in
these the Belles to be hanged, to calle the
people to Seruice, by daie and by night.
Vndre one of these Turrettes, is there
                              commonly

commonly a voulte, whose doore openeth into the quiere. And in this are laid
vp, the hallowed vesselles and ornameit-
tes, and other vtensiles of the church. we
calle it a vestrie. The other parte oughte
so to be fitted, that hauing as it ware on
eche side an arme, the reste maye resemble the bodye with the fete stretched in
breadthe, and in lengthe. On eche side of
the bodye the pillers to stonde. Upon
whose coronettes or heades the vaulte or
rophe of the churche maye reste. And to
the foote beneth, aulters to be ioyned.
Those aulters to be ordrely alway couered with two aulter clothes, and garnisshed with the crosse of Christe, or some
litle cofre of reliques. At eche ende a can-
delsticke: and a booke towarde the myd-
des. The walles to be parieted without,
and within, and diuersly paincted. That
they also should haue in euery parische a
faire sounde stone, made holowe, and
fitte to holde water: in the whiche the wa
ter consecrate for baptisme, may be kept
for the christening of children. Upon the
right hande of the highe aulter, that ther
should be an almorie, either cutte into
the walle, or framed vpon it: in the whi-

L.v.   the

che thei woulde haue the Sacrament or
the Lozdes bodye, the holy oyle foz the
ſicke, and the Chziſmatozie, alwaie to be
locked. Furthermoze thei woulde that
ther ſhould be a pulpite in the middes of
the churche, wherein the prieſte maye
ſtonde vpon ſondaies and holidayes, to
teache the people thoſe thinges that it behoueth them to knowe. The Chauncelle
to ſerue onely foz the prieſtes, and clerkes. The reſt of the tēpozalle multitude
to be in the body of the church. Seperate
notwithſtonding, the men on the ryghte
ſide, and the women, on the lefte. And
eche of them to be ſobze and honeſt in apparelle and behauour. whatſoeuer is cō-
trary to good facion oz chziſtiane religion, with greate diligence to ſhonne it. It
was the maner in the firſt churche, both
amonge men and women to lette their
heare growe, to ſhewe out their naked
ſkinne, and very litle oz nothing to diffre
in apparelle. Sainct Peter put firſt ozdze, that women ſhould couer their heades, and menne rounde their heare, and
either of them to go in ſeueralle and ſon-
dzye apparelle. Mozeouer that to euery
churche, ſhold be laid out a churchyarde,

of

of the grounde adioyning, in the whiche all chzisten mennes bodies mighte indifferently be bewzied. The same to be consecrate, oz halowed by the bisshoppe, and to enioye all the pziuilegies that the churche may enioye.

The funeralle foz the deade, thei kepe not in euery place ylike. Some mourne and kepe dirige and Masse seuen daies continualle together, some .ir. some .rrr. oz fourtye some, fiuetie, and a hundzed, and other a whole yere, wzapped vp in blacke. The coūselle of Toledo ozdeined that the cozps beinge firste wasshed, and then wzapped vp in a shiete, shoulde be caried foz the with singing by menne of his owne condicion oz sozte, clerkes by clerkes, and laye menne of laye menne. And aftre what time the pziest hath sensed the cozps, thzowen holy water vppon it, ₹ said certeine pzayers, to laye it into the graue with the face vpwarde, and the heade into the weaste. Then to thzowe in the earth again, and in token that ther is a chzistiā ther bewried, to sette vp a crosse of wodde, garnisshed with yvie, cipzes, oz laurelle. These be the ozdzes and facions of the Chzistiane religion.

FINIS.

¶ The treatise of Josephus, conteyning the ordres, and Lawes of the Jewes commune wealthe.

¶ To the Reader.

His lytle treatise, good Reader, haue I translated out of a Latine texte, laid worde for woorde, aunswering to the Grieke (for in that tonge Josephus compiled it) as niere as it was possible. And looke howe scrupulous myne Authour was in matching the latine: so scrupulous haue I also bene in deuising myne englysshe. Remembring alway, that thoughe in other writinges of mennes deuyse, an enterpretour maye, eyther to giue lighte to the sentence, or to obserue the naturalle phrase of the tonge that he enterpreteth

preteth in (specially wher ther lieth no
matier of importaunce oz controuersie)
vse a moze libertie of woozdes and sentence: yet in these holy wzitinges deliuered vs fro G O D, in them I saye, and
euery bzaunche of them, we oughte rather to shonne then to seke suche libertie,
asmuche as we maye. Studienge nowe
not so muche to flourishe in painted pen-
ning, as sobzely, and sensibly to giue the
meaninge of those infinite thzeasoures,
with suche woozdes as falle moste feling-
lie foz them, ronne thei neuer so roughe
in the pzose, oz be they neuer so simple
and harde framing with our phzase. If
my doinges therfoze herin shall seme to
the in certeyne places, moze Grekishe
then Englysshe, oz liker the maner of
the Latine then of our owne londe:
impute it to the reuerence that
I owe to these maner
of Authours.

The

Hē Moſes had gouerned the Iſraelites, by the ſpace of fowrtie yeres, but .xxx. daies lackyng: He aſſēbled the people harde vpon Iordane, where the toune now ſtondeth, that is called Abila (ſo named of the plentie of Abeles, theraboute growing) and all the people being gathered together, he ſpake vnto theim in this wiſe. Felowes & companions of my long trauelles, foraſmuche as it pleaſeth God that I departe this life, and myne age is now comen to the nombre of an hundred and twentie yeres: and for that I can be no helpe, ne aide vnto you, in ȳ thinges ye ſhal haue to do on the other ſide Iordeine (the Lorde reſtrainyng me) I thought it not miete, no not euen now at the laſte caſte, to ſlacke myne endeuour towarde you for the aduauncemēt of your wealth But to ſtudie how to purchaſe aſwell to

you

you eternalle enioyeng of prosperitie, as to my self perpetualle memorie emongeſt you, when ye ſhall haue opteined plentie of al bleſſednesse. Go to then, aftre what time I ſhall haue declared, how bothe ye your ſelues maie be bleſſed, and leaue vnto your poſteritie an euerlaſting poſſeſſion of the ſame, I will ſo departe this life. And truly I am worthye me thinckes to be credited, and beleeued of ye, bothe for the earneſt ſtickingin your quarelle ſondrie tymes heretofore, and alſo for that the ſoules of men brought vnto the laſte caſte are then moſt ſtreightly allied and knitte with all vertue.

A good man at no time diſſembleth, and muche leſſe when he lieth at the poincte of deathe.

O Iſraelites, a fauourable GOD, is the onely cauſe of all the good thinges that men poſſeſſe. And he alone can giue vnto the worthy, and take fro the wicked. If ye ſhewe your ſelues towarde him, ſuche as he requireth, and ſuche as I perfectly knowinge his wille and pleaſure admonyſſhe ye to be: he ſhall neuer withdrawe himſelf from you, neither ſhal ye at any time ceaſe to be bleſſed, ꝛ honorable ouer all. Yea the wealth that ye now poſſeſſe, ſhall remaine ſure your owne, and that that is promiſed ye in time to come,

come,ſhall ſpiedely be giuen ye. So that
ye obeie the thinges, whiche God woulb
ye to obeie: and preferre no trade of Ciuile ordre or gouernaunce, befoze the lawes that I preſently giue you: ne ſtraie
vnto ſtraunge maners, contempnynge
the loue and teare, whiche ye now haue
vnto the Lozde. And in folowyng theſe,
ye ſhal be of all menne moſte ſtrong and
valiaunte in fight, and vanquiſheable to
none enemie. Neither is it mete that thei
ſhould feare any manne: foz whoſe helpe
God hath armed hymſelf to battaile.

Greate rewardes are laied befoze ye
foz vertue: if duryng your life ſhe dwelle
continually in you. Foz firſte, ſhe her ſelf
of all goodnes is the beſt: and purchaſeth
haboundaunce of all other thynges that
good are. She truely, vſed emong ye, ſhal
giue vnto you a bleſſed life: make ye to
be praiſed aboue all foreine nacions, and
cauſe ye to be renoumed emōg thoſe that
ſhalbe aſtre your daies. All theſe thinges
maie ye obteine, if ye bee obedience and
kepe well the lawes whiche I haue giue
ye from the mouthe of God, and exerciſe
your mindes in the vndzeſtanding of the
As foz my ſelf, I departe gladde of your

prosperitie, commendyng ye to the rule of sobre discrecion, and to those honeste ordres and Lawes, that I leaue among ye: and to the vertue of your chiefeteines, to whom the aduauncement of your commodities and profites shalbe committed. God also, that hetherto hath gouerned you, & by whose wille I haue bene your profitable minister: shall not yet cease to prouide for ye. But euen as long as ye your selues shall wishe to haue him your gouernour & helper (continuyng in your earneste zeale of vertue) so long shall ye be sure that he wille foresee to deliuer ye from daunger. And the high Prieste Eleasar, and Iosua, the counsaile, and the Officers of the Tribes: shall declare and open vnto you, what is beste to be done. Whiche if ye followe, ye shall haue blessed wealthe amonge you Obeie ye them therefore withoute grudge. vnderstandyng, that the menne whiche praise worthely canne obeie: shall also haue knoweledge how praise worthely to rule, if thei shal ones come to that prerogatiue of dignitie. And iudge it to be franke libertie, not to repine against the thynges whervnto your Capiteines shall require ye.

For

For now ye take this to be libertie. If ye
maie hurte those that haue done good vn
to you: and sette nought by them, whiche
are your welwillers and friendes. The
whiche euill, if ye shall from henceforthe
auoide: the worlde shall go the bettre
with you. Beware I require you, that ye
neuer entreprise suche outrage against
them, as ye haue ofte attempted against
me. For ye knowe that I haue bene oftener in hasarde of my life, throughe you,
then by mine enemies. Wherin I would
ye should not thincke, that I meane in a-
ny wise to attwighte ye, or taunte ye. For
lothe woulde I be, by this my rehersalle
of thinges paste, to leaue in your mindes
any displeasure against me, now, at my
departing. Seing that euē then, when ye
thus dealte with me: I shewed none angre against ye. But by this, to giue ye
warnyng that ye vprightly behaue your
selues heraftre, and offre no iniurie to
your superiours for riches sake. Wherof ye shall haue plentie, beyng ones passed Jordane, and hauyng achieued Chanaan. But if throughe these, vertue shall
become contemptible and fulsome vnto
you, ye shall lose also the fauour of God.

T.ij.   Who

Who becomen your enemie, ye shall also lose the lande whiche ye shall possesse: with shame enough ouercomen of your enemies in the fielde. And being skatered the worlde ouer, ye shall be as thralles and bondemen, in euery coaste and countrie, by Sea and by lande. And as for the remembraunce, and repentaunce of the lawes not obserued: shall then, when ye shalbe fallen into those euilles, stande ye to none effecte. Wherefore, if ye entende to conserue these lawes: leaue ye not an enemie on liue, when ye shall haue vanquished them. But iudge it necessary for your welfares, to destroie theim euery mothers childe. Leste if thei be suffred to liue: ye take sauour in their maners, and corrupte your owne countrie discipline & ordenaunces. I counsaile ye also that ye hewe doune their groues, throwe doune their Altares, and what so euer Churches thei shall haue: and abolishe with fire, the memorialle of theim, and their people. For by that, and none other meanes, shall ye stablishe your selues a sure quiete, in your blisse. And that your nature leade ye not to the worse, for lacke of knowledge of the bettre: I haue bothe

made vnto you Lawes, as I learned thē
at the mouthe of the lorde, & also an ordre
of publique discipline. Acordyng to the
ordenaunces whereof, if ye shall direct
your liues, ye shalbe iudged of all people
the moste happie.

Hauyng spoken these thynges, he deliuered vnto thē the lawes, and the ordre
of their cōmune wealth, writtē in a boke.
But thei vniuersally wepte, and greatly
lamented the departure of their capitein
that so fast approched. Remēbring what
daungiers and carcke, he had suffred for
their sauftie: & muche distrustyng what
should afterwarde come of theim. As the
people that neuer was like to haue suche
a gouernour again. And muche fearyng
least God would withdrawe his tendrenes towarde theim: when there lacked a
Moses to entreate. And thei bewailed
with greate repentaunce, the thynges,
whiche in their angre thei had done vnto
hym in the deserte. So that the teares of
the people, their dole, and sobbyng com-
plaintes: ware greater then could be re-
comforted with wordes. Although Moses did what in hym laie, to perswade thē
that there was no cause why thei should
bewaile

bewaile hym: But rather remembre to put in vse the ordre of the commune welth that he had giuen theim. And so he dissolued the assemblie.

These woordes be spoke in the person of Iosephus

Now then aftre what tyme I shall haue shewed ye thordre of the commune-wealth, miete for the worthines and vertue of Moses, and shall haue described thesame, that it maie appere vnto al men (beyng willyng to reade) what our state hath bene in times paste: I will procede to the declaracion of the other thynges. With suche faithe, that I neither wills penne any thyng other wise then he lefte it, ne adde (either for settyng out of the matier, or other wise) any title of myne owne. Sauyng onely those that he lefte written by piecemeale, as he receiued thē at the mouthe of God: we haue framed toguether into one ordinarie treatise. Wherof I thought good togiue warnig, least some of our bloude happenyng vpō these, might by occasion saie that we had swarued from the truthe

The lawes then perteinyng to the institucion of our citie, are suche as followe. But suche as he lefte vs commune among our selues: those haue I deferred vntill

A

I putte furthe my booke, De moribus & causis, whiche I haue purposed God willyng, to go in hande with next aftre this.

A booke of Iosephus so named.

*What time then ye shall haue achieued the land of Chanaan, and as menne that haue founde laisure to vse their goodes, shal determine from thentefurthe to builde cities: if ye shall accomplishe these thinges, ye shall bothe haue cone a thing acceptable vnto God, and shall winne to your selues a grounded wealthe .

Moses speaketh againe.

See that there be one holie citie, in the mooste goodlie place of all the lande of Chanaan. See that ther be but one churche in it, and one altare: of stones neither squared nor karued, ne yet framed by Masonrie, but handesomely heaped together, as thei be gathered. And lette the same be so plastered ouer, that it maie appere to the sighte, a plaine and comely Altare. But se there be none ascence ther vnto by staiers, but onely a faire vp goyng, by a slope baneque of Turfes. In any other of your cities, se there neither be Churche, ne Altare. For God is but one, and the people of the Hebrues but one. Whosoeuer shal haue spoke̅ * villanie against God, let hym be stoned, and hanged

Blasphemie.

ged

ged fro morowe till nighte, and vilely be
bewried, withoute anye solempnitie.
Thrise a yere the people shal assemble into
the citie where the churche is: fro farre,
and niere, through the whole lande that
the Debrues shal possesse. Bothe to ren-
dre thanckes to GOD, for that he shall
haue sent them: & to make supplicatio for
thinges that are to come. And further,
to thende that with often hauntynge one
with another, and sitting together: there
maie be a friendship engedred emongest
theim. For truely it is miete that menne
of one nacion, and bloude, and coupled
in one trade of lawes: should be acqueinted one with another (as by suche fellowshippe it shal come to passe) and that thei
should cause a remembraüce to remaine
one of another emögest them with suche
repaire, and cöpanieng together. Without the whiche ye shall seme one to a nother moste straunge.

Ye shail also reserue aparte, a tenthe
of all the fruictes of the earthe: beside the
tenthe appoincted to be giuen to the priestes, and Leuites. The whiche ye shall
selle eche man at home in his countrie.
But the profecte comyng thereof, shalbe
spente

ſpent vpõ the feaſtes, and ſacrifices to be made in ẙ holy citie. Foɀ ſo is it mete that men take parte of the fruictes comming of the londe whiche the Loɀde ſhall giue them, to the honour of the giuer . The pɀice that commeth of the commune har lot, ſhalt thou not conuerte vnto the vſe of Sacrifice. Foɀ God delighteth not in the fruites of any kinde of iniquitie: and nothing is moɀe abhominable then ſuch lewdenes of the body. Likewyſe yf anye manne require eyther thy dogge foɀ the folde, oɀ foɀ the chace to lime his bitche, the pɀice comming therof ſhalte thou not conuerte to the ſacrifice of the Loɀd. No man ſhall rayle againſt thoſe that other cities holde foɀ their goddes . Neither ſhall ye ſpoyle oɀ robbe, churche oɀ cha pell of any foɀeine Idolle, ne take away any gifte conſecrate to them . See that none of you be apparelled with a gar mente ✳ of linnen and wollen meinte: foɀ that apperteineth onely to the pɀieſtes. And when the multitude ſhalbe aſſebled into the holy citie, to celebɀate the ſeuẽth yeres ſacrifices, at ſuche time as the feaſt of the Bowthes dɀaweth nighe: lette the byſſhoppe, ſtanding in ſome place alofte

✳ Linſy wolſy.

U.b.   made

made for the purpose, fro whence he may wel be harde, recite the lawes vnto them all . Withholdinge neither woman, ne childe: no not the bondeman from hearing of them . For it behoueth them to haue them writen in their hartes & miudes: that thei may be kepte, neuer to perisshe . For by that meanes shall it come to passe that thei shall not offende, when thei shal haue none ignoraunce to excuse them in the ordinaunces and lawes: and the lawes shal haue ŷ greater authoritie vppon the offendours, in that thei haue warned them afore of the penaltie, and by hearing haue grauen in their mindes what thinges thei commaunde . That thei maye haue the effecte of their meaninge, euen dwelling within them. The whiche neclegted: thei shal offende, and be the cause of their owne euilles . Yea, and let the very children learne the lawes fro their youthe, as being a most goodlye discipline and the cause of blessed wealthe. Twise a daye also, bothe in the morning, and at the houre of bedtime, let them testifie to the Lord, his bounteous goodnes from the time of their deliueraunce oute of Egipte. Forasmuche as

thanckes

thāckes giuinge of very nature is dewe:
and is had aswell to yelde recōpence for
the benefites passe, as to allure the like
in time afterwarde. Let them also write
vpon their doozes, eche most notable benefite receiued of God: and what soeuer
may set forthe his power and fauour towarde them. Lette them beare them for
brothes on their cappes, and braselettes
on their armes, and let them shewe them
to all menne: that goddes tendzenes towarde thē may on euery side be apparāt.

Lette there be chosen for euery citye,
seuen rulers, exercised in all vertue, and
in the waye of equitie . And to euery
of those let ther be giuen two ministres,
of the Tribe of the leuites. And let those
whiche are appointed to ministre the
lawes to the citie: be had in all honour,
and reuerence. So that no man be bolde
to speake any woordes of dishonestie, thei
being present: ne to behaue him self ma-
lapertly . That this their reuerence towarde men of dignitie: may make them
more fearde to offende against God. And
let the iudges haue power to pronounce
their sentēce, excepte any man can shewe
that thei are corrupted with money to
peruerte

peruerte the lawe: o2 can b2ing any other cause to conuince them not to haue iudged a righte. Fo2 it is not miete that such shoulde sitte in iudgement, as will leane to lucre o2 dignitie: but suche as p2eferre equitie befo2e all other thinges. Fo2 so might God seme to be smallie reputed a monge you, and to be iudged of lesse aucth02itie then thei: to whose sentence ye shoulde yelde your consente, fo2 feare of power. The power of GOD is equitie. He then that beareth in anye pointe with them that are of power, fo2 dignities sake: enhaunseth their power aboue the power of GOD.

But if the iudges be not able to determine, in some cace b2ought afo2e thē (as amōge men it oftentimes happeneth) let thē remitte ỹ whole cause to ỹ holy citie. And let the highe p2iest, the p2ophete and the counsell assēbled, giue their sētence. Cleaue not to the Testimonie of one witnes. But of th2e, o2 twaine at the leaste: suche as haue so liued, that fo2 their honestie thei maye be reputed credite wo2thy. The woman shal not be admitted as a witnes, fo2 the lightenes, and disshonest boldenes of that kinde. No the bondmā shall

shall haue no voice in matter of witnes,
for that he lacketh the francque noble-
nes of minde:& either for lucre or feare,
is like to testifie vntruthes. If any shalbe
giltie of false witnes, conuicted therof:
let him suffre the same that the personne
should haue suffred againste whome he
wytnessed.

If ther shall haue bene in any place a
murder committed, and neither the doer can be founde, ne anye man suspected
vpon malice to haue done it : lette serche
be yet made for the doer with al diligece,
appointing rewarde to him who so euer
shall detecte him. But if then neither, no
mã shal disclose it: the officers of the townes nexte vnto the place wher the murdre was done, shall mesure the distaũce
fro the plotte where the deade lieth. And
looke what towne shalbe founde nexte
therunto, the rulers of the same shall
leade a boughte cowe into a valley and
place, neither fitte for ploughe ne plante,
and shal cutte in two the senowes of the
beaste in the boughes. And the priestes
and leuites, and the counseille of that
towne: wasshinge ouer the heade of the
ore, shall with loude voice protest that
their

they neither did it, ne ware present at the
diede. And to desire God to forbeare his
wrathe, and that neuer ther happen so
heinous a diede in the londe agayne.

At this present ye are not gouerned by
any kinge, or any one man alone: but by
a nombre of the beste, chosen out among
ye. The whiche of all gouernaunces is
the beste: and to liue vndre it, passing all
other liues. Wisshe ye not then for anye
other trade of cõmune wealthe, but be ye
cõtented with this: accõptinge your lawes
for your lordes, & doyng al thinges acor-
dig vnto thẽ. For god is sufficiet enoughe
to be your ruler. But if ye shalbe at anye
time desirous to haue a king ouer ye: let
him be of your bloude, and suche a one
as estiemeth righteousnes, and all other
vertues . And let him not sticke to his
owne wisedome, but ordre all matters of
waight by the lawes, and the lorde. And
let him do nothinge withoute the hyghe
priest, and the sentence of the counseille.
Neither let him be giuen to many mariages, ne to seke aboundaunce of money
and horses. Whiche hauing obteined, he
maye ware full of the lawe, and vtterly
contempne it. And if ye perceiue that he
busily

busily seketh suche thinges : lette him be
cutte shorter, that his power encreate
not more thã is expediẽt for you. It shal
be lawful for no man to remoue ÿ bounde
either of his owne londe, or of other men
nes, with whome ye haue peace. But let
it be sene to, that they maye continue in
their steades, as the sure markes of god,
there placed for euer. For therof com-
me the warres , and sedicion: when the
coueitous manne will encroche beyonde
his boundes. Yea who so thus ouerlea-
peth the bounde, will not gretly sticke to
ouerleape also the lawe.

He that planteth an hortevarde, if the
settes bring frute before the fourth yere:
let him neither yelde vnto God the first-
linges thereof, ne occupie them to his
owne vse. For thei are comen in vndue
time, and soner then their nature permitteth. And be nether miete for God, ne the
owner. But in the fourthe frute haruest
(for then are thei seasonable) lette him
beare the whole gather into the holy city,
and let them be spente together with the
tenth of all other frutes: festing with his
frindes, the fatherles childe, and the widowe. And in the. v. yere, he shall haue liberty

vertse to take to him self the profectes of
his plantes. Lette not the vineyarde be
planted oz sowen with aught elies. Foz
it is enoughe foz the grounde to nourishe
the vine, t ro be free fro the labour of the
ploughe. Let the grounde be tylled with
oxen, and let none other beaste be yoked
with them. Pea let the ploughe be hande
somed foz them also, acozding to their soztes. Lette your siede be moste piked and
cleane, pure, and vnmingled: noz lette
them not be sowen by two oz by thze soztes together. Foz nature liketh not suche
felowshtp of sondzy kindes. Deither that
ye put to your cattaile a mate of adiuer-
se, oz contrarye kinde. Foz it is to be feared, lest therby the vnkindlie couplinge
against kinde, passe also at lengthe vnto
men: beginning at thinges of smalle regarde, and so crieping on further. Cer-
tes ther is nothing to be suffr. d foz other
to folowe: wherof mighte pzocede anye
chaunge of your state. But it behoueth
you (foz asmuche as the lawes haue take
charge of the weightyer thinges) to foze-
see with all diligence, that nothing be
blame worthy in these smaller. De that
reapeth his cozne, and gathereth it into

these

thefe: fhall not glene vp the eares as he
goeth. Pea, let him leaue some of the ga-
uelles vngathered: that the niedie male
finde and be relieued by. The clufters of
grapes also, by chaunce (as it happeth)
ouerfene in the gatheryng: fhalte thou
leaue to the poore. See also of thine O-
liue gather, that thou leaue somewhat to
theim that haue not of their owne. For
there cometh not so greate profite to the
owners by the nighe gatheryng : As
there fhall come good wille, at the hande
of the poore. And the goodnes of the lorde
fhall encreafe the goodneffe of the soile,
that the fruictes male abounde: if menne
fhal not onely haue regard to their owne
priuate profecte, but also to the fuftenta-
tion of other. Thou fhalte not mowfeale
thine Ore in the flooze, whileft he treadeth the eares. For it is vnmiete to fhutte
them fro the fruicte: that haue holpen and
laboured for the obteinyng thereof. Neither fhall ye prohibite the waifaryng mã
to tafte of the fruictes that be ripe: but ye
fhall suffre him to eate his fille (as if thei
ware his owne) whether he be an indwel-
ler of the lande, oz a foreiner. Reioifyng
in so sufferyng hym to take his pleasure,

F.j.   of

of suche as be ripe, but none shall he cary
awaie. Neither shall the Grape gathe-
rers, forbidde suche as thei miete: to eate
of the Grapes thei beare to the Presse.
For vnsittyng it is, to grudge the giftes
whiche the lorde hath giuen to the main-
tenaunce of our life: to suche as desire to
take pleasure of their seasonablenes, beyng now at the highest, and sone ready
to detaie, as it pleaseth God to ordeine.
Yea, ifany man of a shamefaced main-
delines, for lacke of audacitie, shal strain
courtesie to take theim, gētly prouoke ye
thē. If thei be Israelites, in the name of
rō paniō or master for your bloudessake.
But if thei be foreiners, as willing them
to take part of suche ghestlan cōmodities
as God hath giuen ye, for the time of the
yere. For it is not to bee iudged as coste,
that thou sufferest a man to take of gētle-
nes: God sending ye plentie and enough
of all good thinges. Not for your owne
vse & welfare alone: but also that ye maie
liberally giue vnto many. To thend that
he mighte this waie declare vnto other,
his fauour and plentuous hande toward
you in suche largenes: That of the ouerplus, ye maie also participate vnto many

And

And he that shall do contrarie herebnto,
let there bee giuen vnto hym by the commune Sergeaunt of the batte. xxxix. stripes with a waster. And lette hym suffre
this moste dishoneste punishemente, for
asmuche as where he was fre by nature,
he hath diminished his owne dignitie, in
becomyng slaue vnto lucre. And a goodly thing is it, and conueniente for you that
haue suffered miserie in Egipte, and in
your passyng the wildernesse: to regarde
theim that suffre the like. And seyng that
ye by the mercifull prouision of GOD,
haue obteined plentie: to geue parte of
thesame vnto the nedie, moued with like
pitie and mercie.

Beside the two tenthes whiche I haue
commaunded ye yerely to paie (the one
to the Leuites, and the other to the fea-
stinges) lette there be a thirde tenthe also giuen the thirde yere, to be distributed
to all widowes and fatherles that lacke.
The firste of all ripe thynges that shall
happen to euery manne to come forthe:
let them beare into the house of the lorde
And there (hauyng giuen thanckes vnto
GOD, for the grounde that bare them,
whiche he gaue theim to possesse; and the

holie Sacrifices beyng finished: let them
giue the strike handseale of the thynges
that the lawe commaundeth them to bring,
to the Priestes. And when any man shal
haue thus done with his fruictes, and tithes, aswell perteinyng to the Leuites,
as other: and shall haue banquetted with
his firstlynges acordingly, and is aboute
to retourne home to his owne: then standing against the Tabernacle of witnesse
let hym giue thanckes vnto God, that he
hath vouchedsaulfe to deliuer them from
the oppressions of the Egipcianes, and to
giue theim a good lande and a large to
occupie, and vse to their commoditie and
pleasure. And protesting that he hath yelded his tithes acordyng to the Lawes of
Moses: let hym beseche God to be alwa-
yes mercifulle and fauourable to hym.
And that it maie please his goodnesse, to
continue indifferently to the vniuersalle
nombre of the Israelites: those benefites
and commodities, that he hath alreadie
giuen theim, and to heape vnto theim what
so euer more ouer maie be giuen.

  Let suche as are come to yeres of mariage, marie with maidens free borne,
and of good parentage or honeste stocke.
And

And who so refuseth to mary with a maiden, let hym not couple to hym one that
hath liued with another manne: neither
suche a one as hath forsaken her former
housebande. But lette not the free borne
couple with the bond, although some one
amonge pe seeme forced therto, with feruencie of loue. For it is mete that menne
should bridle their desire: and it maketh
for your honour. Furthermore, let there
be no mariage made with the commune
harlotte: whose Matrimoniall Sacrifices God wil not admit, for the dishonest
reproche of her body. For by this meanes
the natures of your childrē shal be disposed to honest courage, and towarde to all
vertue: if thei shall not be begotten of dishoneste mariages, neither of the luste of
engendrure with those that are bonde.

If any man hauyng betrouthed hymself to one whom he taketh for a maiden,
shall aftrewarde finde her to bee none: it
shalbe lawfull for hym before a Iudge
to accuse the wenche, vsyng suche proe-
ues as he can alledge. And the father or
brother of the maide, or he that shal seme
most of her kynde, shall defende her. And
if it shall be Iudged that the maide hath

not

not offended, lette her remaine with her accuse, now hauyng no power to putte her from hym, excepte she giue vnto him greate and vehement causes, suche as cānot be gainesaied. But if he haue laied this crime vpon her, of an vnshamefaced boldenes, and without cause: let hym receiue for punishement. xxix. stripes, and paie vnto the father fiuetie Sicles. But if he shall conuince the maiden, to haue lost her maidenheade: if she be one of the communaltie, let her be stoned, for that she did not prudently defende her Uirginitie, vntill her lawfulle mariage. But if she bee a Priestes doughter, lette her bee burnte quicke. If any manne haue twoo wiues, and the one is with him in greate estimacion and fauour, either for loue, or beaultie, or other cause: and the other in worse condiciō or state: If the child borne of the beloued (beyng younger then the child tofore borne of the other) would enioye the prerogatiue of age, for the same fauour of his father toward his mother: and so enioye a double parte of his fathers substance (according to that I haue appoincted in the Lawes) let hym not be suffered so to doe. For it sitteth not with

equitie

As some make compt, aboute tenne ß. sterlyng.

equitie, that the elder should be putte beside the enheritaūce of his father, because thother passeth him, by the mothers side.

Who so defloureth a maide, betrouthed to another, she beyng afore perswaded, and consentyng to thesame: let thē bothe dye together. Because thei are bothe indifferētly wicked. He for his perswasion of the maide, to suffre so filthie a dishonour, and to preferre that wickednes before lawful mariage: and she for that she consented to abandon her bodie to dishonestie, either for pleasure or lucres sake. But if the manne haue done this diede, hauyng gotten her alone in some place where she could haue no defendour, lette him alone die. Who so defloureth a Virgine not yet betrouthed to another, lette thesame marie her. But if the father be not contented to knitte her with hym, let the transgressour paie fiuetie ⚹ Sicles, as a dime tared for the iniurie done.

The Sicle is iudged.iiij. s. sterlyng.

He that will be deuorced frō his wife, dwellyng with hym, for what so euer cause it be (as there happen many vnto men)let him confirme by wryting, thathe neuer had diede of matrimonie with her. That is to saie, that he neuer carnally

F.iiij.   knewe

knewe her, and so shall she receiue power
to dwel with another, whiche afore ware
wickednes. And if also she agree not wel
with the seconde, or that he beyng deade,
the former would marie her againe : let
it not be lawfull for her to retourne vnto
him. The housebande of one that lacketh
issue beyng deade : let his brother marie
the widowe. And the child betwene them
borne , let hym nourishe vp to the succession of the enheritaunce, namyng hym
aftre the name of the dead. For if ye shall
doe thus , it shall make muche for your
commune wealthe , in that the name of
the kindredes shall neuer be extincte: and
the possessions shal alwaies remaine vnto the bloud. And it shall be a comforte of
sorowe vnto the woman, now dwellyng
with the nexte kindesman of her former
housebande. But if the brother wille not
marie her, let the widowe before the Senate or counsaile, thus testifie. That where
she was willyng to remaine stille in the
lignage, and to beare children by him, he
will not admit her. But rather findeth in
his harte to offende against the name &
memorie of his brother . And the Counsaile demaunding for what cause he abhor-
reth

reth the mariage: whether he shall shewe
a cause of weight, or of no weight, lette
them encline therunto . But as for
the widowe of his Brother, plucking of
his shoes, and spittinge in his face: lette
her saye vnto him that he is worthie
to suffre this ignominie at her hande,
for that he hathe founde in his harte
to hindre and empaire the name, and
memorialle of the deade . And lette
him thus departe out of the senate, hauing this reproche during his lyfe: and
let her mary to whome soeuer she wille,
that shall afterwarde require her. If a-
ny manne shall haue taken prisoner in
the warres, a mayden, or maried woma,
and be desirous to haue her fellowshippe
of bodie: let him not touche her bedde, or
body, before that she (being tonsed, and
hauing taken on her mourning wiede)
haue bemoued her kinsfolke, and friendes that perisshed in the warre. That
when she shall haue satisfied and appea-
sed the dolour that she cōceiued for thē:
she may then conuerte her selfe to the bā-
quet and mariage. For it is a goodly and
a decent thing, for a mā that goeth about
to get him selfe an honeste wife: to seke

X.v.   how

how to cure her greued minde: and not
to neglecte her fauour, in pursuing only
his owne pleasure. And thirty daies beinge ones passed thus (for that is enough
to those that are of discretió to bemourne
euen their derest beloued) let her then go
to and mary. Bnt if he, at the first hauing
satisfied his luste, ware full of her, and refuse her to wyfe: let him not haue power
to make her bonde, but lette her go wher
she wille at free libertie.

If ther shalbe founde any younge men
contempninge their parentes, or not yel-
dinge dewe honour vnto them, either of
shamefacednes or sette purpose of des-
pighte: Firste for that the parentes are
wonte to be fittest iudges ouer their children, lette theyr fathers, with woordes
correcte them. Sayeng that thei ioyned
not matrimonie betwiene their mothers
and thé, for pleasures sake, or to encrease
their substaunce in layeng eche others
goodes together in commune: but to op-
teine children that mighte nourisshe thé
in their age, & ministre vnto them what
thei lacke. After thou warte ones come in
to this worlde, we diligétly brought ý vp
with gladnes, & greate thákes vnto god
for

for the, sparinge nothinge that mighte
seme in any wyse to make for thy saufe-
tie, profite, and enstruction in all honeste
knowledge. Nowe therfore (for that it is
miete for men to beare with the faultes
of youthe) lette it suffice the hetherto to
haue neelegted thy dewe reuerence vnto
vs: and come againe nowe into the right
waye. Considering that God him self hai-
nously taketh ẏ that is committed againste
the father: for that he him selfe beinge
father of all mankinde semeth to be offended whẽ offence is committed againste
those that beare the name of father with
him : and can not haue of their children
that whiche is dewe vnto them. And the
law against all suche is an vnmercifulle
iudge: the whiche we wisshe childe thou
shouldest not proue. And if by these admo-
nitiõs, the lewdenesse of the younge man
shalbe redressed and amended: lette them
be quyte of reproche for their misdeme-
anour, and offences. For by this meanes
bothe the lawe maker shal become com-
mẽdable, and the fathers fortunate: whiche shall neither see sonne ne doughter
punisshed. But if the parentes woordes,
and good enstruction to amende, shal not

auaile

auaile, but that thei wyll with continual
dishonours, and oultrages against them,
make the lawes their implacable ennemies, lette him be broughte forthe of the
Citie by the parentes them selues, and
the multitude folowing, and lette him be
stoned to death. And when he hathe lyen
all the daye, for all menne to loke vpon:
lette him be buried in the nighte. So let
them also be handeled that are condempned of any capitalle crime by the lawe, af
tre what sorte so euer it be. Lette euin
the very ennemie be engraued, and lette
no corps lie withoute buriall. For that
ware a punisshement beyonde conscience.

It shall not be laufull for ye to make a-
ny lone to any of the Hebrues, either for
vsury or gaine. For it is not sittinge that
menne of one lignage should seke gaine
with that, that God sente them. But to
iudge it raither gaine, to haue holpē his
necessitie, and to thincke that he shall so
bothe deserue his thancke, and be requy-
ted of God for his gentlenesse. Thei that
haue borowed eyther siluer, or any par-
cell of moyste frutes, or dried: let thē (re-
ferringe the matier to their conscience
that lent them) paye againe their lēders
with

with good will, and gladnesse: thinking
that the thing so restored is laide vp euil
in their owne house and custodye . And
that it shalbe at all times ready agayne
for them when thei lacke it . But yf they
shalbe shameles in profering, & papeng
it home againe: lette them not so muche
as go home for a gauge, before sentence
be giuen vppon them by the iudge .
And as for the gauge lette them requyre
it of some neighbour abrode, and let the
debtour him self without contradiction,
bringe it to the creditour nowe enterpri-
sing vpon him with the aide of the lawe.
And if he that hathe gauged be a manne
of substaunce: lette the creditour kepe the
gauge vntle the restitucio of the lone be
made. But if he be poore, let him rede-
liuer it before the sonne set. Specially, if
the pledge be a garmente, that he maye
haue it to slepe with, according to goddes
tendrenesse that naturally pitieth the
poore . As for his querne or any toole of
his , shalte y not take to pledge: leste thei
should also be disfurnished of the instrumentes perteininge to the necessitie of
their liuinge, and so be driuen for nedi
nesse to greater inconuemence.

Let

Let him that hath robbed a man be punisshed with deathe. But lette him that shall haue picqued either Golde or siluer paye the double. Who so euer shall haue slayne the thiefe in the robbinge of his house, lette him be vnpunisshed. Yea thoughe he ware but vndermininge his house, or makinge his entry therinto.

He that hath stollen any maner of beast, let him restore the value. iiij.folde. But if the same be a labouringe oxe: he shall restore the value.v.folde. And he that shal not be able to paye the somme dewe for the damage: shalbe bonde vnto them to whome the beaste stollen shalbe knowen to apperteine. A manne solde vnto his kindesman, shalbe bonde to him sixe yeres, and the seuenth yere he shalbe free againe. But if he shall fortune to haue a childe by some bondewoman ther, and for the loue and fauour of her, and his childe, be content to serue stille: lette him be made free in the yere of Iubiley (whiche is the fiuetieth yere) & be deliuered with his wife and childern free also.

If any manne shall finde in the hyghe way, either golde or siluer, let him shewe the place where he founde it, and sekinge
after

aftre him that losse it, restore it him a-
gaine. Judginge the profighte which redoundeth vnto him by another mannes
losse, not to be good . Likewyse shall be
done with any kinde of catteille that a
man shal fortune to fijnde a strape in a-
ny place . And if the owner of the same
shall not straight waye be knowen, lette
him kepe it with him at home saulfe. Protesting GOD, that he entended not to
tourne aside, or hide out of the waye, any
thing that is another mannes . Lette it
not be lawfulle for any man to passe by a
beaste in any sorte euil bestadde, or falle
in the myre: but let him helpe and relieue
it , iudginge it to be his owne propre
grief. Let them also shew the waye vnto
them that are ignorante, and not go a-
boute to make them selues game in settinge them wronge , and so hinderinge
their commoditie . In like maner lette no
man laye euil against him that is absent
or deafe. A man hurte in a fraye where
ther was no weapon vsed: shal incontinẽt
be reuenged , he that hurte him beynge
made to suffre the like . But if he shalbe
caried home vpon the hurte, and aftre he
hath lien sicke a good space, shal fortune

ts

to die therof, lette him that hurte him be
vnpuniſſhed. But if he recouer, and haue
ſpent muche in his ſickenes, lette him the
repaie vnto him the whole charges as
ſwell of his lyeng, as to the Phiſicen, and
Surgien. He that ſhall haue with his
foote ſtriken a woman with childe : if
the woman therupon be vntimely diſbur
dened: the iudge ſhal ſet a forfeicte of mo
ney vpon his heade. As one that hathe di
miniſſhed the people in ſo marringe the
frute in the mothers wombe. And he ſhal
giue alſo pꝛiuatly a piece of mony to the
huſbāde of the womā ſo grieued. But if
ſhe die of the ſtripe : let him die alſo, acoꝛ
ding to ẙ lawe that puniſheth life foꝛ life.

No Iſraelite ſhall haue any medecine
of death, ne otherwiſe made to do anye
maner of hurte. And if ther be any one
founde to haue, lette him die foꝛ it : ſuffe-
ring the ſame, he mente vnto them, foꝛ
whoſe deſtructiō ẙ medicine was pꝛepa-
red. Who ſo maimeth let him ſuffre the
like, beyng depꝛiued of the ſame mēbꝛe,
that he him ſelf depꝛiued the other of. Ex
cepte the maymed be content to receiue
recompence in money: wherin the lawe
permitteth him to balewe the recōpence
him

His self, except he therin to muche excede.
The Meate that nourteth with the hozne
shall the owner kille. And if it shall foztune suche Meate to haue slaine in the
Rooze, any man with his Croke, let him
be stoned to death, not so muche as iudged to be manne's meate. Pea, if the owner be tried to haue knowen in the beast
this propretie afoze, and not to haue take
hiede to him, ne kept him vp: let him also
die himself, as the cause of the mannes
death thus slaine. If the Meate shal haue
slaine a bonde seruaunte, the Meate shal-
be stoned to death, and the owner of him   *Sixe pounde
shall paie vnto the Master of the ser-   sterling.
uaunte, thirtie‡Sicles. But if it shall foztune one Meate, thus to be strikrn of a-
nother, so that the one die therof: let them
bothe be solde, and the owners diuide
the prices euen betwene theim bothe.
Who so maketh a welle oz pitte, lette
theim bee circumspecte and take good
hede, to kiepe it couered. Not to with-
holde the watre, oz commoditie of thē
from any manne, but to the ende that
no manne by falling in, take hurte. And
if it foztune any beaste of any mannes,
by suche default of leauing opē the place

P.ij.   to

to falle in, and be marred: let him in whom the faulte is, paie the worth of the beaste to the owner. Let theim be fensed also aboute, to kiepe of suche thinges as otherwise by sliding or rolling, might perishe.

Who so euer hath taken any thing of another mannes to kepe: let him kepe it euen as a relique. And let no persone consente to defraude any manne of thing so betaken to his truste. Neither manne nor woman, no though he might gaine by it thousandes of poundes: as beyng sure that no witnesse could chardge him withall. For out of all peraduenture, it behoueth euery man to deale iustly, euen for conscience sake: as hauing himself a full witnesse against himself. Let euery man therefore doe those thinges, that maie cause him to be praised of other: hauyng before him principally the reuerence of God. From whom no lewdenesse can be hidden. But if it shall fortune this man so put in truste, to lose the thing cōmitted to his custodie, and cannot be founde to meane any practise of knauery, or deceipt in the matier: Let him go vnto the seuen Judges, and there sweare by God that nothing therof was loste by his wille, or

through

throughe his defaulte, nor no piece of is
occupied for him, and so let him departe
acquited therof. But if he haue occupied
neuer so litle a part of the thinge, so deliuered to his custodie, and haue so lost the
same: lette him be condempned to make
recompence for the whole that he receiued.

Like as I haue saied for the saulfe keping of thinges, if any manne shall with
holde the hire of the labouryng manne,
that toileth and drudgeth with his body:
let hym remembre that the wages of the
poore, ought not to be kepte backe. As the
thing whiche god hath giue him (knowe
thou well) in steade of lande and other
possessions. Furthwith therefore contēte
him, without delaie the same daie. For
God wille not haue the labourer defrauded of the profite of his labours.

Punishe not the sonne, for the fathers
faulte: but let the childrē rather that are
founde vertuous, be tendred and pitied
for that thei haue so leude fathers or mothers, and not hated because their parentes be vicious. No, the naughtines of the
sonne, is not to be imputed to the parentes neither: consideryng that young men
will doe many thinges, contrarie to the
P.ij.   discipline

Discipline of their parentes, vppon a sell-
willed wilfulnesse, that thincketh skorne
to be taught. As for the redgeling or guelt
persone, lette him be abhorred, and his
compaignie shonned of al menne: as one
whose manhode is (as a manne would
saie) curtalled or clipped awaie, and the
fruicte of engendrure, whiche God gaue
vnto man for the encrease of our kinde,
for his parte destroied. Yea, let theim bee
hunted out of all mennes compaignie, as
murderers of mākinde, in taking awaie
that, that should haue bene the cause of
issue aftrewarde. For why, it is euidente
that because thei had loste tofore al man-
lines of minde: therefore thei likewise became confor;mable of bodie. So shall ye
also doe with what so euer thing it bee,
that siemeth mōstruous to the beholders
It shall not beholden lawfull emong ye,
to guelde manne, woman, or beaste. And
now let these bee as statutes and lawes,
peaceablie and quietlie to ioine ye into
one commune wealthe. And the tendrenes of God, when he shall see it without
sedicion: shall aduaunce and enhaunce it.
Let the time neuer be sene, that shall altre any one of these, and chaunge theim
into

into contrarie. But forasmuche as there
is no remedie, but that menne shall falle
into busines and troubles, either willing-
lie or vnwillinglie: Lette vs also deuise
somewhat in that behaulfe, that through
foresighte of thinges miete to be done: ye
maie haue wholesome remedies, when
nede is, and not be driuen to sieke remedie at vnsette steuin, when the daungier
lieth in your lappes. But that ye maie
possesse and enioie the lande, that GOD
hath giue ye, banishyng sluggardise, and
kieping your mindes in continuall exercise, to the practise of vertue and manhod
euen whe ye haue gotten it, that ye maie
liue there, without thencursions of straü-
gers, and without any ciuile discencion,
to bere ye or trouble ye. Throughe the
whiche ciuile discorde, if ye shall falle to
doyng thinges contrarie to your forefathers, and lette slippe their ordenaunces
and rules: or shall not continue in the lawes, whiche the Lorde deliuereth vnto
you, moste assuredly good for what so e-
uer affaires of warre ye shal haue, either
now in your time, or your children aftre
you: the Lorde shall throwe the breakers
of the same, cleane out of his fauour and

protection.

protection.

When ye are in minde to warre vpon
any people, and to shewe your force vpon
them: sende firste your Heralde vnto the
though thei be neuer so muche bent to be
your enemies. For before ye lift vp wea=
pon against theim, it behoueth ye to vse
communication with theim, declaryng
that although ye haue an armie of great
power, and horses, harneis, and weapōs
and (that whiche farre passeth all these)
God your fauourer & helper: yet by your
good willes ye woulde haue no warre
with thē. Neither that it ware any pleasure to you, to enriche your selues with
the spoile of their substance: but rather a
thing that ye hate, if it maie otherwise be
If thei shall leane vnto you, then it becometh ye to kiepe peace: Thinckyng with
your selues, that thei are your bettres in
strēgth. But if thei wille endamage you
then leade ye your armie against theim,
vsyng God for your heade capiteine and
gouernour: but for your chiefteine vnder
him, make ye some one of passyng wisedome and courage. For where there are
many gouernours, beside the hinderance
that it causeth when a mannes necessitie
                                    moueth

moueth him to vse spiede: it is wonte allso not to be verie prosperous to theim that vse it . Lette your armie bee piked of the strongest, and hardiest of courage: leaste tournynge their backes when it cometh to stripes, thei profite more your ennemies then you.

Thei that late haue builded, and not yet taken one yeres commoditie of the same, and thei that haue planted either vineyarde or horteyard, and not receiued as yet any fruictes therof: lette theim bee suffred at home. Like wise those that are trouthplite, & towarde mariage, or suche as are newly maried: leaste vpon longing aftre their desires, thei be to tendre ouer their liues. And sparing theim selues to entoie their pleasure, shrincke backe for the nones, and abasse the courage, vppon regard of their wiues. And when ye shal be assembled into campe, lette it be foresene that nothing bee done out of course, to muche against curtesie. And when ye shall besiege any fortresse or toune of defence, and lacke Timbre for the making of your engines and deuises : pille ye not the countrie, cutting doune the trees aboute the citie or fortresse, what so euer

P.iiij.   it

it be: but sparingly vse thē. Remēbring
that the earthe bringeth theim furthe for
the commoditie of manne: and that thei
would laie to your charge, if thei coulde
speake, that vndeseruedly ye hurte them.
As no whitte occasion of the warre, and
those that gladly would haue giue place,
and passed into some other quartre, if it
had bene possible for them. Whē ye shall
haue ouercomen theim in the fielde: slea
ye as many as stande in the battaile a-
gainst ye. The residue reserue ye to paie
tribute vnto ye: the Cananites excepted,
for those it behoueth ye to destroie euery
mothers sonne. And haue ye a specialle
regarde in the skirmishe or battaile, that
no woman, either vse the appareille of
menne, or any manne, the appareille of
women. Suche then was the ordre of the
commune wealthe that Moses left. Beside these he deliuered them lawes in writing fouretie yeres afore, of the whithe
we will treate in another booke.

    Aftre this in the daies folowynge (for
he euery daie continually preached vnto
theim) he deliuered them praiers of blessinge and banning: the one for the fulfil-
lers, the other for the trangressours of

the

the lawe. Therecited he vnto the ῦ verses
that he lefte in the byble, consistnge eche
one of .xii. measures the piece: and contei
ning ῦ forewarning of thinges to come,
acordjng to the whiche all thinges haue
happened. and happe at this present. So
to the poincte, that it can not be said that
he missed the truthe in any thing.

These bookes deliuered he vnto the pri
estes, and the Arcke. In the which he left
the ten articles of the lawe, whiche we
commenly calle the .x. commaundementes
written in two tables, and the Tabernac
le also. And he gaue a lesson to the peo
ple, that when thei had conquered the
lande, and ware satled in the same: they
should not forgettethe iniury of the Ama
lechites, but that thei should make a voy
uge against them, and take reuenge vp
on them, for the damage and displeasure
thei did them, when thei ware in the de
serte. And that when thei should enioye
the contrie of Cananie, and should haue
destroyed the whole multitude of it (as
it behoued, and was miete for them) thei
should buylde vp an altare looking to
warde, the Easte in some place, not farre
from the citie of ῦ Sichemites, betwene

the two mounteines . Gariseo on the
right hande, and Gibalo on the left hade.
And that thei should place their whole
multitude vppon those two mounteines
beinge deuided into two equalle partes.
That is to say on eche hille. vi. tribes, with
the leuites, and priestes and all. And that
thei first, that ware in the mounte Gari-
sin, should wysshe all felicitie, and blessed
nes vnto those that ware deuoute in the
religion of GOD, and the keping of the
lawes, & threwe not at their hieles those
thinges that Moyses had taughte them.
And that then the other in Gibalo, aftre
what time thei had luckely giuen their
good consent vnto thē: should also wishe
like prosperitie, and like blessednes to the
like doers, answerably to the former.
wherunto the firste should againe giue
like lucky consente, with praisinge them.
That done he willed them in like sorte to
do with the cursinges, answering one a-
nother, for the establisshing of the lawes
that should be giuen them. And that the
maner and discipline of this blessinge,
and cursing, mighte neuer falle oute of
vse: he wrate them out the order of bothe
with the prayers, and curses therto ap-
                                    pertinent

pertinente . The whiche also when he died he wrate vppon eche syde of the aulter, where he enioyned also the people to make the sacrifice stondinge, that the Latine calleth Sacrificium Solidum, and aftre, not to offre that daye any moze sacrifice . Foz why he said it was not lawfulle. Thus I saye did Moyses institute these thinges, and the people of the Hebzues from daye to daye obserued them fozthe on.

The nexte daie calling the whole multitude together, in so muche that there was neither woman noz childe, ne bonde body absente: he charged them wondzefully soze to take hede to the lawes, and not to trásgresse them. But that as men that diligently waied goddes minde and wille:thei should spare none that offeded against them, neither foz kindredes sake, ne foz feare. Noz yet as thincking any other cause to be moze to be weighed,then the obseruacion of the lawes . But rather yf any one manne of their kindered oz any whole citie,would go about to disturbe,oz abzogate the ordinaüces of their commune wealthe : that thei should take vengemente vpon them,bothe by officer,

and

and without . And that if in suche case it
fortuned them to haue the bettre of suche
aduersary to the lawe : that thei shoulde
vtterly destroy him or them, not leauing
an agguelet of a pointte for the memo-
rial of such hopelosse persones, if it ware
possible. And in case thei ware not able to
reuenge for lacke of power: that yet they
should so worke, that thei myghte well
shewe that those thinges ware done full
euyll against their wille. And the multitude forsothe did sweare . He taught the
to, howe their sacrifices mighte be made
more acceptable vnto God, and how thei
should when they sette forthe to the warres chose their lucke by stone lottes
as I haue shewed afore. Iosua also pro-
phessed, Moyses yet beyng presente a-
mong them. And Moyses thus wayeng
all those thinges that he had done for the
people, bothe concerning warre, and peace
in makinge them lawes , and teachinge
them an ordre of a commune wealthe, by
the whiche if thei directed their steppes,
thei mighte enioye a prosperous blessednes: signified vnto them, that God had
giuē knowledge that thei should in time
to come forsake his lawes and ceremonies;

nies: and therfore suffre muche affliction
and aduersitie. In sorte that their londe
should be euen filled with their ennemies. Their Cities, and townes beaten
downe smothe to the grounde, the Temple burned, and they them selues beynge
solde, should serue as thralles vnto men
that should take no pitie of their calami-
ties. And that whē thei suffred these thin
ges thei should sore repente thē of their
transgressions, but then in vaine. God
notwithstãding that sourmed, and made
ye shal restore ye againe vnto your 'cite-
zins, bothe their Cities, and the Temple. And the losse of these quoth he shall
happen ofte ner then ones or twyse.

Then Moyses encouraging Iosua to
marche out with the armye against the
Cananites (as one assured to haue God
his ayder in all his entreprises) and prai
enge for prosperous lucke, and successe,
for all the whole multitude, saieth. Se-
inge that I must departe vnto our sore-
fathers, and God hathe appoincted this
the daye of my departure vnto them: I
openly confesse before ye all yet beyng a-
liue, and present with you: the thanckes
that I owe vnto him, and now giue him,
not

not onely for the regarde that he alwaye
had to ye, to tourne fro ye that that was
euill, and to giue vnto ye that that was
good: but also that it pleased him to suc-
coure me when I had niede of his hel-
ping hande, in all my cares and troubles
of minde, for your reformacion, and a-
mendement into bettre, and shewed him
selfe tendre vnto vs in all our affaires.
Or raitther that it pleased him to take in
hande his selfe to leade in, and let out, v-
singe me as a lieuetenaunte, and ministre of the benefites, wherwith he would
blesse your people. For the whiche nowe
at my leaue taking, I thoughte it conue-
nient, and sitting with my duety, first to
prayse and magnifie together with you,
the mighty power of GOD, the whichs
shal also shewe him self carefulle for you
in times to come. And he, yea euē he shal
yelde againe to you a thanckefulnes, of
his gentlenes, for your thanckefulnes of
duetie: wher throughe he shall make you
confesse in conscience, that ye are for his
bounteousnes bounde to reuerence, worshippe, and honour him, and to haue his
lawes in price. Bothe those whiche he
hath giuen vou, and yet hereafter shall,
that

that ye maye kepe him fauourable vnto
you: of all stores the moste goodly trea-
sure. For manne him selfe that is a lawe
maker, becommeth a bittre ennemye,
when he seeth his lawes broken, sette at
noughte, and throwen vndre foote.

But be not ye in wille diere brethren,
for the tendre loue of G O D, to proue
what maner of one he is, when he beginneth to kindle into wrathe for the contempte of the lawes, whiche he gaue vnto you, as the maker of them all. Moses
speaking these woordes, euin to the laste
farewell of his life, and propheciēg the
destenies of euery seuerall tribe, with
manye woordes of good fortune and
chaunce: the whole multitude braste out
into teares, so that the women also wrin-
ginge their handes, and throwinge their
armes abrode, shewed the strōge sorowe
that thei felte for his death now at hāde.
Yea the childrē cryenge, and sobbinge
aboue the rest, as lesse able to bridle their
grief and lamentacion, declared by their
pietifull wailinges that thei vnderstode,
the wonderfulle vertue of him, and the
excellencie of his doynges, aboue the
course of their age. And to saye all, the so-
rowes

rowes of the younger, and the elder ſtraue as it ware in balaunce, foʒ the maiſtery, acoʒding as thei diuerſely felte in their minde. Foʒ the one, knowing by experience what a gouernour, and chiefteine thei loſte: lamented their lacke foʒ the time to come: and the other bothe ſoroiwed foʒ that, and alſo and yet moʒe, becauſe he was beraſte them befoʒe theihad well taſted his pierelesse wyſedome.

A manne mighte geſſe the greatneſſe of the lamentacion, and mone of the multitude: by that that happened vnto Moyſes him ſelfe. Foʒ where he had almoſte aſſured him ſelfe all the daies of his lyfe, that his departure out of this woʒlde ſhould neuer any whitte trouble him (as the thing that he muſte neceſſarily ſuffre by the wil of God, and natures lawe) yet was he by the compaſſion of the dolour of the people cōpelled to let falle the teares. And goynge foʒthe together to the place wher he ſhould departe fro them, thei al folowed him, howling foʒ ſoʒowe. And thoſe that ware fartheſt of, Moyſes commaunded with the beckening of his hādes to ſtaye ſtil ther aloofe. And thoſe that ware nierer, with comfoʒtable woʒdes,

des, he entreated that thei woulde not
bring aftre him their teares any nigher
to make his farewell moꝛe doloꝛous.
And thei thinkinge it miete to geue him
place therin, that he mighte departe his
owne way as him ſiemed beſt: tourned
their heades into eche others boſome &
ſobbed vp their ſoꝛowes with many ſalt
teares among them ſelues, & with many
a longe eye aftre Moyſes. who was accompanied to the place only with the fathers of the Counſelle, the highe pꝛieſte
Eleaſarus, and Joſua now chiefteine.
And when he was comen to the mounteigne named Abary (a very highe bylle
oueragainſt Jericho, geuing a goodli eye
vnto thoſe that are on it, into the pleaſant
londe of the Cananites, farre and wyde
aboute, he willed the counſeil to departe.
And as yet takinge leaue of Eleaſarus
and Joſua, and talkinge with them, he
vaniſſhed in a hoque of the hille, beynge
ſoubdenly ouercaſte with a cloude. He
wꝛate neuertheleſſe in the holye bookes
(whiche we calle the byble) that he was
dead. Fearingleſſe thei ſhould take vp
on them to ſaye that he departed quicke
vnto God, foꝛ the incomparable vertue

z.i.   that

that was in him. He liued in all, a hundred and twenty yeres. Of the which he
cōtinued.xl.in his gouernaunce, lacking
but one moneth . He tooke his leaue
the laste moneth of the yere called of the
Macedonies Dwistre, and of the Iewes
Adar, in the chaunge of the mone. And he
excelled in witte all the menne that euer
ware, and did all that he did with goodly
aduisement & discreciō. He was eloquēt,
and faire spoken in vttering his mynde
to the people . But so bridlinge his affec-
tions that a man woulde haue thoughte
ther had bene none in him. But that he
knewe raither the name of them, by that
he sawe them in other: hen the worcking
of thē, by aught that he felte in him self.
A chiefteine with the best, and moste ex-
pert, but suche a Prophete as none was
againe: so that what soeuer he spake, god
him selfe mighte haue bene thoughte to
haue spoken it. Aftre he was thus with
drawen from this worlde, the people be-
mourned him thirtye daies. with suche
mone, as neuer had bene sene so great a-
monge the Hebrues for any mishappe .
And not onely thei that had had experience of him , ware sorye that thei lacked
                                          him

him : but thei also that redde his lawes
ware muche kindled with the desire
of him , as folkes gessinge by the
woorke, what excellencie was
in the woorkeman. Let
this then suffice after
this maner to haue
declared the pas
sage of Moses
fro this
lyfe to euerlasting
immortali,
tie .

❡ The firste booke
vndre the title of Af=
frique conteineth.

❡ The seconde booke
vndre the title of Asie,
conteineth.

The

The table

Of

The table.

Of the Christianes, of their first co-
minge vp, their Ceremonies and or-de-
naunces. Chapiter.   rij.

A treatyse of Iosephus the Iewe, concerninge the ordenaunces and lawes of
the Iewes commune wealthe.

F I N I S.

¶ Imprinted at London
by Iohn Kyngston and Hen-
rie Sutton. The. rij. daye
of December.
(⁊)

ANNO DOMINI,
M. D. L V.